U.S. East-West Trade Policy

New York University
Center for International Studies
Studies in Peaceful Change

Why Federations Fail: An Inquiry into the Requisites for Successful Federalism Thomas M. Franck, Gisbert H. Flanz, Herbert J. Spiro, and Frank N. Trager (New York: New York University Press), 1968

A Free Trade Association, Thomas M. Franck and Edward Weisband, eds. (New York: New York University Press), 1968

Comparative Constitutional Process, Thomas M. Franck (New York: Praeger; London: Sweet and Maxwell), 1968

The Structure of Impartiality, Thomas M. Franck (New York: Macmillan), 1968

Agents of Change: A Close Look at the Peace Corps, David Hapgood and Meridan Bennet (Boston: Little, Brown), 1968

Law, Reason and Justice: Essays in Legal Philosophy, Graham B. Hughes (New York: New York University Press), 1969

Czechoslovakia: Intervention and Impact, I. William Zartman, ed. (New York: New York University Press), 1970

Sierra Leone: An Experiment in Democracy in an African Nation, Gershon Collier (New York: New York University Press), 1970

Microstates and Micronesia: Problems of America's Pacific Islands and Other Minute Territories, Stanley A. de Smith (New York: New York University Press, 1970

International Business Negotiations: A study in India, Ashok Kapoor (New York: New York University Press), 1970

Foreign Capital for Economic Development: A Korean Case Study, Seung Hee Kim (New York: Praeger), 1970

The Politics of Trade Negotiations between Africa and the European Economic Community: The Weak Confront the Strong, I. William Zartman (Princeton, New Jersey: Princeton University Press), 1971

Word Politics: Verbal Strategy Among the Superpowers, Thomas M. Franck, Edward Weisband (New York: Oxford University Press), 1972

Developing Democracy, William A. Douglas (Washington, D.C.: Heldref Publications), 1972

Turkish Foreign Policy 1943–1945: *Small State Diplomacy and Great Power Politics*, Edward Weisband (Princeton: Princeton University Press), 1973

Classical Liberalism, the Monroe Doctrine, and the Ideology of American Foreign Policy, Edward Weisband (Beverly Hills: Sage Publications), 1973

Secrecy, Democracy and Foreign Policy, Thomas M. Franck and Edward Weisband, eds (New York: Oxford University Press), 1973

U.S. East-West Trade Policy

Economic Warfare Versus Economic Welfare

Thomas A. Wolf
International Institute of
Management, Berlin

Lexington Books
D.C. Heath and Company
Lexington, Massachusetts
Toronto London

Library of Congress Cataloging in Publication Data

Wolf, Thomas A
U. S. East-West trade policy.

A revision of the author's thesis, New York University.
1. United States—Commercial policy. 2. East-West trade (1945-) I. Title.
HF1455.W57 1973 382'.3'0973 73-953
ISBN 0-669-86827-2

Published simultaneously in Canada.

Printed in the United States of America.

International Standard Book Number: 0-669-86827-2

Library of Congress Catalog Card Number: 73-953

To My Mother and Father

Contents

List of Figures

List of Tables

Foreword

Perhaps the most dramatic change in U.S. foreign policy since 1970 has involved relations with Communist countries. From ping-pong diplomacy for Communist China, the successful completion of the SALT talks, and even to the exchanges of environmental control specialists with the Soviet Union, the change in the political environment between the U.S. and most Communist countries has progressed faster and further than most would have imagined possible a few years ago.

In practice, the most concrete steps have been taken in the area of economic relations. This is quite proper since a strong case can be made, as Dr. Wolf does in this book, that the U.S. policies of the earlier postwar period were inconsistent at times, and largely ineffectual in achieving their objectives. In short, the costs exceeded the benefits.

In the spring of 1970, the Center for International Studies held a one-day conference attended by senior business executives of firms actually or potentially interested in expanded East-West trade and by high U.S. government officials engaged in making and executing U.S. policy with respect to East-West trade. Those discussions indicated a need for reevaluating U.S. policy and for additional research in this area. The Center made a commitment to contribute to the latter, and this book is both a manifestation of that commitment and a basis for the reevaluation of U.S. policy.

Using the tools of the economist this study develops the conditions for an optimal policy with respect to East-West trade when economic harm to the Eastern countries is one of the objectives of U.S. policy. Once the optimal conditions are established, the study sets about to evaluate the actual policy measures employed by the United States in the postwar period. At various points, Wolf finds certain policy measures inconsistent with each other, and not infrequently inappropriate for optimizing the overall benefit to the U.S. given the objective of economic "warfare" with the East.

One of the major points made in the study is that political objectives have their economic costs, and as is so often the case, policy measures with respect to trade with Eastern Europe were evaluated in one dimension or the other, but not both simultaneously, as rational policy-making requires.

The study provides keen insights into why the U.S. policy has shifted in the recent past and provides predictions as to the results of those shifts and the likelihood of greater liberalization in the future. By providing a rigorous basis for evaluating a particular set of policies, this study makes a relatively unique contribution to the synthesis of economics and political science. One hopes that it also will improve practical policy-making, but only time will confirm that hope.

THOMAS M. FRANCK

Director
Center for International Studies
New York University

Preface

Until very recently the discussion surrounding U.S. East-West trade policies has been notably lacking in appreciation of the fundmental trade-off between considerations of economic *welfare* and economic *warfare*. This deficiency was revealed to me most forcefully when I undertook some empirical research on this subject as a research assistant to Professor Robert G. Hawkins of the Graduate School of Business Administration, New York University, in the summer of 1970. It was not at all clear what one was to do with the empirical evidence concerning the restrictiveness of U.S. controls on trade with the socialist countries of Eastern Europe and Asia. How was it to be related to the "national security" arguments forcefully put forward for restrictions on United States trade with these countries?

This study attempts in part to remedy this deficiency; to develop a framework for looking simultaneously at trade and "national security" considerations, and to use this conceptual structure to analyze the evolution of U.S. East-West policies over the past quarter-century. My primary goal in writing this book is twofold: to contribute to the general discussion of the formulation of foreign economic policy in a national security context, and to set forth a basis for discussing the East-West trade policy choices facing the United States in the 1970s.

I owe particular thanks to Robert Hawkins, who inspired my interest in East-West economic relations in the first place, and who also served as my adviser for the doctoral dissertation on which this book is based; and to Ingo Walter and David Whitcomb, who as the balance of my dissertation committee provided valuable encouragement, advice, and helpful criticism. I also wish to record my gratitude to New York University for granting me a Marcus Nadler Fellowship, which helped to cover the financial burden of existing in New York City as a mere student.

Thanks are also due to the Center for International Studies at N.Y.U. for its generous financial support of the initial revisions to my dissertation. I am also grateful to the numerous officials at the U.S. Departments of Commerce, Defense, and State with whom I had very informative discussions in the course of writing my dissertation. Finally, I would like to thank Gisela Spivey and Beverly With of the International Institute of Management, Berlin, who together typed the final manuscripts; Sita Ram Mohan for her editorial comments; and Susan and Toby for their familial forbearance.

Berlin,
November 1972

Introduction

As Richard Caves has written, "formal analyses of welfare in terms of national power by economists interested in international trade have been rare; intelligible analyses of international trade by students of nationalism seem to have been rarer."[1] An early contribution to the study of the relationship between foreign trade and national power was Hirschman's *National Power and the Structure of World Trade*.[2] While this book carefully delineated many of the foreign commercial policies a nation should follow in the pursuit of national power, the fundamental trade-off between following such policies and maximizing domestic economic welfare was not really pursued. Although Kemp very briefly discussed some of the economic aspects of "trade warfare" within a framework of international trade theory in his *Pure Theory of International Trade* in 1964, this topic was omitted altogether in his revised and expanded edition of 1969.[3] Kindleberger's *Power and Money* is an interesting survey of the "economics of international politics and the politics of international economics," but no attempt is made in that book to systematically examine the relationship between national security and the formulation of optimal foreign economic policies.[4]

Most of the theoretical literature dealing with the trade-off between economic and noneconomic objectives in the formulation of foreign economic policy has been concerned with such questions as infant industry protection, self-sufficiency, the level of employment, and "industrialization" as national goals.[5] While several of these articles have dealt briefly with the conventional aspects of national security (military preparedness, self-sufficiency in strategic goods or factors of production), they have generally not addressed the implications of "offensive" economic warfare for foriegn economic policy. Furthermore, such studies have omitted one of the fundamental features of national security policy: discrimination by the nation under consideration (which we shall call "Home") *among* foreign countries or groups of countries.

In Part I we attempt to bring these various national security considerations together in a coherent framework. As we shall discuss at some length in Chapter 1, this framework constitutes an elaboration and extension of the notion of a country attempting to jointly maximize its immediate economic welfare and certain "noneconomic" foreign policy objectives. This approach was first propounded by Harry Johnson,[6] and later popularized to some extent by Benjamin Cohen in his *American Foreign Economic Policy*[7]. Such a "theory" of an optimal trade policy will be developed within the context of a national welfare maximization framework, in which we solve for a set of optimal conditions expressed in terms of foreign trade taxes, and, in some cases, domestic taxes or subsidies.

As we shall see, a theory of optimum trade policy in a *national security* context requires us to depart from the assumptions of the conventional optimum tariff analysis. This departure is basically twofold. First, we elaborate on the conventional social welfare function to include various military and "offensive" and "defensive" economic warfare variables. Second, we differentiate the conventional single, "rest-of-the-world" trading partner into separate foreign national (or regional) entities.

In Chapter 2 it is demonstrated that such a departure from the assumptions of conventional optimum tariff analysis leads to a theory of discriminatory optimum tariff policy in which the nation pursuing this policy (our "Home") optimally will take into account both national security and discriminating monopolistic-monopsonistic considerations.

We examine in greater detail, in Chapter 3, the implications of each national security consideration for foreign economic policy. Each of these considerations is found to imply an optimal pattern of foreign trade taxes in general different from one another and from that which would be pursued under a conventional optimum tariff policy. It is further shown that to the extent that "Home" chooses to discriminate among foreign countries, some degree of extraterritorial control over foreign trade is necessary. Finally, we find that if defensive economic warfare considerations embody the notion of *relative* dependence on foreign supplies or export markets, Home should optimally impose both foreign trade taxes and specific tax or subsidy programs in the domestic sector.

Throughout Part I we will be demonstrating the foregoing propositions by means of a generalization of Graaff's mathematical formulation of optimum tariff theory.[8] Recognizing that there may be substantial variation among different readers' interests in algebraic formulations of what are in many cases quite straightforward economic rules, we will formulate in Part I the problem and its solution in descriptive terms (for the policy-oriented reader), and then will follow at the end of the book with a more rigorous mathematical presentation. The reader having little enthusiasm for the latter may simply skip these mathematical appendices without breaking the continuity of the presentation.

In Part II we take a look at the evolution of U.S. trade policies toward the socialist countries of Eastern Europe and Asia[a] in the light of the model developed in the first section. As we shall explain in Chapter 4, our ability to really "apply" our model to actual U.S. trade policies, and to make statements about the "optimality" of these policies, requires us to make some simplifying assumptions concerning the so-called "second-best" qualifications which have come to haunt practically all exercises in applied welfare economics.[9]

---

[a] Defined as Albania, Bulgaria, Czechoslovakia, East Germany, Hungary, Poland, Rumania, and the Soviet Union (the socialist countries of Eastern Europe); and North Korea, North Vietnam, Outer Mongolia, and the People's Republic of China (the socialist countries of Asia).

In Chapters 5 through 7 we trace the evolution of U.S. East-West trade policies in the course of the postwar period. Our more or less chronological discussion of the formulation of these policies is not meant to be a comprehensive historical review. For such a detailed examination the reader is referred to the 1968 study by Gunnar Adler-Karlsson.[10] Rather, our purpose is to indicate the apparent key elements entering into the formulation of East-West policies in each instance—the basic economic and national security considerations.

We have omitted discussion of some of the minor restrictions on trade with the socialist countries, and often devote what might seem to be a more than proportionate amount of attention to other barriers which have been constructed to East-West commerce. Our purpose is simply to throw into relief what after lengthy study appear to be the fundamental considerations operative in American postwar policy making with respect to the Eastern countries.

With regard to each type of restriction on trade with the socialist countries, we will postulate that certain national security considerations enter into American utility functions, whenever possible drawing on declared legislative policies and the surrounding political debate as evidence. Interpreting the various U.S. restrictions on this trade in terms of explicit or implicit foreign trade taxes, we will then compare the pattern of these "taxes" with the theoretically optimum pattern implied by our model.

Chapters 5 through 7 are broken up into three time periods, each roughly corresponding with a basic shift, either in U.S. East-West trade policies as such or in the underlying political-economic environment that ultimately determines the relative success or failure of these policies. The first period, 1948–1953, represented an era of maximum or near-maximum western economic warfare directed towards the socialist countries. The second period, roughly 1953 to 1963, witnessed the beginning of a significant deterioration of the Western economic alliance against the East, following the death of Stalin and the end of the Korean War. This period was characterized by increased apparent "polycentrism" (or independence from the Soviet Union) in the East, notably in the case of China and Rumania, but also by an emerging schizophrenia in U.S. trade policies towards the socialist world. Chapter 7 traces the evolution of U.S. East-West commercial policies since 1963, a period of growing recognition of the fundamental trade-off in foreign economic policy between economic warfare carried out in the name of national security, and domestic economic welfare.

The basic conclusion which emerged from our analysis of U.S. East-West trade policies is that in the beginning they were in part based on some erroneous assumptions, that once these policies were established, however, the problem of "what is an optimum policy" was largely ignored, and that it has been only recently, in response to emerging economic pressures as well as to growing East-West detente, that major steps have been taken to bring these trade policies into line with present international economic and political realities, and to begin to move towards something that could be loosely called an "optimum" set of policies.

In Chapter 8 we examine briefly the available empirical evidence concerning the restrictive effect of U.S. East-West trade barriers, and the potential for expanded U.S. trade with the socialist countries. While most of the evidence concerning the actual trade-inhibiting effect of present or recently liberalized barriers is partial and preliminary, in practically every case it has been demonstrated that the restrictive effect is quite significant. The potential markets in the socialist world possibly lost to American competitors in the West because of the more severe unilateral U.S. controls on the Eastern trade may be significant too, although this represents a measurement problem even greater than the few attempts which have been made at quantifying the static effects of U.S. policy.

Finally, in Chapter 9, we draw on the conceptual framework of Part I and our analysis of the evolution of past U.S. East-West trade policies to set forth certain lessons that should be learned from past U.S. East-West policy making, as well as the basic alternative trade policy choices that the United States faces for the balance of this decade. Not surprisingly, our recommendation is that U.S. economic policy makers should follow a strategy whereby they maximize their flexibility in a world of fast-moving political and economic currents. But more specifically, our examination of past U.S. policies suggests that within such a flexible or "mixed" strategy, unilateral liberalization is most appropriate with respect to certain U.S. trade barriers, while others should probably be removed within a context of negotiated economic concessions on both sides.

The policy of trading economic concessions for often vaguely defined "political" quid pro quos should be looked at with skepticism. There is very little in the history of U.S. policymaking in this area since World War II to suggest that this latter approach is a high payoff strategy. Increasingly, the need is for the United States to replace its "offensive" economic warfare strategy (a response to a bipolar world) with a carefully thought out "defensive" strategy, which would be intended to keep the nation secure in a new era of far more subtle, multipolar threats to future U.S. military and economic strength.

Part I
Towards a Theory of Optimal Trade Policy in a National Security Context

1 The Conceptual Framework

The Objective of Foreign Economic Policy

The concern with "national security" is merely a reflection of the fact that the world is divided into many nation-states. As Cohen has pointed out, these nation-states are

> ... communities of men organized within a particular constitutional order prevailing over some specific geographical terrain. These communities are, in a world of innumerable and overlapping organizations, the focal point of political power. All of them claim the right to exercise complete sovereignty over their own internal affairs. Consequently, no one of them can exercise anything even approximating complete sovereignty except within its own borders. The nation-state individually can attempt only to *influence* the external environment, using whatever instruments are at its command. All such actions intended to affect situations beyond the national jurisdiction represent together the foreign policy of the nation-state.[1]

So as to assure that "sovereignty over their own internal affairs" is preserved, the cardinal responsibility which nation-states give to their foreign policy makers is the responsibility for the *survival* of the nation itself. Consequently, "national security" in a very fundamental sense is the overriding objective of foreign policy. Cohen has observed that "the concept of national security is not a precise, meaningful guide for action; it is subjective rather than objective in content, and consequently rather ambiguous."[2] Nevertheless, while it may be difficult or even impossible for a nation's citizenry to agree on just what "national security" means, it is quite clear that it is enhanced by maximizing the nation's freedom of action in foreign affairs. Again, it has been suggested by Cohen that the "rational" goal for the country seeking to maximize the probability of survival as a nation is "to broaden its range of options—that is, *to maximize its power position*, since power sets the limits to the choice of strategy."[3]

In the ultimate analysis, national power is a function of the wealth of resources at a nation's command (military, economic, and cultural), relative to the resources belonging to and utilized by other competing nation-states. As Cohen observes, "National power can be accumulated to the extent permitted by the resources of the state. These set an upper limit. The problem of the state's foreign policy makers is to maximize national power subject to this constraint—that is, to make most effective use of the available resources in pursuit of the state's proximate foreign policy goals."[4]

Foreign *economic* policy is concerned with those actions of the nation designed to affect the *economic* environment beyond the national border.[5] Yet whatever affects the foreign economic environment likewise affects the domestic economy, either directly or indirectly. The imposition of a barrier to foreign trade in a certain product will not only have an impact on foreign economies; it will also have an effect on the particular production and consumption mix at home. This implicit, yet fundamental, interdependence between the foreign and domestic economic environments is in fact the essence of the continuing dilemma facing the foreign economic policy maker.

Many, but not all, of the policy choices open to the foreign economic policy maker involve a balancing, or trade-off, between considerations of national security and domestic economic welfare. Conventional economic theory tells us that, generally speaking, free trade among the nations of the world will maximize *world* economic welfare by maximizing world production. In a world of scarce resources, free trade would tend to lead to the most efficient world allocation of these resources. From a purely national point of view, of course, this is not always the case. Indeed, the theory of the optimum tariff has shown that countries with inherent monopoly power in world trade may well maximize their *national* economic welfare by restricting trade below its free trade levels, thereby turning the terms of trade against other nations. But rarely would the pursuit of policies designed simply to maximize monopoly power ever lead a country to embargo, say, the export of a "strategic" product to another nation-state. Yet this particular policy might appear "optimal" from the standpoint of "national security." Hence, policies pursued solely in the name of national security may work at cross purposes to policies pursued with the single aim of maximizing national economic welfare.

Drawing on some earlier work by Harry Johnson,[6] which assumed that foreign economic policy makers take into account both *private* consumption goods and so-called *public* consumption goods in making their policy choices, Cohen has been led to a new definition of the objective of foreign economic policy: "The joint maximization of the state's current income and its net influence in international affairs."[7] In this and the following two chapters we attempt to concretize and operationalize this concept, using the theory of the optimum tariff as our framework.

The Maximization Problem

It may be helpful to visualize these dual objectives of foreign economic policy in terms of a $(p + 1) \times (p + 1)$ "product flow" matrix as portrayed in Figure 1-1. For each product entering into international trade this matrix illustrates the quantity flow of that good among the $p + 1$ countries (Home, together with the p foreign countries, $j = 1 \ldots p$).[a] The model elaborated in this study will by and large be concerned with Home commercial policies directly affecting the other p countries; in other words, the first row and the first column of the matrix. We shall see, however, that such policies often have important implications for other elements; that is, trade among two or more foreign countries.

		Exports to			
		Home	$j = 1$	....	$j = p$
	Home				
	$j = 1$				
	.				
Imports from	.				
	.				
	$j = p$				

Figure 1–1

As we have suggested, national security is basically a function of national power or influence over other nations, and may be considered a "non-optional" collective consumption good, in the sense that each citizen of the nation-state has no choice but to partake "jointly of the benefits of any unit."[8] We further assume that national security is an increasing function of: (a) a nation's relative military strength—that is, its relative potential for successfully waging military warfare; and (b) a nation's relative potential for successfully waging economic warfare.[b] Emphasis is placed on "success" here, since the mere potential for warfare, whether military or economic, does not necessarily imply success in achieving the objective, which is increased national security.[9]

While national security is an inherently subjective concept, as mentioned, foreign economic policy making presumably is conducted on a basis of more

[a] The "flow" of products might also be represented in terms of ratios (e.g., imports as a proportion of gross national product) or in value terms.

[b] Obviously national security is also an inverse function of the degree of belligerence of other nations brought about by cultural, political, and other factors. Presumably foreign belligerence is, at least in general, subject to a nation's use or threatened use of military and economic warfare.

objective measures which are considered to be "proxies" of one kind or another for different aspects of national security. The national welfare maximization model elaborated in this chapter seeks to develop an analytical framework around such objective measures, which also may be defined as nonoptional collective goods. Once having set forth the form of our constrained maximization problem, we will proceed in the next chapter to develop and analyze the implications of this "joint maximization" problem for foreign trade policy.

Our welfare maximization model applies to a nation in which an essentially representative government, or benevolent dictator, assumes the responsibility for jointly maximizing national income and national security, subject to the constraint of decentralized economic decision making. That is, economic activity is assumed to be largely undertaken by individuals, entrepreneurs, and private corporations within the context of a market rather than a command economy. Domestic divergences between private and social valuations and costs are assumed either not to exist or to be corrected for through appropriate government imposed tax-subsidy devices.

The welfare maximization problem facing our foreign economic policy maker is based on the notion that he either explicitly or implicitly employs a social welfare *function* in arriving at policy decisions. This function may be visualized as a particular configuration (which we shall define only in general terms) of individual utility functions, each such utility function belonging to a separate citizen in our hypothetical nation-state, "Home." We shall assume that the policy maker has complete knowledge of each individual utility function; that is, he knows the particular indifference surface of each individual, or the personal trade-off that each person experiences among the numerous products and services he can purchase and the services he might render to his fellow citizens. There exists a trade-off among these goods and services because in a world of scarce resources one cannot consume more of everything indefinitely. The choice to consume more of product A means that one must consume somewhat less of product B. A person's "utility function" reflects his system of preferences among these products, indicating what his pattern of consumption would be at any given level of income and relative prices of these goods.[10] Furthermore, we shall assume that the policy maker's social welfare function is of the so-called *Paretian* type: that is, an increase in any one individual's utility (with everyone else's utility level remaining unchanged) increases the social welfare of the nation.[11]

We shall also assume that no *external effects* exist in domestic consumption. Very briefly, this means that each person's consumption preferences are independent of every other individual's particular utility configuration. The fact that you have a color television set presumably has no impact on my relative desire to consume the services of a color T.V. Obviously, this is a gross simplification of reality, but it allows us to formulate our model fairly simply, perhaps at no great risk of presenting misleading foreign economic policy implications. In the terminology of theoretical welfare economics, the overall framework within which our model is formulated, this assumption about the absence of external effects, together with the fact that we have postulated a *Paretian* social welfare function, enables us to derive trade policy rules which are independent of interpersonal comparisons.[12] Other assumptions concerning the social welfare function are spelled out in Appendix A.

We have mentioned that various products or "goods" enter into each individual's utility function. Our concern is not limited, however, to the *private* goods of conventional economic analysis, such as apples, pipe tobacco, or television sets, the consumption of which by one person (or consumption unit such as a family) necessarily precludes their simultaneous consumption by other individuals. We are also interested in certain *collective* consumption goods, of which each individual in Home has no choice but to partake "jointly of the benefits of any unit." Specifically, we wish to take into account those collective good "proxies" which as we mentioned before can be said to represent certain national security considerations.

Let us assume, then, that in general four types of goods enter into an individual's utility function: private goods, collective goods bearing on the nation's relative military strength, collective goods reflecting economic warfare considerations, and other noneconomic "collective consumption" goods. We shall largely ignore the latter category for purposes of this study, although it is recognized that such collective goods can be quite relevant to the formulation of a national security policy.[c] Several such variables, however, will be briefly introduced later in this study.

While the types of goods defined below are meant to reflect major military and economic warfare considerations, the list is by no means to be taken as all-inclusive. The distinction between *offensive* and *defensive* economic warfare considerations rests upon whether the intent is to enhance Home's national security by means of inflicting economic injury on a foreign country (or by increasing Home's potential for inflicting such damage)—the *offensive* consideration; or whether it is intended to enhance Home's national security by means of defending against the other country's attempts to increase its own potential for inflicting economic damage on Home—the *defensive* consideration.

We have already briefly discussed the notion of private goods (such as apples, pipe tobacco, and television sets). Let us simply note that individual consumption of a given private good shall be designated as x_i^k, which denotes

[c] Such domestic collective goods as improvement of the environment, and urban and mass transport considerations, which underlie the present discussion in the United States of "priorities," obviously do impinge upon the formation of policies relating to military preparedness and economic warfare.

the consumption in the current time period of the ith private good by the kth individual, and where we may imagine that there are n such goods ($i = 1, \ldots, n$) and s individuals in Home ($k = 1, \ldots, s$). Furthermore, we follow the postulates of conventional demand theory by assuming that the kth individual receives diminishing *positive* marginal utility from his consumption of the ith good. That is to say, as he consumes more and more of this good, he may desire even further consumption, but as it is always at the expense of consuming some other good, the marginal utility received from consuming incremental units of the ith good diminishes.

We shall designate the consumption of a collective good such as a tank or military aircraft by x_h^k, which denotes the consumption in the current period of the services of the hth *military* good by the kth individual, and where we may imagine that there exist m such military goods ($h = 1, \ldots, m$). We assume that these military goods are *collective* goods, because (if we ignore the unfortunate practice of private stockpiling of weapons), the national security "services" rendered by these goods are simultaneously available to all people living in Home. As with private goods, we postulate that the kth individual receives diminishing *positive* marginal utility from consuming military goods. One might imagine particular situations in which a person receives either negative utility or increasing positive utility from such consumption, but these shall be considered as exceptional cases.

We should also note here the basic difference between so-called private and collective consumption goods. For the kth and $(k + 1)$th persons, their consumption of the ith private good and their marginal utilities from such consumption may, and in general, will be different. But for collective goods, while the utilities that different individuals may attribute to equivalent consumption of the collective good may differ, their consumption is equal. That is to say, each individual receives in an objective sense the same amount of "security" from his nation's military establishment (or other collective good), but individuals will in general differ as to the relative value they place on the existence of these armaments (or other national security "proxies").

Similarly, other nation-states also maintain military establishments, to which individuals in Home are not oblivious. Indeed, in those cases in which the jth foreign country is perceived as either a threat to Home's national security or as an important ally, the existence of a military potential in that country is unlikely to be a matter of indifference to the Home citizenry. This phenomenon is an example of an *international* external effect in consumption;[13] that is, where foreign acquisition of some military weapon has some impact on how individuals in Home perceive their own utility. We shall designate this external effect, or alternatively collective good when perceived from the standpoint of a citizen of Home, as y_{hj}^k, which denotes the acquisition in the current period of the hth military good in the jth foreign country ($j = 1, \ldots, p$) as it enters the utility function of the kth individual in Home.

In this case we assume that the kth individual experiences increasing *negative* marginal utility from the consumption of military goods in the jth country, when that country is considered an "enemy." Basically this means that our Home citizen receives ever greater dissatisfaction from marginal increments to the jth country's stockpile of the hth military good.[d]

Offensive and Defensive Economic Warfare

Turning to the collective goods that may be said to reflect economic warfare considerations, we shall limit ourselves to discussing five such considerations. The first three may be said to be *offensive* in nature, in the sense described earlier. The other two reflect *defensive* thinking.

We have already discussed the external effect in international consumption arising from acquisition by the jth foreign country of the hth military good. But we may also imagine that the consumption in an "enemy" country of certain nominally nonmilitary goods, such as food, clothing, and equipment and vehicles used for civilian purposes, may well cause dissatisfaction in Home. If it is hoped, for example, that deprivation of certain basic consumer goods among the jth country's population may weaken their resolve to support their government, which is hostile to Home, individuals in Home may come to experience increased satisfaction at such deprivation. More formally, we may designate aggregate consumption of the ith nonmilitary good in the jth country as y_{ij}, and y_{ij}^k would represent the presence of this consumption in the kth individual's utility function.[14] Once again we assume that our kth person in Home experiences increasing *negative* marginal utility from aggregate consumption of the ith good in the jth country.[e] Similarly, with respect to the $(j + 1)$th "friendly" country, which might be vulnerable to economic warfare or subversion as practiced by the jth country, the kth individual in Home might experience diminishing *positive* utility from $(j + 1)$th consumption of certain goods, including, obviously, military goods.

---

[d] If the jth foreign country is considered an ally of Home, the kth individual would be expected to experience diminishing *positive* marginal utility from an increase in the jth country's military establishment. But it is also possible that, to the extent that a foreign "enemy" can only build its military strength at the cost of seriously depleting its capacity for consumer goods production, Home citizenry may also experience increasing (or possibly diminishing) *positive* marginal utility from that country's acquisition of military materials. It is assumed in this study, however, that the fear of increased enemy military strength will outweigh this latter consideration. We should also note that our assumption of increasing negative marginal utility for the y_{hj} collective good introduces an apparent asymmetry between this case and that of x_h. This apparent asymmetry would appear to be realistic, however, as explained in footnote c in Appendix A.

[e] See footnote d.

Another offensive economic warfare consideration that might be directed towards an "enemy" country can be defined in terms of the foreign country's earnings of foreign exchange. Because the enemy can augment its supplies of both military and nonmilitary goods through international trade, its potential for importing such goods will be less, the less foreign exchange it is able to earn on the world marketplace.[f] Hence Home citizens concerned with the *j*th country's acquisition of additional military goods and increased consumption of nonmilitary goods could naturally be expected to derive increasing *negative* marginal utility from that country's earning of foreign exchange. We shall designate f_{ij}^k (or f_{hj}^k for military goods) as the *j*th country's earnings of foreign exchange from the sale abroad of its domestic production of the *i*th good, as they enter the *k*th individual's preference function.

A third offensive economic warfare consideration involves the notion of a foreign country's dependence, or potential dependence, upon Home as a supplier of the *i*th good. The thought here would be that the greater this dependence, the greater the political leverage which Home might be able to achieve over the *j*th country, by perhaps threatening to cut its supply of a critical product.[15] This would apply particularly to various raw materials critical to the *j*th country's production effort, but also might be relevant as well to various intermediate or even consumer goods. In this case we shall designate the collective good entering into the *k*th individual's utility function as s_{ij}^k (or s_{hj}^k for military goods), where s_{ij} is the ratio of *j*th country imports of the *i*th good from Home, to total *j*th consumption of the *i*th good. The variable s_{ij} would therefore be a measure of the relative dependence of the *j*th country on imports of the *i*th good to meet its domestic consumption. We shall assume that our *k*th individual experiences diminishing *positive* marginal utility from his "consumption" of s_{ij}^k, when the *j*th country is either considered an "enemy" or for other reasons Home wishes to use this dependence as a means for political leverage. In other words, his satisfaction rises with each incremental increase in *j*th dependence upon Home, but at a diminishing rate.

Alternatively, this same s_{ij}^k consideration might be operative when the *j*th country is a friendly or neutral nation which imports the *i*th product from both Home and the $(j + 1)$th country, the latter being construed as Home's "enemy." In this case Home citizens may see a political advantage to be gained if *j*th dependence upon the $(j + 1)$th nation as a source of supply for the *i*th good is reduced. Such lessened dependence would likely lead to worsened terms of trade for the $(j + 1)$th country, as effective demand for its

---

[f] Alternatively, if the *j*th country maintains a flexible foreign exchange rate, its purchasing power in terms of other currencies will decline if its demand for foreign currencies exceeds the sum of its foreign exchange earnings, depletion of foreign exchange reserves, and net capital inflow.

export of the *i*th good would diminish. Provided $(j+1)$th supply falls with a decline in price, this would reduce $(j+1)$th earnings of foreign exchange available for the purchase of necessary imports. Reduced reliance on the $(j+1)$th country as a source of supply for the *i*th product could be triggered by an increase in the s_{ij} ratio, as Home exports of this good replace the $(j+1)$th product in *j*th consumption. Therefore, to the extent that an increase in s_{ij} implied a reduction in *j*th reliance on $(j+1)$th exports, the *k*th individual in Home could be expected to experience diminishing *positive* marginal utility from increases in this ratio.

Turning now to *defensive* economic warfare considerations, individuals in Home may experience dissatisfaction from Home's becoming increasingly dependent upon some *j*th foreign country for its supply of either military goods or particular nonmilitary goods. This kind of concern would be expected to be greatest with respect to certain raw materials and fuels, the termination of supply of which might cause serious domestic production and consumption bottlenecks.[16] Fearing the possible "blackmail" opportunities such dependence might give certain foreign countries, Home citizenry could be expected to want to steer clear of such situations. This *defensive* national security consideration may be designated by the collective good m_{ij}^k (or m_{hj}^k in the case of military goods), where m_{ij} is the ratio of Home imports of the *i*th good from the *j*th country, to total domestic production of the *i*th good.[g] Fearing greater dependence, past a certain point, the *k*th individual is assumed to experience increasing *negative* marginal utility from increases in this ratio.

A second defensive consideration might apply to certain of Home's export products. For instance, if the production of the *i*th good in Home, which is also a major exportable, is an important source of employment in Home, many people may fear Home's becoming too dependent upon a certain foreign market for sales of this good, particularly if it is believed that this foreign country might try to use such dependence as a basis for exerting political influence over Home. We may designate the collective good operative in such a situation as e_{ij}^k (or e_{hj}^k in the case of military goods), where e_{ij}^k is the ratio of Home exports of the *i*th product to the *j*th foreign market, to total Home consumption of this good.[h] As with the previous *defensive* consideration, we assume in this case that the *k*th individual, over a certain range of values for e_{ij}, experiences increasing *negative* marginal utility from increases in this ratio. In other words, as dependence upon a given foreign export

---

[g] Alternatively, we might define m_{ij} as the ratio of Home imports of the *i*th good from the *j*th country, to total domestic consumption of this good.

[h] Alternatively, we might define e_{ij} as the ratio of Home imports of the *i*th good from the *j*th country, to total domestic production of this good.

market rises, so does the dissatisfaction of our kth Home citizen, and at an increasing rate.

This concludes our brief summary of the various "goods," private and collective, which in general may be said to enter into individuals' utility schemes, and hence into the foreign economic policy maker's social welfare function. In this way we have sought to operationalize the notion that our policy maker is concerned with jointly maximizing economic welfare (as represented by private goods) and national security (as reflected in our collective good "proxies" for national security considerations). Each of these collective good "proxies" is an economic variable, or a ratio of economic variables, defined in terms of conventional economic magnitudes such as production, consumption, exports, and imports. This enables us to express the welfare maximization problem by means of measurable variables. Only the utility parameters relating to each of these variables remain impervious to direct estimation.

The foreign economic policy maker is assumed to maximize his social welfare function subject to the usual constraints embodied in conventional optimum tariff theory. These constraints take the form of domestic production and balance of payments limitations. These constraints or functions are rigorously defined in the appendixes to this book, so we shall only briefly discuss them here.

Home's production (or domestic transformation) function defines the various production "possibilities" existing in Home with respect to our m military and n nonmilitary goods. Since resources employed in the production of, say, the ith good cannot also be simultaneously used in the production of the $(i + 1)$th good (except, of course, in the case of joint products), the domestic transformation function simply suggests the notion of the "opportunity costs" associated with the production of the $m + n$ products. As discussed in Appendix B, we assume diminishing returns to varying factor proportions in the production process. Furthermore, the simplifying assumption is made that the overall transformation function in Home is independent of the domestic distribution of wealth.

The foreign trade transformation function is basically a budget constraint. That is, it is defined simply by the condition that the value of current Home imports less the value of current Home exports must equal the sum of the net capital inflow into Home in the current period and the net decrease in that period of Home's international monetary reserve position. In other words, if we assume that net capital inflow is zero and Home's reserve position remains constant, trade (in money terms) must balance. Certain "curvature" assumptions regarding foreign trade are also made, as explained in Appendix B.

To summarize, the aim of the foreign economic policy maker is to maximize Home social welfare. We have assumed for simplicity that Home welfare is a function solely of conventional economic welfare considerations and certain national security concerns. This function is to be maximized subject to the resources at the disposal of the policy maker; or put differently, subject to the various domestic production possibilities and the balance of payments constraint. This particular constrained maximization problem differs from the problem posed in conventional optimum tariff analysis in two fundamental respects. First, we have allowed national security collective goods to enter explicitly into individual utility functions. Second, we have allowed for the possibility that Home citizens may want to differentiate among foreign countries, precisely because of their national security concerns, rather than to perceive these countries as merely a single, aggregated foreign market. In the next chapter we shall explore the implications of this double departure from conventional optimum tariff theory, and its meaning in terms of formulating an optimum foreign trade policy in a national security context.

2 Optimum Trade Policy in a Discriminatory Context

We have chosen to examine the formulation of optimum foreign trade policies in a national security context within the conventional welfare maximization framework known as "optimum tariff theory." This form of analysis does not, however, refer to tariffs in the narrow sense of import duties. On the contrary, tariff is used in a very general sense of a tax (or negative tax), and includes the possibility of import duties, export taxes, and subsidies on either imports or exports. Moreover, we shall mean by optimum tariffs (or taxes) both explicit import and export taxes or subsidies, as well as implicit taxes such as quotas, embargoes, or other so-called "nontariff barriers" to foreign trade. The point of view adopted here is therefore that of the economist rather than the customs authority or accountant: implicit as well as explicit taxes are considered as components of a nation's commercial policy.

We begin by briefly reviewing the implications for foreign economic policy making of conventional optimum tariff theory. Subsequently, as a prelude to our later discussion of policy making in a national security context, we will examine the optimal trade policy rules for a nation which finds itself in a position of trading with foreign markets that do not trade directly with one another. This is a somewhat unrealistic situation, but the implications it has for optimal trade policy making will be instructive, given our interest in the national security issue. Finally, we shall turn to the case in which we choose to make policy differentiations among foreign markets, and examine in some detail the particular conditions that the discriminating nation (our "Home") must satisfy in order to achieve its national security policy objectives.

For purposes of simplifying the exposition we shall confine ourselves throughout this chapter to discussing just one of our national security variables, y_{ij}^k, which, it will be recalled, represents jth foreign consumption of the ith product, as it enters the kth individual's utility function in Home as an *international external effect* in consumption. (The trade policy implications of the other national security collective goods will be pursued in Chapter 3.) Once again we must make some simplifying assumptions that will enable us to derive the fairly simple mathematical conditions (see Appendixes C and D) underlying the "rules" we derive for optimal trade policy in this and the following chapter. Just how realistic these assumptions are, and what effects their violation may have on our optimal trade policy rules, is discussed at several points later in the book. For the present, suffice it to say that we assume three things: (1) that foreign countries do not retaliate through trade policy against Home's economic warfare; (2) that none of our derived trade policy rules are in actuality unrealizable—that is, "second best" considerations do not apply; and (3) that the optimum tariff (export tax) proceeds are redistributed within Home in some optimal manner—in other words, in accordance with the particular dictates of Home's social welfare function.

Conventional Optimum Tariff Theory

Optimum tariff theory has traditionally been formulated in terms of one country's (Home) facing a single rest-of-the-world market. Graaff's mathematical formulation of optimum tariff theory also takes this approach.[1] This is of course quite reasonable, given the underlying assumption of one world market in each product. Under this assumption any one nation or group of countries faces a single foreign *offer curve*, which is derived by adding together the offer curves of all other nations at each terms of trade. Furthermore, the conventional analysis assumes that individual utility functions include solely *private* goods; the type of international external effect or collective good we have been discussing is not considered. The maximization problem facing the trade policy maker is therefore quite straightforward: he must maximize the social welfare function (which indirectly includes only private goods) subject to the domestic and foreign trade transformation functions discussed in Chapter 1; except that with respect to the balance of payments constraint, Home is considered to face only *one* foreign market, meaning only one foreign price for each product.

As is shown in detail in Appendix C, Home welfare can only be maximized under the assumptions of conventional optimum tariff theory, if the following condition is satisfied with respect to each pair of private goods ($i = 1, \ldots, n$):

$$\left\{\begin{array}{l}\text{Ratio of}\\ \text{domestic}\\ \text{prices}\\ (i\text{th and}\\ i+1\text{th}\\ \text{products}\end{array}\right\} = \left\{\begin{array}{l}\text{Ratio of } k\text{th}\\ \text{individual's}\\ \text{marginal}\\ \text{utilities}\\ (i\text{th and}\\ i+1\text{th}\\ \text{products)}\end{array}\right\} = \left\{\begin{array}{l}\text{Ratio of}\\ \text{marginal}\\ \text{social costs}\\ \text{of domestic}\\ \text{production}\\ (i\text{th and}\\ i+1\text{th}\\ \text{products)}\end{array}\right\} = \left\{\begin{array}{l}\text{Ratio of}\\ \text{marginal}\\ \text{social costs}\\ \text{of importing}\\ \text{(marginal}\\ \text{social revenue}\\ \text{from exporting)}\\ (i\text{th and}\\ i+1\text{th products)}\end{array}\right\} \qquad (1)$$

Provided the second order conditions are also fulfilled (see Appendix B), satisfaction of the above condition (1), also known as the "Pareto optimality" condition, will assure the attainment of the social welfare maximum.

For example, let us assume that the ratio of domestic prices (which we shall assume also equals the ratio of kth marginal utilities and the ratio of marginal costs for the ith and $(i + 1)$th goods) is greater than the ratio of the marginal social costs of importing these two goods; in other words, we assume that the domestic price ratio exceeds the ratio of foreign prices (after tariffs) for the ith and $(i + 1$th) products. Clearly, Home welfare can be increased by substituting *relatively* cheaper foreign supplies of the ith good for domestic production, and concentrating Home resources to a greater extent on the production of the relatively less expensive (at Home) $(i + 1)$th good. This shift in domestic production will mean, under our assumption of diminishing returns in industry, increased marginal costs of production in the $(i + 1)$th sector relative to the ith industry. This process of substitution by imports of the ith good in domestic consumption, and reallocation of Home resources into production of the $i + 1$th product, will continue until the domestic price ratio and ratio of marginal costs has declined to equal the now rising relative costs of ith imports. At this point there is no further incentive to change the patterns of consumption and production.

Given our interest in foreign trade policy making, however, we should examine a little more closely the ratio of marginal social costs (or marginal social revenues) arising from Home foreign trade. As intimated above, in the case of imports, the marginal social cost of importing equals the sum of the foreign price of the good in question and the tariff levied on this product by Home. We may therefore represent the ratio of marginal costs of importing as:

$$\frac{p_i(1 + t_i)}{p_{i+1}(1 + t_{i+1})} \tag{2}$$

where p_i and p_{i+1} are the foreign prices for the ith and $(i + 1)$th goods, respectively, and t_i and t_{i+1} the Home percentage tariff rates levied on the respective foreign prices.

The parameters t_i and t_{i+1} represent the "optimum" tax rates Home should impose on its foreign trade in order to maximize domestic welfare. But as demonstrated in Appendix C, these parameters are actually quite complicated terms which are composed of various foreign elasticities and cross elasticities of supply and demand for these products, as well as reflecting the relative volume of trade in these various goods. Because of the latter fact, but also because elasticities are in general a function of the volume of trade, our tax rates also will differ, in general, for each level of trade.

It can be easily shown that the *lower* the foreign price elasticity of supply (or demand) for the ith product, the *higher* the import duty (or export tax) rate that Home should impose on the movement of this good across the national frontier.[a] In general, the foreign price elasticities faced by Home will be lower the larger is Home, as a producer and consumer, relative to the

[a] See Appendix C, and Graaff.[2]

world market as a whole. In fact as Scitovsky[3] has shown, the theory of optimum tariffs (or export taxes) is analogous to the theory of the profit maximizing monopolistic-monopsonistic enterprise, as developed in the theory of the firm. Just as the firm should optimally reduce output to a point in the elastic range of its demand curve (or supply curve of its factors) at which its marginal revenue (or marginal cost of purchases) is equal to its marginal cost of production; so Home, with respect to those products for which foreign elasticities are not infinitely large, should reduce its exports (or imports) to a point in the elastic portion of its "foreign offer curve," where the marginal social revenue from exporting the ith good (or marginal social cost of importing the ith product) is equal to the marginal cost of producing this good domestically. By restricting trade below free trade levels Home will maximize its own national economic welfare, although world welfare may thereby be reduced.

"Natural" Separation of Foreign Markets

As a basis for interpreting the solution of the welfare maximization problem arising from the inclusion of our so-called "national security" considerations in Home utility functions, it will be instructive to also examine briefly the case of optimum tariff theory when at least one foreign market (the jth) is isolated from other foreign markets. We shall subsume these other countries together under the $(j + 1)$th foreign market. It is of course difficult to imagine a real-world analogue of this case, because it requires a situation to exist in which Home trades with both the jth and $(j + 1)$th markets, but in which for some "natural" (as opposed to "policy") reason, these two markets have no commercial intercourse with one another.[b]

As is discussed in more detail in Appendix C, our assumption of isolation of the jth and $(j + 1)$th markets means that the "rest-of-the-world offer curve" assumption of conventional optimum tariff analysis no longer holds. The "i" and "$i + 1$" subscripts in expression (2) are therefore now replaced by "ij" and "$i + 1j$" subscripts. Furthermore, we have a new optimal condition; namely, that the following equation must be satisfied for each ith good:

$$\frac{p_{ij}}{p_{ij+1}} = \frac{(1 + t_{ij+1})}{(1 + t_{ij})} \tag{3}$$

[b] A slightly more realistic but weaker assumption would be that the jth and $(j + 1)$th markets are not "isolated," but that transportation costs between these two markets are so much greater than between each of them and Home, as to allow Home to buy and sell at different prices in each market for the same good without fear of foreign arbitrageurs' wiping out the entire differential.

Home now faces two distinct foreign markets, and the foreign price elasticities and cross elasticities in these markets will not, in general, be equal in both markets. Consequently, neither will the optimal foreign trade tax rates (t_{ij} and t_{ij+1}), which are a function of these elasticities, in general be equivalent with respect to trade in a given product with these two markets. For instance, we would expect that for many products the price elasticities of supply and demand of a smaller foreign market would be less than the corresponding elasticities for a relatively large market.

Just as in the conventional optimum tariff case, we may make an analogy here to a special case of the theory of the firm. The analogy is to the profit-maximizing behavior of the enterprise which faces two entirely separate markets for its output (or inputs). It has been demonstrated that optimally such a firm should behave as a *discriminating* monopolist-monopsonist, setting different prices in each market so as to equate marginal revenue in each market (or the marginal cost of each source of supply) to its overall marginal cost of production (or overall marginal revenue).[4]

Similarly, Home should act in this case as a discriminating monopolist-monopsonist in foreign trade, in general imposing different optimum foreign trade taxes in each foreign market, so as to equate overall domestic marginal cost with the marginal social revenue from exporting to (marginal social cost of importing from) each market. In analogy to the profit-maximizing firm, the welfare-maximizing nation will, if it is an exporter of the *i*th good, levy a higher export tax rate in the market with the less-price-elastic excess demand for that good, in effect charging a higher price in that market. Similarly, if Home imports the *i*th good, it will levy a higher tariff rate in the market with the less-price-elastic excess supply of that good, in effect paying a lower price in that market.[c] Following a discriminatory optimum tariff policy, Home will achieve a higher level of social welfare than by following the policy of simple monopoly-monopsony in foreign trade suggested in the conventional analysis.

The private monopolist can only successfully discriminate among markets if there is less than perfect arbitrage between them. Similarly, Home can only successfully receive (or pay) different prices in the *j*th and $(j + 1)$th markets if there is not perfect arbitrage (see footnote b). In the case considered here arbitrage will not occur, even by transshipment of goods through the $(j + 1)$th market, because we have assumed perfect isolation of the *j*th and $(j + 1)$th markets. As mentioned, it is difficult to imagine a real-world analogue of this

[c] This may be seen, for example, in equation (3). If the price elasticity of supply in the *j*th market is less than that in the $(j + 1)$th (meaning that t_{ij} is greater than t_{ij+1}), then the foreign price paid by Home in importing from the $(j + 1)$th market will be greater than from the *j*th country. This follows from the fact that Home will be imposing a relatively higher tariff rate (t_{ij}) on imports from the *j*th country, thereby depressing *j*th terms of trade relative to $(j + 1)$th terms of trade.

case, in which two foreign markets are somehow "naturally" isolated from one another but not from Home, in the absence of political considerations designed to insure isolation. This more interesting and (to us) relevant case of the political decision to isolate the two markets is the subject of the next section.

Policy Differentiation Among Foreign Markets

We shall now assume that initially the jth and $j+1$th markets constitute *one* foreign market from the standpoint of Home. We shall further assume, however, that the national security considerations outlined in Chapter 1 are now operative in the kth individual's utility function. So as to simplify our exposition of this case, let us suppose for the time being that the only operative national security variable is the level of consumption of the ith good abroad, y_{ij} $(j = 1, \ldots, p)$. Graaff allowed for this phenomenon in his later general mathematical formulation of optimum tariff theory, in which he defined foreign consumption of the ith good as "y_i".[5] But as we have seen, it seems doubtful that individuals in Home would be affected equally by foreign consumption, regardless of where it takes place. In other words, individuals in Home may in general be expected to geographically differentiate among foreign consumption as a result of various cultural, psychological, and national security considerations. Our maximization problem now is that which we developed in Chapter 1. It differs from conventional optimum tariff analysis in that collective goods enter individual utility functions and general provision is made for differentiation among foreign markets. It is unlike the problem just discussed, the "natural" isolation of foreign markets, in that no such natural isolation is assumed and it allows for collective goods.

A detailed derivation of the so-called "first order conditions" for this problem, which may be interpreted in nonmathematical terms as optimal "trade policy rules," is to be found in Appendix C. These rules are summarized in expressions (4) and (5) below:

$$\left.\begin{array}{l}\text{Ratio of marginal}\\ \text{social revenue from}\\ \text{exporting (}i\text{th and}\\ i+1\text{th goods for}\\ \text{each }j\text{th market)}\end{array}\right\} = \frac{p_{ij}(1+t_{ij})}{p_{i+1j}(1+t_{i+1j})} + \sum_{k=1}^{s}\left[\begin{array}{l}\text{Relative marginal}\\ \text{utility (disutility)}\\ \text{to }k\text{th individual of}\\ \text{increases in }y_{ij}\end{array}\right] \qquad (4)$$

$$\frac{p_{ij}}{p_{ij+1}} = \frac{(1+t_{ij+1})}{(1+t_{ij})}\left[1 - \sum_{k=1}^{s}\left[\begin{array}{l}\text{Relative marginal utility}\\ \text{(disutility) to }k\text{th indi-}\\ \text{vidual of increases in }y_{ij}\end{array}\right]\right] \qquad (5)$$

In both expressions the summed $\left(\sum_{k=1}^{s}\right)$ term reflects the fact that the national security variable "y_{ij}" is now assumed to enter Home utility functions, and that the full effect of this collective good consideration is the result of the sum over all s persons in Home of its impact on each of these citizens individually. Some of these citizens may derive disutility from increases in y_{ij}; others utility; still others may be indifferent. Only if the net result of summing over all individuals is negative is the summed term in (4) and (5) negative.[6]

Except for the presence of this summed term, the ratio of marginal social costs (or revenue) in foreign trade for the ith and $(i + 1)$th goods in expression (4) is identical to that for the previous case of "natural" separation of foreign markets. Similarly, expression (5) is identical to our earlier equation (3), except that once again there is a summed term reflecting the presence of the "y_{ij}" national security consideration.

The effect of the summed national security term is to imply, in general, a different set of optimal tax rates on Home trade than for the previous situations when Home was optimally to act either as a simple monopolist (conventional optimum tariff theory) or a discriminating monopolist ("natural" separation of foreign markets). Let us take, for example, the case in which the jth country is considered by a predominant number of Home citizens to be an "enemy," and in which under normal conditions Home would export the ith product to the jth market. The summed terms in both (4) and (5) are now negative.

Expression (4) tells us that Home must realize an even *higher* price ratio in the jth market $\left(\frac{p_{ij}}{p_{i+1j}}\right)$ than previously, in order to maintain the equivalence of the ratio of marginal revenue from foreign trade to the ratios of domestic prices and marginal costs for the ith and $i + 1$th goods (see expression (1)). This means that the export tax rate ratio for this market between the ith and $i + 1$th goods must be even *higher* than when this national security consideration is absent.

Of even greater interest is the implication following from expression (5). A negative summed term means that the expression in brackets is positive. Therefore the price ratio (and hence the relative export tax rates[d]) for the ith good as between the jth and $j + 1$th markets must be *higher* than that implied by a simple policy of discriminatory optimum export taxes; that is, higher than the price ratio based solely on different values for t_{ij} and t_{ij+1} arising from isolation of the two foreign markets. (The same kind of argument holds for the case in which the ith good is normally imported by Home from the jth country.)

---

[d] A positive export tax rate is represented as a negative t_{ij}.

It will be recalled, however, that we are assuming in this case that Home initially faces one foreign market, a realistic assumption. But in order to achieve a discrepancy between p_{ij} and p_{ij+1} as now implied by expression (5), Home must somehow break up the *one* world market so as to be able to sell at different prices in the jth and $j+1$th markets. If Home can eliminate arbitrage between these markets, this will also mean that in general t_{ij} will differ from t_{ij+1}, as explained in the previous section. Home's ultimate discriminating policy will therefore consist of two elements: first, the discriminating response to the national security variable, which is to separate the two foreign markets from another; and second, the discriminating monopolist-monopsonist's response to the new effective t_{ij}–t_{ij+1} differential arising from the initial discriminating action.

Our assumption that the jth and $(j+1)$th markets are not "naturally" isolated, together with our demonstration that Home must eliminate arbitrage activities between these markets in the ith good, leads to the conclusion that Home must prohibit transshipment of its exports and imports of that good through the $(j+1)$th market. If Home and jth production of the ith good happen to be perfect substitutes in $(j+1)$th consumption for $(j+1)$th production of this good, however, transshipment prohibitions are not enough to guarantee that expression (5) will be satisfied. Home must also cause the $(j+1)$th market to cease *all* trade with the jth market in the target good, since theoretically $(j+1)$th arbitrageurs would otherwise see the opportunity for profiting by the p_{ij}–p_{ij+1} differential by buying in the cheaper foreign market (Home or jth) and selling these foreign made goods domestically. This would free domestic $(j+1)$th supplies for export to the foreign market with the higher prevailing price. Competition among arbitrageurs would eventually eliminate the p_{ij}–p_{ij+1} differential and cause Home's discriminatory optimum tariff policy to be ineffective.[e]

The foregoing transshipment requirement is in theory not too difficult to achieve, since the controls required impinge directly upon Home importers and exporters in the form of certifications of origin or destination.[f] The isolation requirement (forcing the $(j+1)$th market to cease all trade in the ith good with the jth market), however, would probably be not only more difficult of achievement; it would constitute an extraterritorial extension of Home's sovereignty. Furthermore, it is difficult to see how in practice Home could prevail upon the $(j+1)$th country(ies) not to trade with the jth country in the ith good, while maintaining trade itself with the latter country subject

[e] The requirement that the $(j+1)$th market cease all trade with the jth market in the ith good rests on the assumption that any country will not be both an importer and exporter of the ith good.

[f] In practice, however, various techniques for smuggling the target goods into the jth country would undoubtedly be devised.

to the new higher optimal tariff rate. This would probably be a politically (not to say morally) indefensible position, which for practical purposes would likely mean that Home would also have to cease trade with the jth country in the target good.[g]

These considerations suggest that the successful implementation of a discriminatory optimum tariff policy for national security reasons depends to a great extent on either (a) extremely close cooperation with Home by all countries that are not targets of discrimination, or (b) significantly different production capabilities and consumer taste patterns between the discriminating country on the one hand and friendly (but noncooperative) countries on the other. In the first case the *isolation* requirement, which as explained would logically result in more or less of a worldwide embargo on trade with the jth country in the target goods, could be easily satisfied. In the second case, such an extreme policy would be unnecessary because of significant product differentiation; only the less demanding *transshipment* requirement would have to be met.

A Dynamic Consideration

We have shown that if there is imperfect substitution in $(j + 1)$th consumption as between $(j + 1)$th production of the ith good on the one hand and jth or Home production of the ith good on the other, Home can successfully follow a discriminating optimum tariff policy by merely satisfying the transshipment requirement. The isolation requirement need not be fulfilled because arbitrage possibilities will not arise within the $(j + 1)$th economy.

It should be observed, however, that Home's ability to discriminate against the jth market at some given level of trade is *potentially* more fragile in this case than in the event of perfect isolation of the jth and $(j+ 1)$th markets from one another. This is because over time $(j+ 1)$th demand for jth exports of the ith good or $(j + 1)$th supply of jth imports of the ith product may rise considerably. As demonstrated in some detail in the final section of Appendix C, increased $(j + 1)$th demand (or supply) in the ith good with respect to trade with the jth market also implies greater elasticity of jth supply (or demand) with respect to trade with Home. This is because the increased demand (supply) of $(j+ 1)$th consumers (or producers) will be transmitted through trade to jth producers (or consumers), as they relate to commerce with Home. The more elastic is jth supply and demand, the lower will be Home's "optimum" tariff rates, and the less vulnerable will the jth

[g] For this reason it would probably be difficult for Home to "manufacture," say, national security arguments for the purpose of isolating the jth from the $(j + 1)$th market, with a view toward turning in its favor the terms of trade with both markets.

economy be to deterioration of its terms of trade as a result of Home's pursuit of an optimum tariff policy.

If Home's discriminatory policy is based primarily on the existence of "national security" considerations, such a policy will likewise be potentially vulnerable to growing magnitudes of demand or supply in the $(j+1)$th region. For example, let us assume that the operative national security consideration is y_{ij}. The rationale for Home's discriminatory high export tax on the export of the ith good to the jth country is, of course, to raise the price of this product in the jth market, thereby reducing jth consumption of this good, which in turn is assumed to give *positive* utility to individuals in Home. But now we assume that the $(j+1)$th market can produce significantly larger quantities of the ith good—more than needed for domestic consumption—at very little increase in price. The jth country can now substitute imports of this good from the $(j+1)$th market for high-priced Home production, allowing jth consumers to consume at a greater rate at a no higher, and perhaps lower average price level.

This higher price elasticity of jth demand is reflected of course in a lower t_{ij}; hence we now should have a lower "optimal" Home discriminatory export tax rate, if based solely on economic considerations. Nevertheless, if the marginal disutilities connected with y_{ij}^k of individuals in Home are not also now reduced, maintenance of an optimum export tax for this continued national security purpose will lead to diminished Home exports to the jth market, and possibly to an effective embargo on Home exports to this country. In other words, Home exporters may come to be priced out of the jth market.

In this situation, while withholding of Home supply still artificially raises prices and hence the costs of consumption on the jth market, Home loses its power to impose upon the jth country the full economic loss it would wish to effect. Meanwhile, other countries within the $(j+1)$th region are able to realize the traditional "gains from trade" with the jth country, partly at the expense of Home, which by abstaining from the market has thereby created an artificially high export price for the ith good, to the benefit of $(j+1)$th exporters.

A more flexible Home response to increased foreign price elasticities could take at least two forms. First, if individuals' marginal rates of dissatisfaction from increases over time in y_{ij} remained unchanged, Home could try to prevail on the $(j+1)$th region to cease all commerce with the jth country in the target goods. However, to the extent that the willingness of allies or nominally nonaligned countries to cooperate in such an embargo might be, among other considerations, a decreasing function of the elasticity of their own consumer demands and production capabilities, the likelihood of achieving the isolation requirement would be diminished relative to the initial position.

Alternatively, it is possible that Home citizens, when faced with rising levels of consumption in the jth market *in spite of* Home economic warfare, may choose to revise downward their marginal disutilities associated with y_{ij}. This may happen particularly as they come to realize that the *economic* loss to Home of following such a policy is to some extent being increasingly matched by economic gains to $(j + 1)$th countries, and that precisely for this reason the basic national security objective—to limit y_{ij}—is increasingly being frustrated.

3 The Pattern of Optimum Foreign Trade Taxes and Subsidies

Until now we have confined our attention for expository purposes to the case of a particular national security "consideration," namely that in which the utility of individuals in Home is affected by the level of consumption in the jth foreign country (y_{ij}). In the last chapter we used this particular national security variable to develop the theory of the nation as a discriminating monopolist-monopsonist in its commercial dealings with other nations.

We have seen that successful implementation of an optimum tariff policy that takes into account national security considerations, which in general vary from foreign country to foreign country, depends upon either: (1) "natural" isolation of the country which is the target of discrimination with respect to each good deemed to have strategic significance, should there be no product differentiation-by-origin in rest-of-world consumption; (2) agreement by allies to isolate the target country with respect to trade in each strategic good, again under the assumption of no product differentiation-by-origin; or (3) at least extraterritorial control over transshipment in the case of product diffentiation-by-origin in rest-of-world consumption.

While the fundamental solution to the maximization problem of Chapter 1 is similar for each of our national security variables (see Appendix D), it will be worthwhile briefly to examine in turn the implications of these different national security considerations before embarking on our evaluation, in Part II, of United States trade policies with respect to the socialist countries of Eastern Europe and Asia.

Relative Military Strength

Our model includes two variables bearing directly on relative military strength: (1) x_h^k, which represents collective consumption of the hth military good in Home; and (2) y_{hj}^k, which is consumption of the hth military good by the jth country and is also a collective consumption good from the standpoint of individuals in Home.

The variable y_{hj}^k and other collective good aspects of military goods (f_{hj}^k, s_{hj}^k, m_{hj}^k, and e_{hj}^k) are analogous to the collective goods y_{ij}^k, f_{ij}^k, s_{ij}^k, m_{ij}^k, and e_{ij}^k in their implications for an optimum trade policy. We shall therefore not discuss these implications separately, and shall restrict ourselves, with respect to military goods, to considering the collective good x_h^k. Ignoring other collective goods for the present, the interesting optimal conditions is:[a]

$$\sum_{k=1}^{s}\begin{bmatrix}\text{Relative marginal} \\ \text{utility (disutility)} \\ \text{to } k\text{th individual} \\ \text{of increases in } x_h\end{bmatrix} = \begin{cases}\text{Relative marginal} \\ \text{social costs of} \\ \text{domestic production} \\ \text{of } h\text{th military good.}\end{cases} \tag{6}$$

Since the hth good is a purely collective good,[b] however, there will be no price established for it in the competitive marketplace, and without government intervention this good will not be produced. Home policy makers, taking into account the summed term in expression (6), should optimally devise some taxation scheme for raising the sums necessary to subsidize production of the hth good at the level at which expression (6) will be satisfied. This situation is illustrated in more detail in Appendix D.

Before turning to economic warface considerations we should emphasize the fact that for any given good traded with a given target country, only one or two of these considerations will typically be operative. That is to say, most of the collective goods entering the kth individual's utility function will be characterized by total indifference: neither utility nor disutility will be associated with changes in value of these collective goods. Alternatively, slight marginal utility or disutility attached to these goods will be so small as to be dominated by the more "operative" national security consideration for that particular product-country combination. We shall do little violence to reality, therefore, by following the convenient path of taking up each economic warfare consideration separately.

Economic Warfare: Offensive

We have already discussed the offensive economic warfare consideration y_{ij}^k at length in Chapter 2. Let us merely make the final observation that if the summed terms in expressions (4) and (5) are significantly enough negative, pursuit of an optimum export tax policy will cause the price ratios $\frac{p_{ij}}{p_{i+1j}}$ and $\frac{p_{ij}}{p_{ij+1}}$ to become so high as to induce the jth country to cease entirely its import of the ith good from Home. The possibility of this occurring, of course, is greater the lower the price ratio $\frac{p_{ij}}{p_{i+1j}}$ at which the jth country

[a] See Appendix D for the algebraic formulation of this expression.

[b] Under our simplifying assumption that no private traders or consumers are able to uniquely consume units of this good.

becomes entirely self-sufficient (after taking into account excess supply of the $j+1$th market at each price ratio) in the ith good. Now let us take a more cursory look at the policy implications of the other offensive economic warfare considerations, since the basic analysis is similar to that involved with y_{ij}^k.

Our second offensive economic warfare variable was defined in terms of the foreign country's earnings of foreign exchange from its export to Home of the ith product, f_{ij}^k. As explained in Appendix D, the optimal policy conditions necessary for a welfare maximum in this case are similar to our earlier expressions (4) and (5):

$$\left.\begin{matrix}\text{Ratio of marginal}\\ \text{social costs of}\\ \text{importing (}i\text{th and}\\ i+1\text{th goods from}\\ \text{each }j\text{th market)}\end{matrix}\right\} = \frac{p_{ij}(1+t_{ij})}{p_{i+1j}(1+t_{i+1j})} - \sum_{k=1}^{s}\begin{bmatrix}\text{Relative}\\ \text{marginal}\\ \text{utility}\\ \text{(disutility)}\\ \text{to }k\text{th}\\ \text{individual}\\ \text{of increases}\\ \text{in } f_{ij}\end{bmatrix} \tag{7}$$

$$\frac{p_{ij}}{p_{ij+1}} = \frac{(1+t_{ij+1})}{(1+t_{ij})}\left[1+\sum_{k=1}^{s}\begin{bmatrix}\text{Relative marginal}\\ \text{utility (disutility)}\\ \text{to }k\text{th individual of}\\ \text{increases in } f_{ij}\end{bmatrix}\right] \tag{8}$$

It will be recalled that we postulated that in the situation in which the jth country is considered an "enemy," Home citizens would experience *negative* marginal utility from increases in jth foreign exchange earnings. Consequently, the summed terms in the above expressions will be negative. This implies that the price ratios $\frac{p_{ij}}{p_{i+1j}}$ and $\frac{p_{ij}}{p_{ij+1}}$ must be lower than otherwise in order to satisfy the basic optimality condition in expression (1) of Chapter 2. This further means that Home should now levy a *discriminatory, high tariff rate* on the ith good coming from the jth country, relative to the rate of duty on both the $(i+1)$th good imported from this market and the ith good entering Home from the $(j+1)$th region. Furthermore, the previously discussed transshipment or isolation requirements must be met, depending upon whether or not there is product differentiation-by-origin in $(j+1)$th consumption.

Should the negative summed terms in expressions (7) and (8) be significantly large, pursuit of an optimum tariff policy will cause the price ratios $\frac{p_{ij}}{p_{i+1j}}$ and $\frac{p_{ij}}{p_{ij+1}}$ to fall so low as to induce the jth country to cease altogether its export of the ith good to Home. The possibility of this occurring, of course, is greater the higher the price ratio $\frac{p_{ij}}{p_{i+1j}}$ at which the jth country will fully absorb (after taking into account the excess demand of the $(j+1)$th market at each price ratio) its own production of the ith good. We should also note in passing that the f_{ij}^k collective good, when operative as a utility consideration, will be *general* in its application. That is, we would expect that the kth individual would want to deprive the jth country of foreign exchange earnings from the sale of *any* good to Home, not just from the sale of particular goods, since the *product source* of these foreign exchange receipts would typically not have any effect on the jth country's being able to use such earnings for the import of strategic goods. In this sense f_{ij}^k differs radically from the other economic warface considerations incorporated in our model.

We turn now to the national security variable s_{ij}^k, which we defined in Chapter 1 as the relative dependence of the jth country on Home as a source of supply for the ith product. Once again, the optimal policy rules relating to this consideration may be illustrated by two conditions:

$$\left\{\begin{array}{l}\text{Ratio of marginal}\\ \text{social revenue}\\ \text{from exporting}\\ (i\text{th and } i+1\text{th}\\ \text{good to each } j\text{th}\\ \text{market})\end{array}\right\} = \frac{p_{ij}(1+t_{ij})}{p_{i+1j}(1+t_{i+1j})} + \sum_{k=1}^{s}\left[\begin{array}{l}\text{Relative mar-}\\ \text{ginal utility}\\ \text{(disutility) to}\\ k\text{th individual}\\ \text{of increases in}\\ s_{ij}\end{array}\right] \tag{9}$$

$$\frac{p_{ij}}{p_{ij+1}} = \frac{(1+t_{ij+1})}{(1+t_{ij})}\left[1 - \sum_{k=1}^{s}\left[\begin{array}{l}\text{Relative marginal}\\ \text{utility (disutility)}\\ \text{to } k\text{th individual}\\ \text{of increase in } s_{ij}\end{array}\right]\right] \tag{10}$$

In our earlier discussion of this national security consideration we suggested that individuals in Home might experience *positive* marginal utility from increases in s_{ij}, either because the jth country is considered an enemy or potential enemy, or because the jth country is a friendly country which Home citizens would like to see *less* dependent on the $(j+1)$th region for its imports.

In the event that s_{ij} results in positive utility, the summed terms in expressions (9) and (10) will likewise be positive. This implies that the price ratios $\frac{p_{ij}}{p_{i+1j}}$ and $\frac{p_{ij}}{p_{ij+1}}$ must be lower than otherwise in order to satisfy the basic optimality condition of expression (1). This means that Home should now exact a *discriminatory*, *lower* export tax (or possibly even grant an export subsidy) on the ith good when exported to the jth country, relative to the export tax levied on both the $(i+1)$th product exported to the jth market and the ith good when exported to the $(j+1)$th region.

Should this national security variable be operative in the second case mentioned above, namely when Home wishes to reduce the friendly or neutral jth country's dependence upon the unfriendly $(j+1)$th region, this policy of a discriminatory lower export tax on the ith good when sold to the jth market could be seen as "dumping" the $(j+1)$th market's export good on a third market in order to worsen the $(j+1)$th terms of trade.

Expression (10) reminds us once again that following such a discriminatory policy requires extraterritorial control over trade between the jth and the $(j+1)$th markets, either in the form of a general embargo on all trade in the ith good when there is no product differentiation-by-origin in jth consumption, or in the form of prohibition of transshipment when some product differentiation-by-origin exists.

Economic Warfare: Defensive

Our first *defensive* national security variable is m_{ij}^k, where m_{ij} represents Home's relative dependence upon the jth market as a source of supply for the ith product. It should be recognized that our definition of m_{ij}^k is somewhat arbitrary in that it could have been defined simply as $m_{ij}^k = X_i$, or equal to Home production of the ith good. In this case we would postulate that individuals in Home receive diminishing *positive* utility from increases in m_{ij}^k. Alternatively, m_{ij}^k could have been defined as equal to z_{ij}, the latter being Home's aggregate imports of the ith good from the jth country. In this case we would assume that Home citizens experience increasing *negative* utility from increases in z_{ij}.

Our definition of m_{ij}^k as being equal to $\frac{z_{ij}}{X_i}$, or the ratio of Home imports of the ith product from the jth country to Home output of this good, would appear to be a closer approximation, however, to the actual national security consideration that is likely to appear under most circumstances. The objective normally is not merely to increase domestic production of the ith product for its own sake. Neither is the goal to merely restrict or embargo imports of the ith good from the jth country. The national security objective is rather to minimize or at least reduce the *relative* importance of the jth country or region as a source of supply for the ith good.

This concern with the relative magnitudes of z_{ij} and X_i means that Home policy makers should now satisfy optimal conditions with respect to both the domestic economy and foreign trade. This of course is a departure from the earlier *offensive* economic warfare considerations, which implied new policy "rules" only in respect to the foreign trade sector:[1]

$$\begin{array}{l}\text{Relative domestic}\\\text{prices (}i\text{th and}\\ i+1\text{th goods)}\end{array} = \begin{array}{l}\text{Relative}\\\text{domestic}\\\text{marginal}\\\text{costs of}\\\text{production}\\\text{(}i\text{th and}\\ i+1\text{th goods)}\end{array} + \sum_{j=1}^{p}\sum_{k=1}^{s}\left[\begin{array}{l}\text{Relative}\\\text{marginal}\\\text{utility}\\\text{(disutility)}\\\text{to }k\text{th in-}\\\text{dividual of}\\\text{increase}\\\text{in } m_{ij}\end{array}\right] \qquad (11)$$

$$\begin{array}{l}\text{Ratio of mar-}\\\text{ginal social}\\\text{costs of im-}\\\text{porting (}i\text{th}\\\text{and } i+1\text{th}\\\text{goods from}\\\text{each }j\text{th market)}\end{array} = \frac{p_{ij}(1+t_{ij})}{p_{i+1j}(1+t_{i+1j})} - \sum_{k=1}^{s}\left[\begin{array}{l}\text{Relative}\\\text{marginal}\\\text{utility}\\\text{(disutility)}\\\text{to }k\text{th in-}\\\text{dividual of}\\\text{increase in } m_{ij}\end{array}\right] \qquad (12)$$

$$\frac{p_{ij}}{p_{ij+1}} = \frac{(1+t_{ij+1})}{(1+t_{ij})}\left[1+\sum_{k=1}^{s}\left[\begin{array}{l}\text{Relative marginal}\\\text{utility (disutility)}\\\text{to }k\text{th individual}\\\text{of increase in } m_{ij}\end{array}\right]\right] \qquad (13)$$

In our discussion of this national security variable we suggested that Home consumers will experience *negative* utility from increases in m_{ij}, particularly over a certain range of values for this ratio, for certain "strategic" goods. This would result in a negative value for the summed term in expressions (11) through (13). With respect to (11), which refers solely to relations in the domestic economy, this implies that at the optimum the ratio of domestic private marginal costs for the ith and $(i+1)$th products should be greater than the ratio of their relative domestic prices. The implications of expressions (12) and (13) are that the price ratios $\frac{p_{ij}}{p_{i+1j}}$ and $\frac{p_{ij}}{p_{ij+1}}$ must be lower than in the case of no national security considerations. As we demonstrate in some detail in Appendix D, these three conditions taken together mean that: (1) Home should now *subsidize* the domestic production of the ith product, the size of this subsidy equalling the summed term in expression (11); and (2) Home should levy a *discriminatory*, *high* tariff rate on the import of the ith product from the jth country, relative to the tariff rate imposed on both the $(i+1)$th product imported from this market and the ith good when imported from the $(j+1)$th region.

As usual, the transshipment, or isolation requirement, as the case may be, must be met for expression (13) to be fulfilled. Should the negative national security terms in (12) and (13) be significantly enough negative, successful pursuit of an optimum tariff policy will lead to a virtual embargo on the import of the ith product from the jth country, since the price ratios $\frac{p_{ij}}{p_{i+1j}}$ and $\frac{p_{ij}}{p_{ij+1}}$ will fall so low as to make it no longer profitable for exporters in the jth country to export this good to Home.

Finally, let us turn to e^k_{ij}, which represents Home's relative dependence upon the jth country as an export market for the ith Home product. As with our definition of m^k_{ij}, it should be recognized that this particular definition of e^k_{ij} is somewhat arbitrary. Analogous to our discussion of m^k_{ij}, however, neither $e^k_{ij} = \sum_{k=1}^{s} x^k_i$ (aggregate Home consumption of the ith product, where the kth individual would experience diminishing *positive* utility from increases in $\sum_{k=1}^{s} x^k_i$), nor $e^k_{ij} = z_{ij}$ (Home exports of the ith good to the jth country, where the kth individual would experience increasing *negative* utility from increases in these exports) adequately reflect the national security notion of seeking a smaller *relative* dependence upon the jth export market.

As shown in Appendix D, this concern with the relative magnitudes of exports and domestic consumption $\left(e^k_{ij} = \frac{z_{ij}}{\sum_{k=1}^{s} x^k_i}\right)$ means once again that *both* the optimal condition relating to the domestic sector as well as the conditions relating to foreign trade, are affected:

$$\begin{matrix}\text{Relative} \\ \text{domestic} \\ \text{prices} \\ (i\text{th and} \\ i+1\text{th goods})\end{matrix} = \begin{matrix}\text{Relative domestic} \\ \text{marginal costs} \\ \text{of production} \\ (i\text{th and } i+1\text{th} \\ \text{goods})\end{matrix} + \sum_{j=1}^{p} \sum_{k=1}^{s} \begin{bmatrix}\text{Relative marginal} \\ \text{utility (disutility)} \\ \text{to } k\text{th individual} \\ \text{of increase in } e_{ij}\end{bmatrix} \qquad (14)$$

$$\begin{matrix}\text{Ratio of marginal} \\ \text{social revenue} \\ \text{from exporting} \\ (i\text{th and } i = 1\text{th} \\ \text{goods to each } j\text{th} \\ \text{market})\end{matrix} = \frac{p_{ij}(1+t_{ij})}{p_{i+1j}(1+t_{i+1j})} + \sum_{j=1}^{p} \sum_{k=1}^{s} \begin{bmatrix}\text{Relative marginal} \\ \text{utility (disutility)} \\ \text{to } k\text{th individual} \\ \text{of increase in } e_{ij}\end{bmatrix} \qquad (15)$$

$$\frac{p_{ij}}{p_{ij+1}} = \frac{(1 + t_{ij+1})}{(1 + t_{ij})} \left[1 - \sum_{j=1}^{p} \sum_{k=1}^{s} \left[\begin{array}{l} \text{Relative marginal} \\ \text{utility (disutility)} \\ \text{to } k\text{th individual} \\ \text{of increase in } e_{ij} \end{array} \right] \right] \tag{16}$$

In Chapter 1 we postulated that in certain cases, when domestic production of the ith good is a significant employer in Home, that Home citizens may experience, over a certain range of values for this ratio, *negative* marginal utility for increases in e_{ij}. This would mean that for the ith product the summed term in each of the foregoing expressions would be negative. For equation (14), which refers to the optimal condition for the domestic economy, a negative summed term means that Home policy makers should enact a subsidy on domestic consumption of the ith product, in order to assure an excess of domestic private marginal costs of production over the relative domestic prices of the ith and $(i+1)$th goods. Expressions (15) and (16) suggest that Home should levy a *discriminatory, high* export tax on exports of the ith product to the jth country, relative to the export tax rate imposed on both the $(i+1)$th good sold to the jth market and the ith good when exported to the $(j+1)$th region.

Again, Home policy makers can only satisfy expression (16) by assuring that either the transshipment or isolation requirements are met, as the case may be. Should the national security terms in expressions (15) and (16) be significantly large, successful pursuit of an optimum export tax policy will mean a virtual embargo on Home sales of the ith good to the jth country, since the price ratios $\frac{p_{ij}}{p_{i+1j}}$ and $\frac{p_{ij}}{p_{ij+1}}$ will rise so high as to make it no longer profitable for importers in the jth country to import this good from Home. The possibility of a cessation of trade is greater, the lower the price ratio $\frac{p_{ij}}{p_{i+1j}}$ at which the jth country becomes self-sufficient in the ith good (after taking into account the excess supply of the $(j+1)$th market for the ith good at each price ratio).

Conclusions

We have shown that the introduction of proxies for national security considerations into individual utility functions implies an optimum pattern of explicit or implicit export and import taxes in general different from the pattern of taxes which is optimal in the absence of such considerations. This optimum pattern of export and import taxes should discriminate among foreign countries or regions to the extent that the impact of these various countries or regions on a nation's security differs. Furthermore, the optimum pattern of taxes varies, depending upon the nature of the operative national security consideration(s).

The introduction of *relative military strength* as a national security consideration optimally implies the need for government subsidization of domestic production of appropriate military goods. Furthermore, restrictive or prohibitive export taxes should be imposed on the export of such goods to those countries constituting the national security threat.

The introduction of *offensive* economic warfare considerations optimally implies policy intervention in foreign trade. Should the object be to deprive a certain foreign country or countries of certain target commodities (the y_{ij}^k consideration), higher export taxes on those goods exported to the target of discrimination are in order. Should the consideration be to deprive these countries of foreign exchange earnings in general (the f_{ij}^k consideration), a pattern of higher tariffs on all goods is implied by our optimal conditions. Finally, should the object be to increase the target countries' reliance on the Home nation for their supplies of certain commodities (the s_{ij}^k consideration), lower export taxes or even export subsidies on such goods would be optimal.

Whenever national security is thought to be enhanced by defensive actions aimed at reducing a nation's *relative* economic dependence on a foreign country or region, policy intervention in *both* foreign trade (through export and import taxes) and domestically (through taxes or subsidies on domestic consumption or production) is required. Reduction of the Home country's dependence on foreign sources of supply (the m_{ij}^k consideration), is optimally achieved through a combination of higher tariffs on the import of and subsidization of domestic production of the target goods. If less dependence on foreign markets as an outlet for domestic production is desired (the e_{ij}^k consideration), optimal foreign policy intervention will consist of higher export taxes on the export of and subsidization of domestic consumption of the commodities in question.

To the extent that a competitive world market exists and there is no product differentiation according to origin in foreign consumption, discriminatory export or import taxes can only be successfully implemented by gaining the agreement of other countries not to trade with the target of discrimination in the relevant commodities, or as an extreme measure, by isolating one's own nation from the rest of the world with respect to the relevant goods. If product differentiation according to origin is present in foreign consumption, discriminatory export or import taxes may more easily be successfully implemented, but only if the discriminating nation is able to prohibit transshipment of its exports to or imports from the country which is the target of discrimination. Over time, however, simply satisfying the transshipment requirement alone will become less and less adequate if the relevant production and consumption elasticities in third countries increase significantly, resulting in a diminished reliance of the target country on the discriminating nation for imports or as an export market.

Finally, the analysis of the past two chapters has brought out the fundamental trade-off between short-term economic welfare and national security considerations. Each of the foregoing "optimal" policy responses to national security considerations, with the exception of the subsidization of domestic production of military goods (x_h) and the response to the collective good s_{ij}^k, results in some kind of restriction on Home's foreign trade below the level that would be optimal if solely economic considerations were taken into account. Such intervention in the foreign trade sector also has in each case an impact on the ratio of domestic prices and marginal costs of domestic production, and hence also an effect on the levels of consumption and production. In the case of the *defensive* variables m_{ij}^k and e_{ij}^k, this indirect effect on the domestic economy is reinforced by direct domestic subsidization measures.

Although the impact of the x_h and s_{ij}^k considerations is not to restrict foreign trade, an optimal policy response to both of these collective goods impacts the domestic economy. With respect to military goods production, such weapons and armaments can only be produced at the expense of domestic consumption of various private goods. The response to the s_{ij}^k variable, on the other hand, which is to subsidize (relatively) exports of the ith product to certain target markets, results in a higher level of domestic production of this product and a lower use of the nation's worldwide monopoly power, than would be optimal were this particular national security consideration to be absent.

In brief, there is a short-term "economic cost" attached to each of these policies pursued in the name of national security. This cost may be long-term as well if the implementation of such policies has an impact on the long-run economic structure in Home or in foreign countries. Of course this long-run, or dynamic, cost may be negative (a "benefit").[c] But ignoring these more dynamic, and therefore less tractable considerations, we may characterize the pursuit of policies designed to enhance national security as an *investment* designed to maximize Home's present and future degrees of freedom in a world of competing nation-states. As with all forms of investment, it can only be actuated through abstention from current consumption. And, as with the conventional analyses of investment versus consumption, decision makers in a national security context are constantly faced with the problem of how much current consumption to forego in return for a less certain future consumption stream, the latter being at least in part a function of the "security" of the national economy.

---

[c] For example, heavy current expenditures on defense may diminish current consumption of private goods or certain public goods, but the eventual technological spillover of such spending into the private sector in terms of enlarged production possibilities and new products may make it possible for the nation to achieve higher welfare levels in the future than in the absence of such military expenditures.

Part II
U.S. East-West Trade Policy

4 Bases for Evaluation and Qualifications

Bases for Evaluation

There are at least four basic questions we might ask concerning United States policy making with respect to trade with the socialist countries of Eastern Europe and Asia,[a] within the context of the theoretical model developed in Part I:

1. Do U.S. foreign economic policy makers really employ some kind of explicit or implicit welfare maximization model in their formulation of trade policies toward the socialist countries?

2. If such a welfare maximization framework is utilized, is the political process efficient in transmitting individual utility preferences to policy makers?

3. Providing the answers to both of the above questions are in the affirmative, how has the *actual* pattern of U.S. trade restrictions compared with the so-called optimum pattern when our model is applied to the various utility considerations reflected in the evolving public debate surrounding trade with the East?

4. Has the public discussion of the conceptual trade-offs implicit in the underlying utility functions been adequate, and has the quality of the empirical information available to policy makers on the question of trade with the socialist countries been adequate to the foreign policy significance of this issue?

The first two questions can probably be most rigorously examined within the framework of organization theory and political science, rather than of economics. For purposes of this study of U.S. trade policies toward the

[a] The socialist countries of Eastern Europe and Asia are defined as Albania, Bulgaria, Czechoslovakia, East Germany, Hungary, Poland, Rumania, and the Soviet Union (the socialist countries of Europe); and North Korea, North Vietnam, Outer Mongolia, and the People's Republic of China (the socialist countries of Asia). At times Cuba will also be considered as a member of this grouping of countries, but Yugoslavia is usually excluded, since this country has been treated by U.S. trade policy basically as a "Western" country since the late 1940s. Unless otherwise specified, the terms "socialist countries," "Eastern countries," "Communist countries" and "the East" are interchangeable in meaning throughout this study.

Eastern countries, we shall assume that both questions are answered in the affirmative. That is, we shall assume that U.S. policy makers attempt to pursue some welfare maximization objective similar to that developed in Chapter 1, in an organized, rational manner, and that there are not unreasonable lags between changes in individuals' utility functions and policy makers' recognition of and reaction to such changes.

Our predominant concern in this Part will be with the third question, which is concerned with examining the divergences of the actual evolving pattern of policies from the theoretical optimum pattern. In addressing ourselves to this question we shall continually have to maintain our guard against a kind of circularity of reasoning. This problem arises because the underlying utility considerations are not "givens," in the sense that the various national security collective goods in our theoretical model are given. On the contrary, we will seek to establish *inductively* the underlying utility considerations by drawing whenever possible on the political debate surrounding enactment of legislative and executive regulations prescribing actual U.S. trade policies, and by examining the declared intent of Congress in enacting such legislation.

Were we merely to posulate the underlying utility considerations on the basis of the actual pattern of trade policies, we would be forced to conclude simply by the logic of our model that there are no divergences from the optimum. By drawing instead on the political debate and declarations of legislative intention as the basis for postulating the operative utility parameters, we establish a means for analyzing the *efficiency* and *consistency* of the various policy instruments.

Once having established the basic utility considerations underlying U.S. policies, we shall proceed to discuss the impact on these considerations of major political-economic trends which have characterized the period since the initial discriminatory trade policies toward the socialist countries were developed. These major trends are well documented, but obviously any discussion of their probable effect on underlying U.S. utility considerations is open to disagreement. In this regard we will once again strive to draw directly on utility considerations as reflected in the continuing political debate concerning economic relations with the East.

Within this framework of national security considerations we shall place the United States in the position of "Home" in our model. We will then proceed to compare the actual pattern of U.S. East-West trade policies as they evolved over time, interpreted in terms of explicit and implicit export and import taxes, with the theoretical optimum pattern of trade policies derived in the model in the form of the necessary first order conditions for a welfare maximum. This particular process of analysis and evaluation will comprise Chapters 5 through 7.

In Chapter 8 we shall also very briefly examine the fourth question raised above, concerning the quality of the conceptual and empirical "feedback" to individual utility functions with respect to East-West trade issues. In the final chapter we shall use our model and our analysis of past U.S. East-West trade policies to explore the basic alternative trade policy choices facing the United States in the 1970s.

Qualifications and the Theory of the Second Best

It is important to emphasize what we *cannot* conclude from our comparison in the following chapters between actual and theoretically optimum policies. First, since most of the various utility parameters and elasticities embodied in our theoretical model have no empirically verified content, we are not here judging whether various implicit or explicit taxes and subsidies are "too high" or "not high enough." While such an examination is theoretically possible, it is not practically feasible.[b] In our evaluation we are merely asking whether the general *pattern* of actual taxes and subsidies has tended to correspond to the general *pattern* we would expect were policy makers to follow a welfare maximization procedure similar to that developed in Part I.

Second, whenever we observe divergences of the actual pattern of taxes and subsidies from the ideal pattern, we must be careful *not* to imply that piecemeal correction of nonoptimal policies will necessarily move us closer to the general optimum. According to the general theory of "second best," as first put forward in rigorous mathematical form by Lipsey and Lancaster,[3] should any one or more of our innumerable[c] optimal conditions be constrained to nonsatisfaction, we cannot in general suppose that satisfaction of some or all of the remaining conditions will move us any closer to the optimum position. For example, in the model presented in Part I we tacitly assumed away various economic and institutional barriers to perfect competition. Obviously many of our optimal conditions, which depend upon such assumptions, are constrained to nonsatisfaction in the U.S. economy.

We should point out that we are here using the concept of second best in a more general sense than usually employed. The term is normally used when it is assumed that various constraints make it impossible to achieve the usual

[b] Also, Graaff[1] notes that "we have an infinity of optimum tariff structures, each corresponding to a different initial distribution of wealth, but all determined by the same rule. We cannot judge between them without making interpersonal comparisons; and their existence makes it rather difficult to attach significance to attempts at discovering the 'probable height' of an optimum tariff." Also see Nath[2] on the impracticality of the "optimum tariff" concept.

[c] That is, considering all possible combinations of our m military goods, n nonmilitary goods and p foreign countries.

Pareto optimal condition (i.e., expression (1) for conventional optimum tariff theory) throughout the economy.[4] In such a case one must define a second best solution, which in general means a different set of optimum conditions than in the absence of such constraints.

In our model, however, we have incorporated various national security constraints as variables entering our utility functions. Hence the set of conditions necessary for attaining our optimum are already different from those in the conventional case. Our second best concern thereby revolves around the possibility that certain of our own, somewhat different optimal conditions may also be constrained to nonsatisfaction because of economic or institutional realities that we have not taken into account in our simplified model. Therefore, not only such domestic "imperfections" as monopoly, but also institutional barriers to achieving the "optimum" pattern of discrimination among foreign markets could be construed as second best constraints.

Recent contributions to the literature on second best have indicated, however, that Lipsey and Lancaster were overly pessimistic in their conclusions as to the implications of second best theory for applied welfare economics. Indeed, it has been shown that it is possible to make judgments concerning the relative desirability of alternative situations in which some optimal conditions are constrained to nonsatisfaction.[5] Furthermore, numerous demonstrations have been made that to the degree that there is separability among decision units (among producers and consumers, and between these two groups), a reasonable assumption for a large economy, the derived optimal conditions, and hence trade policy rules, will hold for that part of the economy not directly affected by the second best constraints.[6]

A significant second best constraint in our analysis of U.S. trade policies is the quite obvious de facto renunciation of the full use of its monopoly-monopsony position in world trade by the United States. It will be important to examine briefly some of the probable causes of this policy and its implications for our analysis. There appear to be at least three possible causal factors.

First, the experience of the leading trading countries of the world with retaliatory tariffs in the 1930s evidently has led to a realization among these nations that, in general, the national welfare of each could most probably be enhanced by mutually moving toward rather than away from free trade. U.S. adoption of the highly restrictive Hawley-Smoot tariff structure in 1930 is generally agreed to have inspired retaliatory tariff measures on the part of other leading trading countries.[7] This was an obvious example of the retaliatory propensity analyzed by Scitovsky,[8] although the underlying motivations were probably derived more from protectionist and beggar-thy-neighbor factors than from conventional optimum tariff considerations. Whatever the motivations, there is little doubt that the tendency toward higher tariff structures in this period exacerbated the employment and confidence problems of the international economy.

This trade restrictive trend was reversed with United States enactment of the Reciprocal Trade Agreements Act in 1934. The basic intent of this legislation was to stimulate domestic employment by encouraging bilateral negotiations aimed at reciprocal lowering of tariff barriers, with attendant most-favored-nation (MFN) provisions.[9] The new trend toward liberalization was strengthened and broadened by the multilateral bargaining framework established under the General Agreement on Tariffs and Trade (GATT) in 1947.

Second, the basic rules of the GATT convention include the provision that protection should be afforded domestic industries only through import tariffs, and this is generally backed up by national antidumping legislation aimed at protecting domestic industry from foreign export subsidies. Therefore to the extent that the collective consumption of "industrialization" is deemed to be of high social utility, the attempt to subsidize such industrialization through domestic or export subsidies is discouraged by GATT and by national legislation. Export subsidization for balance of payment reasons is also frowned upon by the international community.[d] Johnson[10] has shown that this bias against domestic and export subsidies logically points to reciprocal bargaining down of tariffs as an alternative means to expanding exports of industrial goods.

Third, it is possible that mutual renunciation of optimum tariff policies on the part of many nations has been caused by their implicit realization that for a broad range of goods there may be little difference in the price elasticity of demand for most imports among these countries. (Whether there are only small differences in price elasticities among these countries is, of course, an empirical question.) Johnson has shown for a two-country model that only one country can possibly increase its welfare if both nations are following an optimum tariff policy, and that both countries will be worse off if their price elasticities of demand for imports are not significantly different.[11] This theoretical finding, of course, could help to explain the adverse economic effects typically attributed to the retaliatory tariffs of the 1930s. The distinction between this argument and the first causal factor discussed above is that in this case we are concerned with factors that might dissuade nations from embarking on an optimum tariff policy in the first place, while in the previous case we are concerned with the notion that reciprocal liberalization might be deemed worthwhile by nations once the retaliatory cycle had occurred.

The net effect of these and possibly other factors has been the *general* renunciation of optimum tariff policies in the conventional sense, or even tariff

---

[d] Export subsidization in the form of government credit support for exports is not generally discouraged, however, although there have been unsuccessful attempts from time to time to establish basic "rules of the game" with respect to such support (e.g., the Berne Union experiment).

and export subsidy structures designed to protect or subsidize certain domestic industries. Generally the pressures for protection and subsidy have been channeled (at least until recently) into reciprocal bargaining down of tariffs and, to a much lesser extent, into domestic adjustment assistance policies.

The implications of this particular second best consideration, the general failure to impose conventional optimum tariffs, are not really significant for our purposes. Indeed, this involves only making a simplifying assumption about the elasticities that implicitly enter into our conventional optimum conditions, and allowing for some form of *protectionist* "collective good" to enter into domestic utility functions so as to account for the existing structure of protectionist tariffs.[e] In any event, the actual pattern of foreign trade taxes we will be interested in will be the *differential* treatment of trade with countries presumably posing national security problems for the United States, and of trade with all other countries.

It should be kept in mind, however, that the tax structures that *do* exist for trade with countries which are not discriminated against for national security purposes will in general reflect protectionist and subsidization pressures rather than the conventional optimum tariff considerations. With respect to domestic second best constraints, we shall be implicitly assuming a considerably high degree of separability among decision units, and that the deviant units or industries (i.e., those which do not approximate our simplifying assumptions as to equivalence of relative price ratios, ratios of commodity substitution, and domestic marginal cost ratios) are a distinct minority. In other words, we shall be assuming that our optimal policy rules do in fact hold for most products.[f]

Another basic assumption underlying the development of our welfare maximization model in Part I was that other countries do not retaliate against Home (U.S.) optimum tariff policies. This of course was a simplifying assumption used for expository purposes. Given the fact that countries in general do not follow optimum tariff policies, as discussed above, this assumption does not turn out to be a problem in practice. The further question is whether foreign countries which are targets of national security–inspired discrimination will retaliate. The mathematical complexities of this question rule out a definitive answer at this time as to the relative height of the "optimum" foreign trade taxes in the event of retaliation, but suffice it to say that the

[e] More specifically, mutual renunciation of optimum tariff policies may be interpreted as meaning that policy makers implicitly assume infinite foreign price elasticities for most goods, implying that the various optimum tariff rates (the t_{ij}) approach zero. As we shall see in later chapters, protectionist considerations in the *i*th industry may be represented by a collective good such as m^k_{ij}.

[f] This is basically an empirical question, of course, and is really beyond the scope of this study.

resultant taxes will still be discriminatory and higher than in the absence of economic warfare. Consequently, the question of retaliation is not really an important issue for us here, inasmuch as we are mainly interested in the optimum *pattern* (not the precise height) of foreign trade taxes, and in their general relationship to the actual evolving pattern of U.S. taxes on East-West trade in the postwar era.

5 Maximum Economic Warfare, 1948–1953

Strategic Export Controls

The United States employed a comprehensive system of export controls throughout World War II as a complement to the American military effort. The President was granted these sweeping export control powers under authority of Section 6 of the Act of July 2, 1940, which was extended and amended every several years thereafter:[1]

> Whenever the President determines that it is necessary in the interest of national defence to prohibit or curtail the exportation of any military equipment or munitions, or component parts thereof, or machinery, tools, or material, or supplies necessary for the manufacture, servicing or operation thereof, he may by proclamation prohibit or curtail such exportation, except under such rules and regulations as he shall prescribe . . .

The control system was perpetuated after the War primarily for "short supply" and foreign policy purposes. The short supply controls were necessary for certain commodities in great demand by reconstructing countries, as it was believed that unrestricted export of these products could in time cause severe shortages and inflationary pressures in the United States. In a sense, this policy consideration was a variant of the defensive national security variable e_{ij}^k discussed in Part I. In this case, however, e_{ij}^k was simply equal to z_{ij} (aggregate exports of the ith product to the jth region), where U.S. citizens experienced negative utility from increases in exports (over a certain range of values) because of resultant domestic scarcity and inflationary pressures. The optimal policy response to this consideration was to impose a higher export tax (in this case in the implicit form of controls) on the sale of these products to reconstructing countries. Furthermore, certain exports in great demand abroad were controlled for the foreign policy objective of treating allies impartially yet in accordance with Marshall Plan commitments.[2]

A more aggressive U.S. policy of export controls, aimed at the Soviet Union and its presumed "satellites," as well as at the increasingly dominant Communist forces in China, began to emerge in late 1947 and early 1948. Soviet unwillingness to cooperate in the Marshall Plan and other schemes for postwar reconstruction and in the new international organizations, as well as evidence of Soviet expansionism in Europe, led to formulation of a policy of "containment" of the "Communist bloc" in general and of the Soviet

Union, as the driving Communist power, in particular.[3] As Cohen has observed:[4]

Our main objective was the economic equivalent of political "containment": to minimize our own and our allies' trade contacts with the bloc in order to deny to the Soviet Union and its presumed satellites the major benefits of an international division of labor. East-West trade, we reasoned, was of much greater importance to the Communists than to ourselves. Hence, correct or not, it seemed possible for us to enhance our own national security at relatively little cost to ourselves in terms of income foregone.

The underlying motivations for a containment policy were not as simple as one might think. Undoubtedly there were strong emotions working here which saw "communism" as an evil and immoral force which, if it were impossible to erradicate, must at least be contained. Undoubtedly there was also some sense of betrayal, in that the wartime friend, the Soviet Union, seemed to be launching out on its own expansionist adventure now that the Germans and Japanese had been vanquished. Moreover, the totalitarian character of the Communit regimes was particularly odious, after years of fighting an all-out military battle against the Axis dictatorships.

But there were also other arguments for the economic containment policy, although they may in several cases have been predicated upon erroneous assumptions. The basic purpose was to reinforce the overall containment policy by depriving the socialist world of military and strategic goods, which, it was believed, would keep the Soviet Union in a position of relative military and economic inferiority, thereby minimizing Soviet flexibility in foreign affairs.[5] Moreover, there appears to have been a feeling that by keeping the centrally planned, Communit dominated countries economically weak and vulnerable to production bottlenecks, internal rebellion in these countries would be encouraged, or at least their leaders made more amenable to compromise with the West.[6] This containment consideration may be represented, in terms of our model, by the *offensive* economic warfare variable y_{ij}^k. In the Cold War thinking that emerged in the 1947–1949 period, the Soviet Union and its presumed satellites, as well as the Communist dominated sections of China, were basically the jth region, and y_{ij} represented this region's aggregate consumption of a whole range of military and nonmilitary goods.

There is little evidence that this more aggressive economic warfare posture against the East had really been implemented before early 1948, although at least one student of this subject has argued to the contrary.[7] As the Cold War intensified in 1948 and 1949, however, with the Communist takeover in Czechoslovakia in February 1948, the Berlin Blockade of 1948–1949, and the victory of the Communist forces over Chiang Kai-Shek, as well as the first Soviet explosion of an atomic bomb in late 1949, the United States began to put this "economic equivalent of political containment" into effect. On

March 1, 1948, the control apparatus was extended so as to require that all commercial shipments to Europe must have individual licenses. This represented the first official extension of the control scheme beyond the "short supply" scope which had existed after the War.[8]

The broadening of export controls under authority of the amended wartime legislation was given a firmer legislative underpinning in the Export Control Act of 1949 enacted in February of that year. This legislation declared that it was the policy of the United States to utilize export controls to the extent necessary:

(a) to protect the domestic economy from the excessive drain of scarce materials and to reduce the inflationary impact of abnormal foreign demand; (b) to further the foreign policy of the United States and to aid in fulfilling its international responsibilities; and (c) *to exercise the necessary vigilance over exports from the standpoint of their significance to the national security.*[9]

The Executive's discretionary authority with respect to enforcement of this policy was also maintained:

To effectuate the policies set forth in section 2 hereof, the President may *prohibit* or *curtail* the exportation from the United States, its Territories, and possessions, of any articles, materials, or supplies, including technical data, except under such rules and regulations as he shall prescribe . . .[10]

Clearly Congress, in enacting this legislation, had in mind a range of goods for which from the standpoint of Americans there existed clear diseconomies in international consumption (the y_{hj}^k and y_{ij}^k considerations). As our analysis in Part I has shown, the presence of diseconomies in international consumption of the ith good, when consumed by the jth region, would imply in most cases an optimal policy consisting of the imposition of a *discriminatory, higher* export tax on this good when sold to jth region. It is also clear that Congress envisioned an *implicit* tax structure on exports that would effectively embargo the export of all goods to countries which might be deemed to use these goods in a fashion detrimental to the national security of the United States. Since the national security significance of many nonmilitary goods could only be determined after careful examination, this legislation in effect mandated the President to "exercise vigilance" over many nonmilitary as well as military goods exported to the target socialist countries. The collective disutility parameter for y_{hj}^k was clearly prohibitively negative for all military goods ($h = 1, \ldots, m; j =$ the East), and the parameter for y_{ij}^k was significantly negative and perhaps also *prohibitively* negative for many nonmilitary goods that might directly or indirectly contribute to the national security threat posed by the socialist world.

In actuality the Export Control Act of 1949 merely represented congressional confirmation of the policy of national security–oriented export controls which had been in effect since March 1948. The Export Supply Branch of the Office of International Trade, Department of Commerce (now the Office of Export Control) continued to have responsibility for export controls, under authority delegated by the President in accordance with the Export Control Act of 1949 (and earlier export control legislation).

Very simply, the control authorities had established a compendium of export regulations that effectively separated all goods into two categories. Goods deemed clearly nonstrategic were allowed to be exported under open general license; no application for official approval was necessary. All other goods and technical information of a strategic nature required a validated license for export.[a]

The Export Control Act further required the Administrator (now the Office of Export Control, or OEC), to consult with appropriate government departments and agencies with respect to the composition of the export control list and exceptions to embargo.[11] As a result, a hierarchy of interagency committees composed of representatives of the Departments of Commerce, Defense, State, and Treasury, and various agencies such as the Central Intelligence Agency, was formed to assure the necessary policy coordination.[12]

The Office of Export Control effectively controls all commodities and technical data not controlled by other agencies. The other controlling agencies and their commodity jurisdictions are:[13]

1. Arms, ammunition, implements of war, and other classified material; regulated by the State Department, Office of Munitions Control, under authority of the Mutual Security Act of 1954, section 414;

2. Narcotics; regulated by the Bureau of Narcotics of the Justice Department, under authority of the Narcotic Drugs Import and Export Act and the Marijuana Tax Act of 1937;

3. Gold; regulated by the Treasury Department, under authority of the Gold Reserve Act of 1934 and Section 5(b) of the Trading With the Enemy Act (1917, as amended in 1933);

4. Nuclear source materials, facilities, and related technology; regulated by the Atomic Energy Commission, under authority of the Atomic Energy Act of 1954;

---

[a] More than two categories have existed at various points in time. But the distinction between "general" and "validated" license has continued to be the critical one, for purposes of our analysis.

5. Vessels; regulated by the U.S. Maritime Administration, under authority of the United States Shipping Act of 1916;

6. Tobacco seed and plants; regulated by the Administrator of the Agricultural Marketing Service of the Department of Agriculture, under authority of the Tobacco Seed and Plant Exportation Act of 1940.

As we saw in Part I, a nation seeking to carry out a discriminatory export policy against some *j*th market must satisfy either the *transshipment* or *isolation* requirements, depending upon whether or not the target goods are characterized by product differentiation-by-origin in rest-of-the-world consumption. The transshipment requirement was recognized by the policy makers in the Executive branch who had the responsibility for developing the detailed export control regulations. Destination control provisions were eventually established for the export of *all* commodities (including technical data) to *all* countries, whether exported under a validated or general license.

Violation of these provisions was of course punishable under the law. Violations of the spirit but not the letter of the licensing regulations were often punished by blacklisting.[14] Exporters shipping under a general license were required to certify as to ultimate destination of the goods (or technical data) in their Shipper's Export Declaration, bill of lading, and commercial invoice. Exporters shipping under a validated license faced the additional requirement of obtaining the certification of the ultimate consignee as to the ultimate destination of the exported goods (or technical data).[15]

In addition, the following kinds of products and transactions were eventually brought under the scrutiny of the export control authorities: (i) domestically produced commodities used as materials or components in foreign made end products; (ii) transshipment of goods through a target country(ies) en route to a nontarget country, and (iii) reexports of technical data or foreign made commodities that were direct products of U.S. technical data, or that were produced by any plant or major component thereof which was a direct product of U.S. technical data, if such goods or technical data would ordinarily require a validated license for direct export from the United States.[16] (The numerous ways in which these various regulations were violated, either in the letter or the spirit, are discussed in Adler-Karlsson.)[17]

From our analysis in Part I we know that satisfaction of the transshipment requirement is sufficient, at least in theory, to permit a nation to successfully pursue a policy of discriminatory economic warfare with respect to those products which are subject to considerable product differentiation in third country consumption. For example, as long as there was a large qualitative difference between American made electronic devices with possible military applications and similar instruments manufactured in Western Europe, the American products embodying the latest technological advances could be effectively barred from the East by prohibiting their direct export from the U.S. and their transshipment via allied nations.

For a range of military and nonmilitary strategic goods, however, such product differentiation may have been slight. Furthermore, the logic of an *embargo* policy, which resulted from significantly negative y_{hj}^k and y_{ij}^k utility parameters across the whole range of military goods and a wide list of "nonmilitary" products, suggested that the United States should also attempt to achieve agreement by other nonCommunist countries not to export the target products to the East. Finally, while transshipment controls could easily be satisfied in theory, policy makers could only be certain that their economic warfare goals were being achieved if they knew that foreign countries which could possibly be used as transshipment points also were embargoing the sale of the target goods to the socialist world.

As a result of this recognition that a mere transshipment prohibition policy was insufficient, U.S. policy makers took several actions to obtain the cooperation of friendly nations and even neutrals in the strategic embargo policy. A first step was taken in connection with legislation authorizing Marshall Plan aid to Europe in early 1948. Section 117(d) of the Foreign Assistance Act of 1948 directed the Administrator of Marshall Plan assistance to refuse delivery to recipient nations of U.S. goods "which go into the production of any commodity for delivery to any nonparticipating European country, which commodity would be refused export licenses to those countries by the United States in the interest of national security."[18] In this way, Marshall Plan aid was used as an instrument to gain compliance of the Western European allies with the U.S. export control policy.

As we shall discuss later on with respect to other foreign aid programs of the United States, "foreign aid" itself arises out of international external effects in consumption, or the "y_{ij}^k" and y_{hj}^k national security consideration. Just as these external effects were negative for a very wide range of goods when consumed in the East, so U.S. citizens derived *positive* satisfaction from Western European consumption of many military and nonmilitary goods. Our earlier analysis of negative "y_{ij}^k" effects implies that a *positive* utility parameter associated with this variable means a discriminatory, *lower* export tax (which often means an export subsidy) on the export to the jth friendly country of the ith product subject to this effect. The foregoing legislation regarding the attempt of the United States to force compliance with its strategic embargo policy merely reflected the fact that the so-called positive external effects arising from the jth Western European country's consumption of the ith product were nullified, or perhaps became negative, if the jth nation used the product in the manufacture of the $(i + 1)$th good for sale to the Communist countries, whenever the $(i + 1)$th good was embargoed by the U.S. itself for sale to the East.

A second initiative in the policy of isolating the Communist world involved a series of negotiations with the other principal Western industrialized countries regarding a collective embargo of strategic exports to the East. Discussions in this regard began in 1948 and culminated in November 1949 with the establishment of COCOM (Consultative Group–Coordinating Committee). This group is now composed of fourteen of the fifteen NATO countries (Iceland excluded) and Japan. Each item on the COCOM list of embargoed exports to the socialist countries must be agreed to unanimously, and exceptions to the embargo likewise must receive unanimous approval.

It appears that there was considerable opposition in Western Europe, however, to such a massive, bloc-wide embargo policy. The West Europeans had historically engaged in East-West trade to a far greater extent than the United States, and therefore the U.S. presupposition that the East had more to lose than the West from a decline in this trade was questioned. European policy makers were also less sanguine than their American counterparts that all the coordinative and technical problems involved with such an extensive embargo policy could be satisfactorily resolved. Furthermore, they regarded Eastern, and particularly Soviet, dependence upon the West as of far less importance than did the American architects of the COCOM machinery. Finally, there undoubtedly was resentment in West Europe that the U.S. was using its immense immediate postwar power superiority to obtain compliance by the Europeans in a policy that would be economically far more injurious to them than to the United States.[19]

Interestingly enough, even some American observers were skeptical, and believed that the embargo policy, if successfully coordinated, would backfire on those who wished to hold Soviet power in check, particularly in its relations with its Eastern European "satellites." For example, Spulber argued that "the trouble with the embargo is simply that the more efficacious it becomes with respect to the small countries of the Soviet orbit, the greater becomes the bargaining position of the U.S.S.R. in its intrabloc relations."[20]

While the cooperative embargo machinery of COCOM was aimed primarily at military goods, nonmilitary products of "strategic" importance were also included. The Battle Act of 1951, the U.S. legislative underpinning for American participation in COCOM, specifically embargoed any "shipment of arms, ammunition, and implements of war, atomic energy materials, petroleum, transportation materials of strategic value, and items of primary strategic significance used in the production of arms, ammunition, and implements of war to any nation or combination of nations threatening the security of the United States, including the Union of Soviet Socialist Republics and all countries under its domination . . ."[21]

The United States could never obtain the assent of its COCOM partners, however, to extend the cooperative embargo list so as to encompass the entire range of goods embargoed unilaterally by the U.S. under authority of the Battle Act and the Export Control Act. Only about 90 to 95 per cent of so-called "primary strategic goods" embargoed by the U.S. were ever included in the COCOM lists.[22] Furthermore, the United States maintained tight control, which often meant effective embargo, over many more commodities which could hardly have been considered to be of "primary strategic significance" in the sense of the Battle Act. Moreover, while the COCOM list was continually expanded in the three to four years immediately following the establishment of this cooperative machinery, particularly under the stimulus of the Korean War, which broke out in June 1950, it has been suggested that the extensions of the list in a sense camouflaged from congressional sponsors of the Battle Act the fact that many exemptions from the embargo were being granted to the Western European nations.[23]

In summary, it can be said that as a result of the COCOM arrangement, the United States was able, at least officially, to totally isolate the target socialist countries with respect to an inner core of military and strategic nonmilitary goods. In addition, the U.S. maintained *unilateral* control over an additional list of products for which it was not able to obtain the unanimous consent of its COCOM allies to control on a multilateral basis. As we noted earlier, U.S. controls over this "extra-COCOM" list (or so-called "COCOM differential") did extend, however, to transshipment of these products.

To the extent that there existed product differentiation-by-origin in allied consumption for these extra-COCOM goods, the United States was successful in raising the costs to the socialist world of obtaining these items, or as the case might be, and usually was, in completely embargoing U.S. exports of the target products. Whenever product differentiation according to origin did not exist, however, it was at least theoretically possible for businessmen in allied countries to purchase the original U.S. excess supply at an unchanged (or lower) world price, substitute this U.S. supply for locally produced goods in their domestic consumption, and sell their resulting surplus domestic production at that price to the Communist countries.

In practice, however, such substitution in allied consumption was probably minimal during the first postwar decade. The economies of many of the Western industrial countries had been ravaged by the war and were unable to provide adequately even for domestic demand, regardless of price.[b] In addition, the Eastern countries themselves began to follow a basically autarkic policy with respect to the industrialized West.[24] Furthermore, the level of U.S. trade with most of the socialist controlled countries was relatively small to begin with, and thus the potential for the substitution effect to work in foreign consumption was limited.

Transport costs undoubtedly also made such substitution difficult.

---

[b] Marshall Plan aid to Western Europe and extensive U.S. "short-supply" export controls in the immediate postwar period are testimony to the demand-supply imbalance in Western Europe following World War II.

Nevertheless, some evidence of "substitution" of this nature does exist, as witnessed by the declared need of the U.S. control authorities to refuse licenses for shipments to COCOM members and other friendly countries in cases in which such U.S. exports would be prohibited if made directly to the East and it was known that in fact the recipient Western nation exported similar products to the socialist countries.[25]

A third step toward a comprehensive embargo of the East involved the attempt by the United States to enlist the support of the non-COCOM, principally nonindustrialized remainder of the western world. Generally speaking, it is probably reasonable to conclude that with the exception of various strategic raw material exports of some of the developing countries, satisfaction of the *transshipment* requirement was sufficient with respect to the non-COCOM countries. This is because a high proportion of the goods subject to the COCOM embargo were highly technologically intensive, and not really produced in the less developed countries at that time.

Whatever the precise degree of product differentiation in rest-of-world consumption for the targeted strategic goods, it apparently became standard practice for the United States to incorporate in its bilateral foreign aid agreements with dozens of countries provisions that attempted to coordinate the export controls of recipient countries with those of the United States.[26] Indeed, the Battle Act of 1951 provided for sanctions against third country violation of the U.S. embargo policy set forth in that legislation:[27]

> All military, economic, or financial assistance to any nation shall . . . be terminated forthwith, if such nation . . . knowingly permits the shipment to any nation or combination of nations threatening the security of the United States, including the Union of Soviet Socialist Republics and all countries under its domination of any such item . . . included in any of the following categories: Arms, ammunition, and implements of war, atomic energy materials, petroleum, transportation materials of strategic value, and items of primary strategic significance used in the production of arms, ammunition, and implements of war.

The threat of terminating all "military, economic, or financial assitance" to any nation violating the unilateral U.S. embargo policy, was predicated on the same notion of external effects in international consumption (y^k_{hj}, y^k_{ij}) present in the Marshall Plan aid sanctions mentioned earlier. In this case, however, the scope of the threatened sanctions was far greater.

Finally, the United States chose to supplement the foregoing instruments aimed at insuring foreign compliance with the COCOM embargo policy by issuance of the Transaction Control Regulations in 1953. These regulations are enforced by the Treasury Department, Office of Foreign Assets Control (OFAC), and are issued under authority of the Trading With the Enemy Act (1917), as amended in 1933. Section 5(b) of this Act gives to the President broad and flexible powers to control international transactions. These powers originally applied to the "war emergency" of World War I, but were amended in 1933 to apply to cases of "national emergency."

The Transaction Control Regulations now apply to transactions with all socialist countries, with the exception of Cuba and Yugoslavia.[c] They prohibit, unless licensed by the OFAC, any person within the United States, and foreign firms controlled by such persons, from purchasing or selling or arranging the purchase or sale of COCOM controlled goods located outside the U.S. for ultimate delivery to the target Eastern countries. Obtaining credit in connection with such a transaction is also forbidden.[28]

We may conclude that the *general* pattern of implicit export taxes as initially established in the late 1940s and early 1950s conformed quite well to what we might call an "optimum" pattern, given the apparent underlying utility considerations. While the precise bases for distinguishing between goods subject to general license and goods subject to validated license can certainly be debated, it does appear that the general *pattern* of discrimination, ranging from outright embargo on military goods and many "strategic" nonmilitary goods to little or no control over many nonstrategic items, conforms to an optimal pattern of export taxes based on underlying differences in utility (or "disutility") parameters associated with y_{ij}^k and y_{hj}^k across the range of exports.[d] Furthermore, the Marshall Plan and other foreign assistance to nonCommunist nations also reflected the y_{ij}^k and y_{hj}^k external effect considerations, except that in this case the marginal utilities associated with these variables were typically positive, unless the potential aid recipient failed to coordinate its East-West trade policies with those of the United States.

That this "optimum" pattern of export taxes took the form of controls over exports (which meant either outright embargo or an implicit tax on exporters), rather than explicit tax rates, only suggests that the costs (not to say the impossibility) of attempting to estimate all the true collective utility parameters associated with y_{ij}^k and y_{hj}^k as well as all the various foreign trade elasticities, clearly outweighed the combined costs of: (1) the administrative and private costs arising out of the export control procedure, (2) the net welfare loss from failing to impose precisely optimal taxes, and (3) that part of the implicit export tax which was not recoverable from the jth target nation in the form of a higher foreign export price because of the jth country's relative strength in what was essentially a bilateral monopoly situation.

The implications of our optimal trade policy rules regarding *transshipment*

---

[c] Transactions with Cuba are now subject to the Cuban Assets Control Regulations; see Chapter 6.

[d] The continual review of export license applications and the wide degree of differential treatment of such applications in terms of information required and approval delay, may be interpreted as approximating the more or less continuous distribution of export control decisions implicit in our algebraic formulation of the "necessary optimal conditions."

requirements were at least theoretically observed by the new export control structure; and through the COCOM machinery, the Battle Act provisions covering foreign aid, and the Transaction Control Regulations, the United States attempted to meet the *isolation* requirements. Disagreement among COCOM members as to the need for prohibiting the export of all those items embargoed by the U.S., however, meant that the target countries in the East could only be isolated with respect to an inner core of strategic goods. The logical requirements of the "optimum" trade policy rules were therefore breached in regard to those extra-COCOM goods not subject to product differentiation-by-origin in rest-of-world consumption. As we have observed, however, the extent of arbitrage in these goods through substitution in foreign consumption probably was negligible, as a practical matter, in the early years of the embargo policy.

To the extent that export sales to the target socialist countries were actually consummated for goods requiring validated licenses, it can only be concluded that the various tax elements arising from the approval procedure (clerical and administrative costs, uncertainty, lost opportunities in other markets, etc.) fell upon the American exporter initiating the transaction. Presumably the exporter was able to recover, in general, whatever additional costs he incurred by an add-on to his normal export price. Otherwise, the business would not have been worth pursuing. His success in recovering these costs, however, was most likely greater in the case of goods characterized by significant product differentiation-by-origin, or in extremely inelastic supply in competing countries; in other words, in respect of products for which competitive pricing was not the key marketing factor.[e]

Import Restrictions

The existence of negative international external effects in consumption (y^k_{hj}, y^k_{ij}) over a very broad range of products would naturally give rise to negative reactions among Americans concerning accumulation of foreign exchange (f^k_{hj}, f^k_{ij}) by the Eastern "bloc." The logical connection between these two collective good considerations was pointed out in Chapter 1. As the Cold War and the containment policy developed, it became apparent that

[e] We should point out that for a wide range of strategic or marginally strategic nonmilitary goods, as well as for military goods, U.S. exports to most nonCommunist countries also required (and still require) validated licenses. While the approval procedure in these cases undoubtedly also involved various "costs" to U.S. exporters, these costs were probably negligible compared to those involved in the typically more lengthy and complex approval procedure for exports to the Communist world requiring validated licenses. That the costs involved in obtaining validated licenses for exports to nonCommunist countries were negligible seems apparent from the relative lack of criticism of such requirements by exporters testifying before the 1968–1969 hearings on East-West trade.[29]

providing the Communist nations with an additional source of hard currencies would enable them to more easily purchase extra-COCOM controlled goods elsewhere, or at least to obtain nonstrategic goods more easily so as to release internal resources for development of local strategic goods producing industries.[30]

As we shall see, certain domestic import-competing interests undoubtedly saw the popular antiCommunist mood in the U.S. as conducive to furtherance of their own protectionist aims. In the case of these individuals, reinforcing the (f^k_{hj}, f^k_{ij}) consideration was another collective good variable which basically represented aggregate imports of competing products from the *j*th region (z^k_{hj}, z^k_{ij})[f], for a subset of the *n* nonmilitary goods. Furthermore, the popular distaste for Communist ideology and methods undoubtedly led many to want to boycott Communist made goods on ideological and moral grounds.[31] Again, this suggested distinctly negative utility, arising from increases in imports from the East, for some subset of individuals in the U.S.

As could easily be demonstrated, analogous to the analysis in Part I, the implication for the general *pattern* of optimal implicit or explicit import taxes on trade with the socialist world was the same regardless of whether (f^k_{hj}, f^k_{ij}) or (z^k_{hj}, z^k_{ij}) or both types of collective good considerations were operative in American utility functions. Possibly (f^k_{hj}, f^k_{ij}) was the predominant consideration. To the extent that (z^k_{hj}, z^k_{ij}) was also operative, for either protectionist or ideological-moral reasons, it will be enough to remember that the presence of this consideration merely *reinforced* the direction of policy action implied by the optimal foreign trade policy rule concerning the foreign exchange variable.

It will be recalled from Chapter 3 that the optimal policy "rule" when the (f^k_{hj}, f^k_{ij}) variable is operative is to impose a discriminatory, higher import tax on the *h*th military good or *i*th nonmilitary good when imported from the *j*th region. In addition, it was observed that the logic of this particular collective good, unlike the other national security "proxies" discussed in Part I, is that such a discriminatory, higher tax should be levied on *all* potential imports from the region which is a target of discrimination. In other words, an optimal policy toward imports from the socialist world would have been a pattern of discriminatory, higher tariffs (or possibly an embargo, were the collective marginal disutilities from eastern earnings of foreign exchange quite large) on all imports from these countries. Moreover, the highest explicit or implicit tax rates would have tended to be levied upon those goods which were particularly susceptible, as well, to the aforementioned protectionist or ideological-moral considerations.

In the 1951 congressional hearings that dealt with the extension of re-

---

[f] Note that the z^k_{ij} collective good is merely a variant of m^k_{ij}, where $m^k_{ij} = z^k_{ij}$, (see Chapter 3, page 31).

ciprocal trade agreements legislation, there was a curious thread of national security–protectionist–moral reasoning which characterized the testimony of some participants with respect to trade with the socialist world. On the one hand, there was the clear line of reasoning embodied in the concept of negative utilities attached to the foreign exchange variable (f_{hj}^k, f_{ij}^k): "... There is no mix-up in the general proposition that we are providing dollar exchange to be used against our national security interests."[32] On the other, it was argued that if the Communist nations were "enemies," why should the U.S. admit imports from these countries that might *harm* domestic industries.[33] This latter argument embodied both the protectionist and ideological-moral motivations for restricting imports.

The Administration warned that denial of most-favored-nation treatment (MFN) for the imports of the Eastern countries would break treaties with Poland and Hungary, violate U.S. obligations to Czechoslovakia under GATT, and otherwise weaken the moral position of the United States with respect to Soviet treaty-breaking in the early postwar period. The Administration also further argued that import restrictions "would not contribute to our military security, for we already have strict controls over exports to the Soviet countries which may possibly contribute to their military potential."[34] The latter reasoning failed to take into account, of course, that many extra-COCOM controlled goods were at least theoretically available abroad, and could be purchased with foreign exchange earned from exports to the United States. Also, the practical difficulties of collectively embargoing even military goods were often great.[35] Moreover, this argument overlooked the fact that the ability to earn hard currencies (thereby allowing purchase of non-strategic goods in the West), gave the East increased flexibility with respect to releasing internal resources for local strategic goods production.

Despite the oppostion of the Executive branch, discrimination against exports of Communist controlled countries was established as a policy objective with enactment of the Trade Agreements Extension Act of 1951. Section 5 of this Act directed the President to "suspend, withdraw or prevent the application" of MFN treatment to "imports from the Union of Soviet Socialist Republics and to imports from any nation or area dominated or controlled by the foreign government or foreign organization controlling the world Communist movement."[36]

In accordance with this legislation the United States withdrew MFN treatment for the designated countries in the course of 1951 and 1952.[37] As the Administration had predicted, this action created a problem with respect to Czechoslovakia, which had acceded to GATT just prior to the 1948 coup that brought in a Communist regime in that country. The United States was forced to invoke Article 35 of the GATT accords, which enables members of GATT to abstain from adhering to GATT rules with respect to one another.[38]

Revoking MFN treatment for the socialist countries meant that they were to be denied the tariff concessions agreed to by the United States in reciprocal trade agreements negotiated over the period since enactment of the Reciprocal Trade Agreements Act in 1934. The new tariff rates for these countries, referred to as the "Column 2" duties, approximated the generally higher duties prescribed by the Hawley-Smoot Tariff Act of 1930.

There were only several cases in which the resulting import restrictions were more severe than as prescribed by the Hawley-Smooth tariff structure. An example of the protectionist consideration at work, which was translated into specific policy intervention partially by means of appealing to national security worries, concerned the embargo on the import of seven specific types of fur skins from both the People's Republic of China and the Soviet Union, as enacted in Section 11 of the Trade Agreements Extension Act of 1951.[39] The President was given no discretionary authority in this regard, and in accordance with this legislation the prescribed action was taken with respect to the P.R.C. in 1951 and the Soviet Union in 1952.[40]

Another example, which presumably arose principally from ideological-moral considerations, was the provision in the Tariff Act of 1930 which excludes entirely importables known to be produced by convict or forced labor.[41] Crabmeat imported from the Soviet Union was subject to embargo on these grounds in the 1950s.[42]

The imposition of higher duties, resulting from the denial to Communist countries of most-favored nation treatment, conformed to the dictates of our "optimum" trade policy rule. But as we have seen, the logic of the offensive economic warfare consideration (f_{hj}^k, f_{ij}^k) suggests that the marginal utility which a given individual in the discriminating nation experiences from an increase in jth foreign exchange earnings should be *uniformly negative* for all goods. Yet the pattern of higher duties under the Hawley-Smoot tariff structure does not apply to all goods. Many products have identical duty rates for both Column 1 and Column 2 origins.[g]

Furthermore, to the extent that we have appropriately defined the dominant national security variable operating in this situation (i.e., foreign exchange earnings of the target region), and if we assume that the marginal disutility related to (f_{hj}^k, f_{ij}^k) is equal, for any given individual, across the entire range of importables, the particular configuration of this national security consideration as it enters our optimal conditions[h] indicates that the tariff should be higher, the higher the final jth export price for the ith or hth good. While this requirement conceivably might in fact be fulfilled by the Hawley-Smoot tariff structure, it is extremely doubtful, since this particular tariff pattern was established as a result of congressional logrolling methods

[g] Column 1 duties apply to all countries other than Column 2 countries.
[h] See Appendix D.

rather than national security considerations, over twenty years before these national security factors became operative.[43]

We are forced to conclude that the "second column" tariff schedule was at best an attempt to approximate an optimal tariff structure with what constituted an institutional datum—the old Hawley-Smoot schedules. There is little to indicate that this approximation had anything to recommend it other than the ease with which it was effected. It is in fact doubtful that the resulting tariff pattern could even be defended as a "second best" solution which took into account the obvious administrative costs and problems involved in ascertaining the precise magnitudes for all the relevant utility parameters; this is because it is not at all clear that an outright embargo on imports from the Communist world would have been less successful in *approximating* the principal aim of U.S. Cold War policy at that time, namely the isolation and containment of the East.

Given the alleged general noncompetitiveness of most eastern European and Russian products in nonsocialist markets, from a standpoint of quality, the need for satisfaction of the *isolation* requirement embodied in expression (8) of Chapter 3 (page 29) was probably minimal in the early 1950s. The *transshipment* requirement, however, was explicitly acknowledged in the tariff schedules; the Column 2 duties were made applicable to products "whether imported directly or indirectly" from the target socialist nations.[44]

Restrictions on Private Capital Exports

The restrictions on the export of private U.S. capital to most of the socialist countries, as embodied in the Johnson Act, are the result of other than national security considerations per se. Following aggressive securities selling in the late 1920s and the international economic and monetary collapse of the early 1930s, over $3 billion or 37 per cent of the outstanding foreign government and foreign privately issued securities held by Americans were in default by 1933.[45] The collapse of the international securities market together with the imposition by many foreign governments of restrictions on the transfer of profits and capital repatriation led to congressional hearings in 1931 and 1932 aimed at investigating the sale of foreign securities in the United States and proposing remedial legislation.[46] These hearings apparently reflected the significant negative marginal utility of many Americans asociated with the net export of private capital to foreign countries whose governments happened to be in default on securities held by American citizens.

It can be easily shown that the trade policy implication of such disutility arising from capital exports is similar to that following from international external effects in consumption of capital (or more precisely, capital services). That is to say, the trade policy rule when capital exports are the collective good (z_{ij}^k, where the ith "good" is private capital) is similar to the optimal condition when y_{ij}^k enters individual utility functions; namely, a discriminatory, higher export tax on the export of private capital to the jth target country.[i]

As a result of the 1931–1932 hearings, the Johnson Act was enacted in 1934 with the purpose of protecting American investors from income and capital losses on aggressively distributed securities of less than creditworthy foreign borrowers.[49 j] The act (as amended) provides that:[51]

Whoever, within the United States, purchases or *sells the bonds*, securities, or other obligations of *any foreign government* or political subdivision thereof or any organization or association acting for or on behalf of a foreign government or political subdivision thereof, issued after April 13, 1934, *or makes any loan to such foreign government*, political subdivision, organization or association, except a renewal or adjustment of existing indebtedness, *while such government*, political subdivision, organization or association, *is in default* in the payment of its obligations, or any part thereof, to the United States, shall be fined not more than $10,000 or imprisoned for not more than five years, or both.

This section is applicable to individuals, partnerships, corporations, or associations other than public corporations created by or pursuant to special authorizations of Congress, or corporations in which the United States has or exercises a controlling interest through stock ownership or otherwise. *While any foreign government is a member both of the International Monetary Fund and of the International Bank for Reconstruction and Development, this section shall not apply* to the sale or purchase of bonds, securities, or other obligations of such government or any polictical subdivision thereof or any organization or association acting for or on behalf of such government or political subdivision, or to making of any loan to such government, political subdivision, organization, or association.

This prohibition on the export of private U.S. capital to foreign governments in default on obligations to U.S. citizens or the U.S. Government does not apply to Albania or Bulgaria, as neither country is in default. Nor does the prohibition apply to Yugoslavia, which is a member of both the IMF and the World Bank. Neither does it apply to public corporations, such as the Eximbank. Furthermore, as provided in Section 11 of the Export–Import Bank Act of 1945, as amended, private credit transactions in which

---

[i] The distinction between the export of capital goods and money capital has only recently received significant attention in the literature on the theory of optimal capital movements.[47] Although this distinction may well result in analytically different solutions, we have assumed in this study (along with Kemp) that "international borrowing and lending can be viewed as the purchase and sale of the services of capital."[48]

[j] Mikesell, however, argues that while the Johnson Act "was purported to be a measure for the American investor against loans to poor credit risks engendered by greedy American bankers ... It was in fact an expression of angry resentment on the part of isolationist-minded American congressmen who had little sympathy for the problems of foreign countries and no appreciation of America's responsibility in world economic and political affairs."[50]

the Eximbank participates are exempt from the provisions of the Johnson Act.[52] All other Eastern countries are, however, affected by this legislation.

Several U.S. Attorneys General rulings have fairly recently been made relating to the proper interpretation of the Johnson Act prohibition of the making of "loans." The most recent ruling states that this prohibition does not apply to financing arrangements which "are directly tied to specific export transactions, if their terms are based upon bona fide business considerations, and if the obligations to which they give rise 'move exclusively within the relatively restricted channels of banking and commercial credit.'"[53] This and other rulings by the Attorney General have led to the common interpretation[54] that even medium term export credit and deferred payment schemes are allowable, with respect to exports to the affected socialist countries, as long as such terms are "within the range of those commonly encountered in commercial sales of a comparable character."[55]

With respect to private credit transactions carried out by foreign affiliates, subsidiaries, or branches of U.S. banks or corporations, Giffen cites a 1939 Attorney General ruling to the effect that such transactions can normally be considered as lying outside the coverage of the Johnson Act.[56] This ruling appears to have relied, however, on the notion that foreign branches, subsidiaries, and affiliates operate more or less independently of their U.S. parents.[k]

When the ith good is private capital it seems reasonable to assume that this "good" is basically not subject to product differentiation-by-origin in nontarget country foreign consumption. This would mean that the *isolation* requirement would have to be fulfilled for the optimal conditions to be met. But to the extent that financial intermediation occurs across national boundaries, and foreign institutional and individual lenders and investors are not prohibited from exporting capital to the target Eastern countries, arbitrage will in theory occur and our optimal conditions will not be satisfied. In practice, however, the isolation requirement is in general satisfied with respect to the East. This is because, with few exceptions, the socialist countries have prohibited the import of private capital, as private capital has no place in their ideological system. In other words, their demand for foreign private capital is perfectly inelastic at zero.

It should be noted, however, that even were the import of private capital acceptable to these countries, and perfect arbitrage through the $(j + 1)$th market (that market not affected by the Johnson Act prohibitions) possible,

---

[k] See, however, Pisar on this question: "It is important to note that the Johnson Act does not extend to foreign subsidiaries or offshore licensees of American corporations if the transactions subject to financing are wholly effecuated outside the United States. In consequence, subsidiary companies formed or licensed in Western Europe, Japan or elsewhere have generally been free to supply goods on credit, often underwritten by local state export insurance instrumentalities. . . ."[57]

U.S. policy aims as envisioned in the Johnson Act might still be met despite the nonsatisfaction of the isolation requirement. This is because the initial purported aim of this legislation was to protect the American investor from foreign defaults on American held foreign securities. Therefore even if there is transshipment or substitution of American private capital abroad, the American investor or lender is not hurt unless the foreign financial intermediary or issuer of primary securities itself becomes a poor credit risk because it has invested a large portion of its portfolio in worthless securities issued by the jth target country(ies).[1]

We have seen that the prohibition against private capital exports to the jth defaulting country prescribed by the Johnson Act apparently reflected prohibitively negative utility parameters associated with the export of private capital to such countries in the early 1930s. Given closer regulation of securities sales and an improved international monetary climate after World War II, it was highly questionable whether the same motivations that would make this collective utility parameter significant were still operative. It would appear that the principal motivation after the War, with respect to the export of capital (whether private or public) to the socialist countries, was the desire to deprive these nations of capital for consumption. In other words, there were now prohibitively negative utility parameters associated with y_{ij}^k; that is, the consumption of credit or capital unattached to an underlying commodity transaction. As we have seen, a prohibitively negative value for these utility parameters implies an embargo on all exports of the ith good to the jth region. This line of reasoning would not account, however, for the fact that Albania and Bulgaria were both "permitted" targets of private capital exports under the Johnson Act, while Poland and Rumania, which came to receive more liberal export control and cargo preference treatment (see Chapters 6 and 7), were not. We must conclude that either this national security consideration was not that significant; or if it was, that it was not adequately reflected in existing legislation.

Initial Differentiation Among the Socialist Countries

While the U.S. "containment" policy tended to view the socialist countries as a Soviet dominated "bloc," some differentiation was made *among* these countries even during the early years of maximum economic warfare. In the case of Yugoslavia, this differentiation seemed to be based upon a phenomenon which has more recently come to be called "polycentrism." The in-

---

[1] Assuming that the fears of jth country default underlying the negative utility considerations involving z_{ij}^k are well founded, then the probability of the $(j+1)$th obligor defaulting on its obligations will be greater, the less diversified its portfolio.

creased U.S. economic differentiation with respect to both the People's Republic of China and North Korea, however, apparently was a direct response to military warfare in Korea.

Apparent increased independence of the smaller socialist countries from the Soviet Union, or what Cohen has labeled "polycentrism,"[58] has often had an effect upon how these countries are viewed by individuals in the United States. To the extent that Americans fear the military potential of the Soviet Union rather than the separate potential and intentions of her presumed "satellites," and to the degree polycentrism reveals a lessened willingness of these countries to lend support to Soviet military and economic warfare, their increased independence would imply diminished U.S. disutility arising from their consumption of nonmilitary goods. Polycentric trends would therefore imply a diminished negative collective utility parameter associated with y_{ij}^k for the jth polycentric satellite, or possibly even a positive value for this collective utility parameter.

Yugoslavia was the earliest example of the impact of "polycentrism" on American utility functions. This country began to show its independence from the dominant "bloc" country, the Soviet union, as early as 1948, as a result of which she was expelled from the Cominform. United States policy makers made the foreign policy decision at the time to treat Yugoslavia more or less as a "Western" country with respect to economic relations.[59] Consequently, Yugoslavia has continued to receive MFN treatment on its exports and to be exempt from most of the onerous export controls applying to trade with the East. This decision appears to have reflected significantly diminished collective disutilities for the (f_{hj}^k, f_{ij}^k) and y_{ij}^k national security considerations with respect to Yugoslavia, and was the first case of U.S. policies aimed at rewarding and encouraging "polycentric" movements within the Communist world.

With respect to belligerents in a "hot" war, such as the Korean conflict, which began in 1950, it is only natural for most individuals in a belligerent nation to have decidedly negative feelings concerning any trade with the enemy. (This "natural" reaction may only really apply to the ideological nature of twentieth century conflicts, however, and may also result from the fact that modern wars usually much more directly affect the civilian population than did eighteenth or nineteenth century wars.)[60]

While the Communist dominated regions in China apparently became increasingly subject to a U.S. trade embargo in the course of driving the nationalist forces from the mainland in 1949, the total embargo on trade with the mainland was not imposed until after commencement of armed hostilities in Korea in June 1950.[61] In late 1950 the Foreign Assets Control Regulations were issued under authority of Section 5(b) of the Trading with the Enemy Act (see *supra*, page 55). These regulations, enforced by the Treasury Department's Office of Foreign Assets Control, placed an embargo on virtually all commercial and financial transactions by U.S. or U.S. controlled firms with the People's Republic of China and North Korea.[62] These virtual embargo measures undoubtedly reflected prohibitively negative collective utility parameters in the U.S. for the entire range of potential belligerent consumption (the y^k_{hj}, y^k_{ij} consideration), as well as for the companion foreign exchange collective good (f^k_{hj}, f^k_{ij}).

Keeping in mind the usual *transshipment* and *isolation* requirements, as the case may be, we observe that the success of this differentiated treatment of the belligerents depended not only upon cooperation from U.S. allies and "nonaligned" countries, but also upon whether destination certifications made with respect to exports to other socialist countries, which themselves presumably constituted some national security threat to the U.S., were credible.

With respect to the other Western nations, the previously mentioned sanctions of the Battle Act applied in the case of the PRC and North Korea as well. Furthermore, the United States pressed for the establishment of separate machinery within the COCOM framework to coordinate the more extensive embargo on trade with the Asian Communist countries. As a result, an additional coordinating committee, "Chincom," was set up in September 1952. This group established a broader export control list for China and North Korea that came to be known as the "China Differential."[63] Finally, the U.S. was also successful in persuading the United Nations General Assembly to adopt a "China embargo" resolution, calling for a cooperative effort among member nations, who were of course also supporting a U.N. military force in Korea, with respect to the embargo of strategic exports to the PRC. The Soviet dominated countries did not vote on the embargo resolution, as they considered the entire UN posture on the Korean conflict to be illegal.[64]

With regard to possible transshipment of "China Differential" goods through Eastern Europe to China, U.S. control authorities were apparently concerned enough to impose stricter controls on the Eastern Europe trade, including a provision enacted in early 1951 that *all* U.S. exports to Eastern Europe would require a validated licence.[65] Additional assurance against transshipment was provided by subjecting the Southeast Asian commercial centers of Hong Kong and Macao to a virtual embargo policy. On the import side, the Foreign Assets Control Regulations went to great length in seeking to prohibit indirect imports originating either in the PRC or North Korea.[66] While in theory this satisfied the transshipment requirement, the isolation requirement applicable to those products which were perfect substitutes in third country consumption was not met. Whether arbitrage through substitution of Chinese goods in foreign consumption actually occurred is of course an empirical question.

6 Deterioration of the Cooperative Embargo and U.S. Policy Contradictions, 1953–1963

Deterioration of the Cooperative Embargo

The scope of the Western strategic embargo list was expanded significantly in the several years after the establishment of COCOM, primarily as a result of increased allied unity following the outbreak of the Korean War.[1] But as this conflict came to an end in 1953, allied pressure upon the United States to reduce the embargo's coverage became quite intense. This led to negotiations within COCOM in late 1953 and early 1954, resulting in considerable shortening of the embargo lists. Further cuts in the COCOM lists were made in the period 1955–1958, after which time relative stability returned to the cooperative embargo, as the lists had by 1958 been pared to a point where unanimity as to which goods were really of "strategic" importance was not as difficult to achieve.[2]

The increased allied pressure on the United States with respect to the scope of the COCOM lists was not solely in response to the cessation of military warfare in Korea. There were many political and economic forces working towards a breakdown in the western embargo alliance. Most of these forces are discussed at some length by Adler-Karlsson;[3] consequently we shall merely note them and devote ourselves to analyzing their implications for the United States policy of offensive economic warfare against the East.

The year 1953 not only marked the end of the war in Korea. It also was characterized by a slight turn away from a policy of economic autarky by the Soviet Union. There is evidence that this change in Soviet policy, which meant an increased willingness to trade with the West, occurred even before the death of Stalin.[4] Furthermore, there appeared to be increased recognition in the West that a power stalemate had evolved in Europe, implying that the opportunities for "chipping away" at the Soviet bloc through economic and even military warfare had greatly diminished. The idea of bringing the Communist regimes "to their knees" now seemed less and less realistic. This new realization came in the wake of the lack of tangible response by the West at the time of the East German riots in June 1953, the stalemate in Korea, and the successful testing of the first airborne H-bomb by the Soviet Union in August of that year.

At the same time most of the industrialized world was dragging through a recession, and evidence began to appear that the West's embargo policy was becoming increasingly economically costly to the cooperating nations.[5] This undoubtedly became ever more evident to the Western Europeans as many of the postwar domestic supply bottlenecks began to disappear, and these economies became increasingly outward looking. Furthermore, as Adler-Karlsson has noted, " suspicion was widespread that a great amount of illegal trade, perhaps more than the normal trade, took place which never entered the official statistics."[6] Finally, Marshall Plan aid was terminated in 1953, and the sanctions incorporated in this program for forcing compliance with the U.S. embargo policy ended with it. As the Western European economies proceeded with reconstruction, the force of the Battle Act sanctions on these countries also diminished. Continued American attempts to force compliance with the larger embargo list, in the face of these various forces which implied its reduced effectiveness as a political instrument, in turn led to increased dissension and "polycentric" talk within the NATO alliance.

The Western European attitude of this period can be characterized as an early recognition of the fundamental trade-off between economic *warfare* and short-run economic *welfare* considerations. Negative international external effects in consumption (y_{hj}^k, y_{ij}^k) existed for them, too, but the number of products which they saw as being "strategic" for the enemy's purposes was simply much smaller for them than for the Americans. This may have been due to their greater skepticism as to the feasibility of a massive program of economic warfare directed towards the East, as well as to a greater appreciation for the relative invulnerability of the Soviet and Soviet dominated regimes in the smaller socialist countries. But this smaller concern with Eastern consumption levels over a wide range of products, as well as basic indifference towards Eastern foreign exchange earnings (the f_{hj}^k, f_{ij}^k consideration),[a] undoubtedly reflected as well their awareness of the great economic costs to themselves of restricting trade with the East.

As Western Europeans negotiated reductions in the COCOM embargo list, the degree of U.S. *unilateral* export restriction by definition increased. Consequently, the United States' ability to deprive the East of all those commodities that appeared on the COCOM differential list depended upon (1) enough product differentiation in third countries so as to make substitution in these countries' consumption difficult, and (2) tighter controls on transshipment. The latter condition was apparently fulfilled, at least officially.[7] But the former requirement became increasingly more difficult to satisfy. This is because the lengthening of the "extra-COCOM" U.S. unilateral control list occurred at the same time that Western European

---

[a] The Western European nations never invoked a discriminatory import policy to the same extent as the United States. Furthermore, it may be said that to the degree the Western Europeans realized how important a constraint inconvertibility and the consequent shortage of hard currencies was to the socialist countries' own ability to import, they might well have experienced positive utility from increases in Eastern foreign exchange earnings.

(and Japanese) domestic bottlenecks were being overcome and businessmen in these countries were increasingly looking abroad for markets. In fact, the pressure from the allies for a reduction of the cooperative embargo (i.e., a lengthening of the extra-COCOM list) was itself a positive function of increased Western European and Japanese interest in, and ability to supply, the Eastern markets.

The situation that the United States increasingly encountered from the early 1950s on was therefore similar to that portrayed in the final section of Chapter 3: "A Dynamic Consideration." It was shown there that reliance upon product differentiation-in-foreign-consumption in the absence of an outright cooperative embargo of the target region is *potentially* a very fragile means of assuring the success of an offensive economic warfare policy. This is because third country supply and supply elasticities may increase over time, meaning that third countries will merely take away target markets from the discriminating nation and frustrate its policy objectives. As some of the evidence gathered together in Chapter 8 shows, this is apparently what happened to the United States over the past twenty years. In fact, it should have been expected, as Western European and Japanese elasticities were only artificially low in the immediate postwar period, as a result of the tremendous wartime damage and loss of life.

We also observed that the successfully discriminating nation has two basic options in the face of the foregoing dynamic consideration. Either it can press its allies and the nonaligned to cease all trade with the target countries in the affected products, or it can revise its own preference scheme as regards the importance of depriving the target region of certain products and foreign exchange earnings. The first option was of course out of the question—indeed, United States allies were pressing for a relaxation of the cooperative embargo. Therefore more, not fewer, goods became subject to the dynamic consideration we have mentioned. The second option was available, but the Americans were in no mood to revise downward their disutilities arising from Eastern consumption of the wide range of products subject to extra-COCOM control. On the contrary, the mid1950s witnessed a strong upsurge in "anti Communist" feelings in the United States, as exemplified by the various McCarthy-inspired purges. The United States was therefore locked into a policy which was becoming less and less possible to implement successfully.

The disparity between the U.S. and allied trade policies toward the People's Republic of China became particularly severe after 1957. As a result of the initial downward COCOM revisions in 1954, which the U.S. insisted should not apply to China, the so-called "China differential" actually was greater than ever before, and was subscribed to by all the COCOM nations. In 1957, however, the United Kingdom unilaterally revoked the "China differential" and was quickly followed by the other COCOM countries, with the exception of the United States.[8] For the next fourteen years the

U.S. continued to maintain a complete embargo on exports to and imports from the People's Republic of China.

The more extensive and severe external effects that U.S. citizens supposedly experienced from Chinese consumption and earnings of foreign exchange are difficult to explain. One reason might have been the continued political instability of the Southeast Asian countries bordering on or near Mainland China, together with the influence of the "China Lobby" which kept alive the hope of a nationalist reconquest of the Mainland. This is in contrast to the relative power stalemate in Europe and an evolving de facto acceptance of Soviet hegemony in Eastern Europe.

Signs of Policy Differentiation

Although the broad outlines of American East-West trade policy remained unchanged throughout the fifties and early sixties, there were several further instances of U.S. policy differentiation among the socialist countries in this period. On the one hand, the United States embarked upon a more liberal policy vis-à-vis Poland after 1956; on the other, Cuba was singled out for extremely severe policy treatment after the accession of the Castro regime in 1959.

The new position toward Poland resulted from the "polycentric" policy consideration which we observed in the last chapter in connection with Yugoslavia. It will be recalled that this consideration involves Americans attaching positive utility to evidence of "satellite" independence from the Soviet Union. With respect to Poland it was believed that the advent of the Gomulka regime following the political upheaval in late 1956 might well result in significant and favorable (to the West) changes in that country's internal and foreign policies. Indeed, the President responded immediately with a statement assuring U.S. assistance to the "freedom-loving peoples" in Eastern Europe. This was followed by a declaration of the U.S. Secretary of State that U.S. economic aid to the fledgling Polish regime would be immediately forthcoming.[9]

While it is possible that an inclination toward favoring Poland as against the other socialist countries might also have existed because of the relatively large American constituency of Polish descent,[b] it is very likely that Poland was selected for special treatment precisely because the "successful" upheaval there was a tangible polycentric symbol to which the polycentric policy could be easily associated.[10] Moreover, there was considerable polycentric thinking in Congress in the late fifties, as dramatized by the so-called

[b] In other words, there existed a large subset of Polish-Americans with zero or even positive utility parameters associated with Polish consumption of a wide range of products.

"Captive Nations Resolution" of July 1959, which declared it to be a U.S. objective to break up the Soviet "empire."[11] Senator Kennedy's 1960 statement in connection with his proposed (but unsuccessful) 1957 bill to amend the Battle Act so as to allow granting of aid to Communist countries showing polycentric tendencies should be quoted in this regard.[12]

We must arm ourselves with more flexible economic tools. We must be willing to recognize growing divisions in the Communist camp, and be willing to encourage those divisions. My amendment to the Battle Act would permit the President to use our economic strength to promote peaceful change behind the Iron Curtain wherever this would help wean the so-called captive nations away from their Kremlin masters. In the 85th Congress this amendment was defeated by one vote. In the 86th Congress, it passed the Senate and died in the House. In the 87th Congress, under new Presidential leadership, it must become law.

We have already discussed the implications which the polycentric consideration appears to have for our national security variables. It will be recalled that the basic effects are: (1) to attribute a lower level of disutility to consumption of a wide range of nonmilitary (and possibly even some military) goods in the polycentric country, and (2) to experience less satisfaction from depriving such a country of foreign exchange earnings. In response to these modified utility functions with respect to Poland, U.S. policy makers undertook to effect major trade policy changes in three areas: foreign aid, export controls and imports.

The foreign aid initiative was taken under the aegis of the Agricultural Trade Development and Assistance Act of 1954 (PL 480) framework. The PL 480 program has two basic objectives, the sale of surplus agricultural commodities, and the provision of foreign aid by selling these products at less than world prices and by authorizing the use of foreign currency proceeds arising from such sales for the purpose of foreign economic development.[13] As we discussed at several points in Chapter 5, the motivation for granting foreign aid springs basically from *positive* international external effects in consumption, whether for military goods (y^k_{hj}) or nonmilitary products (y^k_{ij}).

Although one of the basic purposes of the U.S. foreign aid program was to bolster economically or militarily vulnerable countries lying outside the Communist sphere and to help the less developed economies to achieve an atmosphere conducive to free institutions,[14] provision was also made in the PL 480 program to reward or encourage polycentric movements within the Communist world. Section 103(d) of PL 480, as amended, allows the Executive to "enter into agreement for the sale of agricultural commodities for *dollars* on credit terms" to any socialist country or area not "dominated or controlled by a world communist movement."[15] Moreover, the extension of dollar credits under this program to certain Communist countries is, to the degree that it is "assistance," an exception to the general prohibition of assistance to such countries under the Battle Act.[16] As noted earlier, Yugoslavia was determined by the President to be independent of the "world Communist movement" as early as 1949, and Poland was also determined by the President in January 1957 to be independent of the Soviet Union, with respect to eligibility for PL 480 exports for *dollars*.[17] Actual agricultural exports on these terms began in 1957.[18]

We should also observe that sales of subsidized agricultural commodites at world prices, often on credit, by or with the support of the Government's Commodity Credit Corporation (CCC), are permitted to those socialist countries for which trade is not embargoed. Such sales and attendant credit extensions are also not deemed to be "assistance" for purposes of the Battle Act.[19] After the basic policy turnabout in 1956–1967, Poland purchased hundreds of millions of dollars worth of such CCC-financed products over the course of the next decade.[20]. In summary, the PL 480 and CCC programs effectively subsidized the export of certain agricultural commodities to Poland, in response to positive utility parameters associated with the consumption of these commodities (y_{ij}) in this country.

With respect to export controls, the discrimination in favor of Poland, which began in August 1957, took the form of a gradual decontrolling of goods from the extra-COCOM control list.[21] This meant that many items which still required a validated license for export to the other target countries could now be exported to Poland on open general license. It is also altogether possible that approval of validated license applications became easier to obtain in connection with exports to this country.

This lowering of the implicit export tax rates on the export of certain products to Poland raised the same type of *potential* problem that we noted in the last chapter with respect to the higher level of discrimination against China. That is to say, successful discrimination in favor of Poland against the other socialist nations depended upon whether the United States could rely on the certifications made as to the ultimate destination of exports made to Poland under general license, which would require a validated license if shipped to other target countries. Presumably the belief in the credibility of these certifications was in some sense a positive function of the perceived "independence" of the favored country.

Another rationalization for the taking of this risk could have been to decontrol for Poland only those items that would probably be approved for export to the other target countries anyway, with maintenance of the distinction in the control list serving to "give notice" to the world of which countries were favored. The difference from the point of view of U.S. exporters, however, in terms of the aforementioned "costs" of coping with export control procedures, would of course have been significant (see *supra*, p. 57).

The third basic reward to Poland for its apparent "polycentric" behavior related to U.S. imports from that country. As we have argued throughout this study, consistent with diminished marginal disutility from jth country consumption of a wide range of goods would be diminished marginal disutility of individuals in the discriminating nation with respect to jth earnings of foreign exchange (the f_{hj}^k, f_{ij}^k consideration). This linkage appears to have underlain U.S. policy towards Poland after the accession of the Gomulka regime. That is, granting the Poles additional means for earning hard currency would be an obvious form of reward for polycentric behavior.

This consideration, rather than the emerging interest of Poland in joining GATT, seems to have been the predominant factor in leading the President in 1960 to restore MFN treatment to Poland.[22] While Congress had prescribed denial of MFN to all nations "dominated or controlled by the foreign government or foreign organization controlling the world Communist movement," it left with the President the discretion to determine which such countries were in fact so dominated. The President made the determination in late 1960 that Poland was not Soviet dominated within the meaning of the 1951 legislation. MFN treatment for Poland was extended unilaterally and was not the subject of a new trade agreement.[23]

The other case of policy differentiation among socialist countries during this period involved American trade relations with Cuba. This island economy had long been basically a monoculture as far as its export trade was concerned. In 1958, for example, sugar exports made up roughly 80 per cent of Cuban exports by dollar volume. Cuba's trade was also heavily concentrated geographically; over two-thirds of Cuban trade volume was transacted with the United States.[24] One of the reasons for reliance upon the U.S. as an export market was the system of tariff preferences which the United States had historically accorded a number of Cuban products.[25] Furthermore, the U.S. sugar quota for Cuba was quite important, accounting for a significant part of Cuba's exports to the mainland.

After the Castro regime came to power in early 1959, U.S.-Cuban political and economic relations began to deteriorate. The introduction by Castro of foreign exchange controls and a program of agrarian reform seemed to discriminate particularly against U.S. exports of various manufactured consumer goods to the island on the one hand, and the sizable American-owned investments in Cuba on the other. U.S. policy makers began to consider a reduction in the Cuban sugar quota as a means of influencing Cuban economic policies. The growing Cuban flirtation with the Soviet Union, and expropriations of American industrial property, only accelerated the deterioration in U.S.-Cuban relations. A detailed analysis of the cause-and-effect relationships in these early relations between Castro's Cuba and the United States are beyond the scope of this book. It is interesting, however, to note that sometime later Secretary of State Dean Rusk was to describe U.S. objectives in regard to Cuba as follows:[26]

(1) To reduce Castro's will and ability to export subversion and violence to other American states; (2) To make plain to the people of Cuba that Castro's regime cannot serve their interests; (3) To demonstrate to the peoples of the American Republics that communism has no future in the Western Hemisphere; and (4) To increase the cost to the Soviets of maintaining a Communist outpost in the Western Hemisphere.

The particularly intense American irritation and fear of the new Cuban regime can only be understood in the light of both the tangible economic losses suffered by American exporters and investors as a result of Castro's economic "reforms," and the fears of spreading Communist inspired subversion in the Western Hemisphere resulting from Castro's turning away from the United States and towards the Soviet Union for the "special relationship" so necessary to Cuban economic well-being. Given the historic trade preferences allowed Cuba, its proximity to the mainland, and the particular antiAmerican nature of the Castro regime, many Americans undoubtedly felt a special sense of betrayal against the Cubans who stayed and supported the new government.

Finally, the Cuban economy, with its great historical dependence on one export commodity (sugar) and one export market (the United States) must have seemed particularly vulnerable to U.S. economic sanctions.[27] Translated into the collective good considerations of our model, the American collective utility parameters associated with Cuban consumption of a wide range of military and nonmilitary goods were undoubtedly negative. Consistent with this would have been negative utility parameters in connection with Cuban earnings of foreign exchange.

The United States carried out a policy of gradually escalating economic warfare against Cuba over the period 1959–1963. In 1960 the U.S. lowered its Cuban sugar quota for the first time.[28] Later that year a virtual embargo was placed on exports to Cuba. Exceptions to this embargo included certain medicines and medical supplies and nonsubsidized foodstuffs.[29] The embargo was made more complete through issuance in 1963 of the Cuban Assets Control Regulations. These regulations, like those applying to economic relations with the People's Republic of China and North Korea, were effected under authority of the Trading with the Enemy Act, and are enforced by the OFAC. They also place severe restrictions on financial transactions involving Cuba.[30]

In spite of existing legislation directing the President to deny MFN treatment to "any country or areas dominated or controlled by communism" (see *infra*, p. 59), MFN was not denied to Cuban imports. This was only because certain bilateral agreements concluded under the auspices of GATT, together with trade preferences for the Phillipines, had historically been geared to the *lowest* duties levied by the U.S. on certain products, and in many cases this meant those duties payable under the preference system formally accorded Cuban imports.[31] In actuality, however, imports from Cuba have been subject to a total embargo since February 1962.[32] Since 1963 these imports have been embargoed under authority of the Cuban Assets Control Regulations.[33]

As with the strategic embargoes directed against the socialist countries of Eastern Europe and Asia, the United States in this case also attempted to use its foreign aid program to force allied compliance with its own economic warfare policy. This particular policy was undertaken at the initiative of Congress rather than the Administration. In the Foreign Assistance Act of 1963 Congress directed the President to terminate aid to any countries which did not curtail shipments to Cuba, except in those cases in which the President found it to be in the national interest to waive the sanction.[34]

As we have seen, the export and import embargoes could only be effected to the extent that transshipment through third countries was eliminated for those products that were not subject to perfect substitution in third country consumption. For all other goods, the United States had to ensure that no trade in such products took place between Cuba and the rest of the world. With respect to the embargo on imports, the transshipment requirement was generally satisfied, in theory, by the quite comprehensive coverage of the Cuban Assets Control Regulations.

Implementation of the export embargo provided greater problems. Once again the allied members of COCOM refused to embargo anything more than the COCOM list of products. Furthermore, threatened "blacklisting" of ships calling at Cuban ports and termination of foreign aid was not wholly successful in detering allied commerce with Cuba. The waiver given the President with respect to termination of foreign aid under the Foreign Assistance Act of 1963 was used quite often. Moreover, "the American endeavors to strain Communist shipping facilities by blacklisting were counteracted in the East by chartering Western ships for tranport between European and Russian Communist ports, thereby releasing the Communist-owned cargoes that were normally traveling these routes, e.g., between Leningrad and Vladivostok, for trade with Cuba."[35] Ironically, the more successful the American embargo of Cuba, the more the Cubans were forced to rely on the other Communist nations both for imports and as export markets.

Two Policy making Bodies and Policy Schizophrenia

The hint of an emerging U.S. East-West trade policy making problem was contained in the previously mentioned 1963 amendment to foreign aid legislation, which was designed to force foreign compliance with the U.S. policy of total embargo of Cuba. The basic problem lay in the fact that there were effectively two decision making bodies with respect to East-West trade policy, Congress and the Executive. Whenever Congress chose to tie the hands of the Administration in certain facets of this policy, a curious schizophrenia resulted with respect to U.S. policies toward the socialist countries. Some policies came to reflect the slightly liberalized attitude of the Executive, while other policy actions seemed to merely reinforce the old "containment" attitude.

The legislation providing for termination of foreign aid to countries shipping goods to Cuba was passed by the Congress without the Administration's having requested such authority. Continued utilization by the President of his waiver under this legislation with respect to cutting off aid, demonstrated that the Administration did not generally consider use of this policy instrument to be appropriate, given its own perception of international political and economic realities and the national interest. Indeed, one can say in general that Congress throughout the postwar period had collectively taken a harder, less flexible "containment" position than the successive administrations. This was apparent, for instance, in our discussion in Chapter 5 of the withdrawal of MFN treatment for U.S. imports from socialist countries, as well as of the more rigid congressional interpretation of the Battle Act legislation and its implications for the COCOM cooperative embargo. Congress also seemed to be more skeptical regarding the implementation of specific polycentric policies in the late fifties and early sixties. As we have seen, Congress did pass a "Captive Nations Resolution" in 1959. Nevertheless, it was unwilling to permit a general relaxation of Battle Act restrictions on aid to individual Communist countries. Finally, it will be recalled that the liberalizing steps taken by the Eisenhower Adminstration with respect to Poland in the late 1950s and 1960, including PL 480 aid, selective decontrolling of exports and the granting of MFN, were all taken without the necessity of seeking congressional approval.

Of course it would be silly to expect Congress and any administration to always agree on all issues. Each senator or congressman has a particular state or local constituency to which he is responsible, as well as having obligations to the "national interest." The President, on the other hand, is responsible, in theory, to all the people. Consequently each member of Congress takes into account most intensely those preference systems of his own, narrowly defined constituency, whereas the President supposedly responds to the entire "national" constituency. Of course, another reason for divergence between congressional and presidential perceptions of the world might also lie in their implicitly applying different weighting schemes to the preference systems of their constituents.

Unfortunately, all to little attention has been focused upon the determinants of congressional and executive policy making as regards commercial policy issues. One recent study has implied, however, that *Congress* may well be influenced to a greater degree by special interest groups, because such groups are typically well organized and are thereby geared to influencing congressional behavior on issues affecting their narrowly defined economic interests.[36] It is difficult, however, to explain the less differentiated congressional policy posture with respect to East-West trade that characterized this period. Perhaps all that can really be said is that the degree of emotionalism regarding this issue seems to have been greater in Congress than in the successive administrations, resulting in a less discriminating congressional attitude towards economic warfare levied at the socialist world.

The fundamental problem of two decision making bodies did not really exist, of course, as long as Congress was content with passing legislation similar to the Export Control Act of 1949, Section 5 of the Trade Agreements Extension Act of 1951, or the aforementioned Foreign Assistance Act of 1963. That is to say, as long as Congress allowed the President discretion concerning export controls, denial of MFN or foreign aid, the Administration could continue to orchestrate a policy on all fronts that contained the precise amount of differentiation among foreign trading partners that it thought appropriate to accomplishing its policy objectives. The real conflict came—and the era of schizophrenic policy making really began—when Congress decided to remove Presidential discretion in some areas while permitting continued discretion in others. This is what happened in the heightened Cold War atmosphere of the early 1960s. The problem was exacerbated later in the decade as a result of the intensification of the war in Vietnam.

During the 1950s the Soviet Union and its Eastern European satellites had been able to narrow the margin of military superiority heretofore enjoyed by the United States and its NATO allies. Over the same period most of the socialist countries had demonstrated a pronounced ability to achieve rapid economic growth.[37] By the end of the decade Soviet Leaders were in fact predicting that they would soon surpass the United States as the preeminent world economic power.[38] The rapid military and economic growth of the socialist world contrasted sharply with a picture of relative sluggish economic growth in the United States. Indeed, the U.S. experienced three recessions in the seven year period 1954–1961. As the sixties opened, the Soviet boasts of future economic supremacy and the triumph of their economic system gained credibility. Against this background, together with heightened military-political tension between the two superpowers as a result of the U-2 reconaissance plane affair, building of the Berlin Wall, and increased Soviet-American confrontation over Cuba, Congress passed several important trade restrictive measures in the early sixties.

With respect to exports, Congress extended and amended the Export Control Act of 1949. The principal amendments explicitly reflected the predominant congressional belief that the national security of the United States was threatened by the increased economic strength of the socialist countries, as well as by their relative military strength. Congress felt it was important to state quite clearly that it perceived that the collective utility parameters in the U.S. associated with Communist consumption were prohibitively negative for a wide range of nonmilitary goods, the consumption of which (the y_{ij}^k consideration) would contribute to the economic strength of the socialist world.[39]

The more important 1962 amendments to the Export Control Act of 1949 were as follows:

1. The finding that "the unrestricted export of materials without regard to their potential military and *economic* significance may adversely affect the national security of the United States."[40]

2. An explicit declaration of policy with respect to economic warfare: "The Congress further declares that it is the policy of the United States to use its economic resources and advantages in trade with Communist-dominated nations to further the national security and foreign policy objectives of the United States."[41]

3. The President was granted the authority to prescribe rules and regulations which "shall provide for denial of any request or application for authority to export articles, materials, or supplies, including technical data, or any other information . . . to any nation or combination of nations threatening the national security of the United States if the President shall determine that such export makes a significant contribution to the military or *economic* potential of such nation or nations which would prove detrimental to the national security and welfare of the United States."[42]

4. Finally, the penalties for violation of any provision of the Act or any regulations, orders or licenses issued under authority of the Act were stiffened.[43]

Although the Administration apparently had not requested an extension of the scope of this Act, the amendments to include goods primarily with *economic* significance may have had some effect on the export control system. As these amendments were interpreted by the export control authorities, the burden of proof was on any one who would argue that a good contributing significantly to the economic potential of one of the target socialist countries was not detrimental to U.S. national security. But the authorities did claim to take foreign *availability* of the good into consideration.[44]

It is not at all clear whether passage of these amendments had an effect on the relative treatment of Poland by the export control authorities. But Presidential discretion with respect to Poland as well as Yugoslavia was in fact taken away by Congress in 1961 in connection with grant and loan aid to these two countries.[45] One observer has suggested that the inclusion of

Yugoslavia in this action was in response to "a particularly antiWestern speech by Tito."[46]

A more important, and, as it has turned out, a more enduring limitation on the President's East-West trade policy making powers, involved the 1962 congressional legislation on imports from the Communist countries. The President's message accompanying the introduction in Congress of the proposed Trade Expansion Act of 1962 asked for continued *discretionary* authority with respect to the Presidential determinations allowed under the Trade Agreements Extension Act of 1951.[47] It will be recalled from the last chapter that Section 5 of the 1951 Act directed the President to deny MFN treatment to imports from the Soviet Union and from any nation or area determined to be "dominated or controlled by the foreign government or foreign organization controlling the world Communist movement." President Truman had immediately determined that Yugoslavia was not so "dominated or controlled" and, as we have seen, President Eisenhower made a similar determination with respect to Poland in late 1960.

In spite of the President's request, more restrictive language emerged in the substitute bill that was introduced in Congress after initial hearings.[48] This language presumably reflected the congressional feeling that there now existed negative collective utility parameters with respect to the earning of foreign exchange by all the socialist countries, regardless of whether they had or might be expected to show evidence of "polycentrism" within the Soviet orbit. Possibly some of the same kinds of protectionist considerations which seemed to figure in the 1951 import legislation also were at work.

This substitute bill was enacted into law despite the Administration's objections to its treatment of trade with the socialist countries.[49] Subsection 231(a) of the Trade Expansion Act of 1962 removed the discretion of the President in the matter of MFN treatment, and required denial of MFN to "products whether imported directly or indirectly, of any country or areas dominated or controlled by communism."[50]

Presidential action on this score was to be effected "as soon as practicable." There continued to be strong support within the Executive Branch, however, for continuing to grant MFN to Yugoslavia and Poland for foreign policy reasons.[51] Finally, congressional proponents of this point of view managed to affix Section 402 to the Foreign Assistance Act of 1963, which added the following new subsection (b) to Section 231 of the Trade Expansion Act of 1962:[52]

> The President may extend the benefits of trade agreement concessions made by the United States to products, whether imported directly or indirectly, of a country or area within the purview of subsection (a) which, *at the time of enactment of this subsection*, was receiving trade concessions, when he determines that such trade concessions would promote the independence of such country or area from domination or control by international communism, and reports this determination to the Congress.

As of the time of enactment of this subsection (December 1963), MFN treatment for Poland and Yugoslavia had not yet been terminated. In March 1964 the President made the determination specified in this subsection that permitted continuation of MFN treatment for these two countries.

Although subsection 231(b) explicitly recognized the "polycentrism" consideration operating in American utility functions, this factor was allowed to influence policy only with respect to the two Communist controlled countries which had already been accorded more favorable treatment for their polycentric behavior. MFN could henceforth be granted to other socialist countries only through new legislation.[c] A basic asymmetry seems to be inherent in subsection 231(b) which, as we shall see, has had unfortunate implications for the consistency of U.S. trade policies toward the socialist world. In effect, while the President continued to have discretion with respect to export controls, at least as far as differentiation among socialist countries was concerned, no such discretion existed now with regard to import policies.

Undoubtedly this more detailed congressional supervision of the precise height of import tariffs is an expression of Congress's constitutional power "to lay and collect taxes, duties, imports, and excises."[54] Export controls, on the other hand, are only *implicit* taxes from the government's point of view. While the economic and national security impact of the two kinds of taxes may be similar in important respects, from a legal standpoint they are dissimilar, and the relative lack of interest shown by Congress in the discretionary management of export controls is understandable. Furthermore, Congress is even less well prepared to do a satisfactory job in "setting" or reviewing the implicit export tax rates embodied in export controls than it is in establishing or approving tariff rates, even if it were to see the former as its constitutional duty. This is because the pattern of controls is continually being reviewed and modified, in response to the constant flow of applications for validated licenses to export. We have also noted the particular leverage which well organized economic interest groups have in Congress. There is some historical evidence that these groups have tended to develop most frequently with respect to import policies, possibly because the threat of competition from abroad is a more unifying force than the appearance of export opportunities.[55] Consequently, it is understandable that Congress should be more preoccupied with import policies. What is less understandable is the refusal of Congress after 1962 to even grant the Executive the same basic discretionary powers in respect of East-West import policies, as it has been allowed to exercise with respect to trade agreements with non-socialist nations.

---

[c] Nations considered as coming under the control or domination of Communist regimes after passage of the 1963 legislation would not lose their MFN treatment unless the President chose not to make the determination required by Section 231 (b).[53]

7 Growing Recognition of the Trade-Off, 1963–

In the last chapter we saw that U.S. East-West trade policies in the late fifties and early sixties were marked by three pronounced characteristics. First, as the cooperative embargo lists were shortened, the effectiveness of the U.S. "containment" policy likewise deteriorated. As the embargo effort became increasingly a unilateral U.S. exercise, the "gains from trade" with the East that were formerly almost totally denied the West now began to be realized by the other Western allies, often at the expense of the United States.

Second, the Eisenhower and Kennedy administrations had shown some signs of wishing to differentiate among the socialist countries for trade policy purposes. This movement towards greater differentiation was predicated primarily upon "polycentric" motivations; that is, the desire to encourage increased independence of the various "satellite" countries from the Soviet Union. The only socialist country favored by the U.S. in this manner was Poland, although Yugoslavia had long benefitted from the polycentric consideration in U.S. policy.

Finally, we noted an emerging schizophrenic phenomenon in U.S. policy, which resulted from a curious asymmetry that evolved between American export and import policies in East-West trade. This asymmetry arose from the fact that there are two policy making bodies, Congress and the Executive, and the former chose in 1962 to deny the President discretion only with respect to liberalization of imports from the socialist world. Before 1964 this was basically only a potential problem, however, because Poland, the principal benefactor from the polycentric policies, was eligible both for liberalized export controls and MFN treatment.

Search for a More Realistic Policy

Although the Kennedy Administration was somewhat inhibited by the 1962 export control and import legislation from pursuing new East-West trade policy initiatives, it cautiously embarked on a course designed to provide positive leadership to those who were urging a reversal of the economic containment policy.[a] This policy was pursued even more vigorously by the

[a] Adler-Karlsson notes that "in 1961 President Kennedy tried to amend the Battle Act in a way that would give him greater flexibility to continue the policy which had been started in Poland in 1957. His proposed amendment was approved by the Senate on May 11, 1961 but was never passed by the House. There are no indications that Kennedy pressed the issue very vigorously."[1]

Johnson Administration in later years, although the Johnson efforts in this regard were increasingly frustrated by the congressional response to the war in Vietnam. The new course seems to have been predicated upon acceptance of at least three new strategies by which the West could hope to contain Communist expansionism, while at the same time backing away from the less and less effective isolationist policies embodied in the massive offensive economic warfare against the East. The three new notions were what we shall call "coexistence" (embodying here also the idea of increased contacts between East and West), "polycentrism," and "internal liberalization."[2] Often they were subsumed together under the umbrella concept of "building bridges" to the Communist world.[3]

A prerequisite for acceptance of these new strategic notions was the gradual recognition that several of the basic assumptions underlying the basic Cold War embargo policy were perhaps unrealistic. That is to say, the severe and indiscriminate diseconomies experienced by Americans in connection with Communist consumption had arisen out of a lack of appreciation for the resilience and relative invulnerability of the Soviet dominated regimes. A fairly persuasive case could be made for the relatively limited aims of the COCOM embargo as it evolved after 1953: to preserve the gap between NATO and Eastern *military* strength by embargoing the export to the Communist countries of what in most cases were clearly *military* goods and technology.[4]

But it was doubtful that by depriving nonmilitary products to the Soviet Union and its presumed satellites, the military strength of the Eastern countries would be severely sapped. As the so-called "Miller Report" observed in 1965: " . . . gains from nonmilitary trade with the United States are unlikely to release additional resources for Soviet military expenditures. The U.S.S.R. accords overriding priority to military expenditures. Any change in total resource availability in the U.S.S.R. through trade would, under present policies, affect its civilian economy, not its military budget."[5]

While practically any degree of trade embargo raises economic costs for the embargoed society (and, as we saw in Part I, reduces the purely *economic* welfare of the embargoing nation), it is not at all clear that the U.S. extension of the embargo to many nonmilitary products really severely damaged the Eastern economies. Indeed, it was noted earlier in this study that most of the socialist countries had been able to achieve dramatic economic growth in the 1950s, and this was accomplished by and large without substantial help from the West as a whole, let alone from the United States. The immense untapped resources of the socialist world as a "bloc" were too great to hope to create long-run bottlenecks in their productive system by means of an embargo policy. Moreover, economic cooperation among most of the socialist countries was undoubtedly only encouraged by the Western embargo policy. The establishment in 1949 of the Council for Mutual Economic Assistance (Comecon) by the socialist countries of Eastern Europe, and the erratic but gradually evolving pattern of economic and technical cooperation among Comecon members, was in large part a response to the emerging postwar "Western" economic alliance.[6] This intrabloc cooperation, under strong Soviet guidance, only reduced the chances that the economic and political (as distinguished from the military) goals of the embargo policy would be realized. Furthermore, Soviet hegemony over this area could only have been enhanced by the Western embargo strategy.[7]

Finally, it must have become apparent to many careful observers that even *successful* attacks on civilian welfare levels in the Eastern countries by means of near-maximal offensive economic warfare would be unlikely to result in an overthrow of their communist regimes.[8] As long as these societies remained in many crucial respects totalitarian, little internal dissent was even allowed. The regimes in these countries seemed to remain in power regardless of the economic burdens placed on large internal groups.[b]

For those Americans who were actually rethinking their assumptions regarding East-West trade policy, such considerations apparently led to a downward revision in their subjective estimates of the national security value of depriving nonmilitary goods to the East. In other words, for a wide range of civilian products the collective disutility associated with Communist consumption (y_{ij}) diminished, which implied, as we have seen, a lower level of implicit export taxes on the sale of these goods to the socialist countries.

Acceptance of the new strategic notions of coexistence, polycentrism and internal liberalization represented more than just a grudging recognition that the old policy was ineffective. The attractiveness of these ideas sprang from the same basic belief that supported the earlier embargo policy; namely, that the United States could utilize the instruments of trade policy to accomplish political as well as economic objectives. The basic difference between the old-style "containment" policy and the new argument for "building bridges" was the greater degree of subtlety of the latter. Only time will tell whether the basic assumptions underlying the new strategy were any more realistic than those prevalent earlier. We shall argue in Chapter 9, however, that some evidence has already accumulated demonstrating that several of these notions may rest on oversimplified assumptions.

In March 1964 the Senate Foreign Relations Committee held hearings on U.S. East-West trade policy which "for the first time . . . were clearly designed to bring about a new consensus on Capitol Hill in favor of the building bridges policy."[9] The following year President Johnson created the Special Committee on U.S. Trade Relations with East European Countries and the

---

[b] The change of regimes in Poland in 1956 and 1970 would seem to be the exceptions that prove the rule, although even in these cases the ideological orientation of the governing regime remained the same.

Soviet Union, which returned to the President with the celebrated "Miller Report" in April, 1965. Several excerpts from this report summarize quite concisely the manner in which the notions of peaceful coexistence, polycentrism, and internal liberalization were combined to suggest a new strategy of broadening trade relations with the socialist countries of Europe:[10]

The possibilities of "peaceful coexistence" and mutually advantageous trade do not sound convincing coming from those who speak of "burying us." We know very well that coexistence means something different to Soviet leaders from what it means to us. Within the framework of a policy so labeled, they believe they can still pursue hostile actions against the free world so long as major war does not result. But they have found it necessary to change their view of coexistence over the past decade and the conditions of the modern world will cause it to change further over the next decade. Much the same may be said of Soviet motivation and desire, and that of most of the East European nations, for increased trade with the United States. This Committee, therefore, has come to believe that in a larger time perspective the possibilities of "peaceful coexistence"—in the genuine meaning of that expression—can be made to grow. We conclude this in spite of Soviet professions and not because of them.

. . . We believe that men and nations function best in an open society. There are signs that pressures for greater openness within Soviet society are mounting. The reasons may be pragmatic rather than ideological, but they are nonetheless real. The Soviets want a modern and technically advanced society. Their own experience shows that the building of such a society can be severely handicapped by a closed and tyrannical political order and a rigid, centrally directed economic system.

The case for expanding peaceful trade comes down to the proposition that we can use trade to influence the internal evolution and external behavior of Communist countries. Trade provides us with a policy instrument to encourage the movement toward greater national independence in Eastern Europe and the trend toward greater concern for consumer needs in all the European Communist countries. By refusing to trade we put ourselves in a posture of hostility that could be at odds with these developments as well as with other elements of our overall strategy toward these countries. Our refusal to trade cannot importantly limit Soviet military power but it can help to reinforce their doctrinal belief in the need for self-sufficiency. A willingness to trade, on the other hand, would be concrete evidence of our belief in constructive and peaceful relations. The benefit done our relations with the underdeveloped world by evidence that we genuinely believe in the efficacy and ultimate triumph of open societies far outweighs the disadvantages of any enhancement of Soviet legitmacy. In sum, this argument holds that the gains are significant and the risks are negligible.

Clearly, these *positive* notions that trade should be used as a "policy instrument" to open the socialist societies to Western ideas, to influence their "internal evolution" toward greater economic and political decentralization, and to encourage "the movement towards greater national independence in Eastern Europe," reflected sharply diminished disutility associated with these countries' consumption of nonmilitary goods, which only reinforced the implications of the realization that the massive embargo policy had been unsuccessful.[c] To the extent that expansion of trade was seen as a desirable objective, consistency would also have dictated a downward realignment of disutilities associated with Communist foreign exchange earnings (the f_{hj}^k, f_{ij}^k consideration). Indeed, the Eastern countries could only significantly expand their imports from the United States if they could also raise their own exports to the American market, because of their necessity for bilateral balancing of trade arising out of the inconvertibility of their currencies. The extension of export credits by the U.S. to the socialist countries would also have helped solve the Eastern foreign exchange problem.

We should also mention another consideration, which suggested that the U.S. needed to realign its policies more closely with its Western allies. This involved the problem of *extraterritoriality*, and was the result of the U.S. attempts to enforce its own unilateral export controls on trade with the East. It will be recalled from Chapter 5 that the United States sought to prohibit effective transshipment of embargoed products and technology by means of regulations under authority of the Export Control Act that subjected various exports of foreign-based companies incorporating such technology or products to validated license requirements. Furthermore, the Transactions Control Regulations were used to bring all foreign operations "controlled" by Americans directly under the purview of the U.S. export control authorities, thereby attempting to assure compliance of the COCOM members and non-COCOM states with the COCOM regulations.[d]

In the course of the fifties and sixties this extraterritorial reach of the U.S. control machinery increasingly brought allegations from foreign countries that the United States was meddling in affairs that fell exclusively under their own sovereign jurisdictions. These problems were perhaps most acute with respect to Canada and France.[13] So as to avoid severe polycentric movements within the Western alliance, and to head off the possible spillover into other commercial and foreign investment policy spheres of foreign resentment of U.S. policies, U.S. policy makers increasingly realized that a less all-encompassing export control policy was necessary.[14]

---

[c] In the language of welfare economics, the new policy of attempting to influence the "internal evolution" and "external behavior" of the Communist countries in the direction of a relatively greater emphasis on economic development and less on relative military strength than in the past, could be represented as attempting to change the configuration of the so-called "Bergson social welfare function" in these countries. The new Bergson function would give greater weight to the utilities of those internal groups favoring economic goals. This represented a shift, for Americans, from the old policy of attacking the socialist countries' "Scitovsky contours," in the sense of trying to erode the utility levels of individuals within these countries.[11]

[d] In addition, the Commerce Department controls the shipment of various products on U.S. flagships and aircraft, even in trade between third countries; and as we have seen, the Government also maintains a blacklist of ships carrying cargoes to Cuba (and, now, to North Vietnam).[12]

Increased pressure from U.S. businessmen, basically those with a strong exporting interest, also began to be placed upon Congress and the Administration in the early sixties to lower the East-West trade barriers. This concern on the part of private traders did not really begin to exert a powerful force until later, however, as will be shown in subsequent sections.[15]

Implementing the New Policy

The Kennedy and Johnson administrations found that to shape a new policy of "building bridges" was one thing; to implement it was another. Not only had Congress historically been less liberal with regard to East-West trade policy than the successive administrations, it had only recently explicitly expanded the purview of the Executive's export control authority to cover goods of "economic significance," and had eliminated Presidential discretion with respect to extending MFN treatment to additional socialist countries. In the period 1963–1966 the two administrations did take several new initiatives, however, which improved the climate for a fundamental reevaluation of American East-West trade policy, but which also brought out the latent schizophrenia of U.S. policy in this area. The first major initiative was the Soviet-American wheat deal of 1963–1964, followed by selective decontrolling for Rumania beginning in July 1964. In 1966 the Johnson Administration sponsored legislation designed to return to the President discretion as to extending MFN to additional Communist countries. Later the same year, the Commodity Control list applying to all the socialist countries of Eastern Europe was shortened.

In several respects the announcement by the Kennedy Administration that it was willing to conclude a $140 million wheat sale to the Soviet Union was a watershed in U.S. East-West trade relations. On the one hand, the sheer size of the transaction was enormous by postwar standards, being greater than the total U.S. exports to the entire socialist world in every year (except two) since 1948. On the other, President Kennedy's close personal identification with the transaction gave East-West commerce a form of high level, official blessing, which had basically been withheld in the past. In sum, the wheat sale was a symbol of the economic *possibilities* of East-West trade and its *legitimacy*. In addition, it appeared to be a commercially *profitable* deal for American business.[16] While the Administration maintained that the sale of foodstuffs to the East represented no basic change in policy, as it had seldom embargoed such transactions in the past,[17] the sheer magnitude of the 1963–1964 wheat deal served to make it a symbol of the beginning of a new era.

Ironically, this massive transaction also led to two new restrictions being placed on U.S. trade with the East, one of these reluctantly being imposed by the President, the other by Congress. The Presidential limitation consisted of a new "cargo preference" regulation, which required that one-half of any shipment of wheat and feed grains to certain socialist countries be carried in U.S. flagships. The congressional action involved restricting the activities of the Export–Import Bank (Eximbank) in East–West commerce. We shall digress here to consider the historical background of the "cargo preference" concept, as it has long embodied a curious blend of protectionist and national security considerations, which has tended to make it an extremely useful instrument for certain domestic interest groups.

The notion of cargo preference as a major policy instrument became popular in the depression environment of the 1930s.[e] In 1934 Congress passed the following resolution:[19]

That it is the sense of Congress that *in any loans made by the Reconstruction Finance Corporation or any other instrumentality of the Government to foster the exporting of agricultural or other products*, provision shall be made that such products *shall be carried exclusively* in vessels of the United States, unless . . . vessels of the United States are not available in sufficient numbers, or in sufficient tonnage capacity, or on necessary sailing schedule, or at reasonable rates.

The increasing pressure for measures designed to promote a strong U.S. merchant marine were quite clearly motivated by both protectionist and national security considerations. President Roosevelt's 1935 message to Congress concerning merchant marine legislation amply demonstrates this conjunction of motivations:[20]

I present to the Congress the question of whether or not the United States should have an adequate merchant marine.

To me there are three reasons for answering this question in the affirmative. The first is that in time of peace, subsidies granted by other nations, shipping combines, and other restrictive or rebating methods may well be used to the detriment of American shippers. The maintenance of fair competition alone calls for American flagships of sufficient tonnage to carry a reasonable portion of our foreign commerce.

Second, in the event of a major war in which the United States is not involved, our commerce, in the absence of an adequate American merchant marine, might find itself seriously crippled because of its inability to secure bottoms for neutral peaceful foreign trade.

Third, in the event of a war in which the United States itself might be engaged, American flagships are obviously needed not only for naval auxiliaries, but also for the maintenance of reasonable and necessary commercial intercourse with other nations. . . .

In terms of the model developed in Part I, both the protectionist and national security considerations relating to the *i*th good "shipping services"

---

[e] Although the requirement that *all* U.S. military shipments must be carried on U.S. ships dates from 1904.[18]

may be conveniently summarized in our collective good m_{ij}^k, where m_{ij} is the ratio of U.S. imports of shipping services to total U.S. production of such services, and Americans are presumed to experience disutility from increases in this ratio over a certain range of values for m_{ij}^k. That the configuration of this collective good reflected the *relative* dependence on foreign shipping services, as denoted by $\frac{z_{ij}}{X_i}$,[f] is suggested by the notion of "a reasonable portion of our foreign commerce" in the foregoing message from the President, and by the fact that the proposed Merchant Marine Act of 1935 declared it a national policy that the U.S. "shall have a merchant marine . . . sufficient to carry at least one-half of the foreign commerce of the United States."[21] With respect to the *i*th good (shipping services) we know from Chapter 3 that the introduction of the protectionist-defensive economic warfare consideration m_{ij}^k into individual utility functions optimally implies government intervention in both the domestic and foreign trade sectors. In most cases such intervention should consist of a domestic production subsidy for shipping services and a discriminatory, higher tariff on the import of shipping services from the *j*th country.

Maritime legislation was finally enacted in 1936 in the form of the Merchant Marine Act of 1936.[22] In this Act the policy that one-half of all foreign commerce of the United States had to be transported in American-owned vessels was diluted to the provision that the United States should have a merchant marine "sufficient to carry its domestic water-borne commerce and a *substantial portion* of the water-borne export and import foreign commerce of the United States."[23] The requirements of our optimal policy rules were at least in general met through provisions for production subsidies covering the differential cost of building ships in the United States and operating subsidies covering the differential operating costs involved in American shipping.[24] We should note that the utility consideration $m_{ij}^k = \frac{z_{ij}}{X_i}$ apparently did not discriminate *among* foreign countries in the 1930s. In other words, $j = 1$ and $m_j^k = \frac{z_i}{X_i}$. This implied, of course, that any tariff imposed on the import of shipping services should have been nondiscriminatory (see expressions (11) through (13), pp. 32). But the 1936 legislation made no direct attempt to satisfy the trade policy rule of a higher tariff on the import of shipping services.

When legislation was enacted in the 1950s which did constitute policy intervention in the foreign trade sector, however, Title VIII, section 809 of the Merchant Marine Act of 1936 was referred to as a precedent of sorts for

---

[f] *Supra*, p. 31 for a discussion of different possible definitions for m_{ij}^k.

such policy intervention. That section provided that "preference shall be given" to U.S. citizens "who have the support, financial and otherwise, of the domestic communities primarily interested," with respect to operating differential and production subsidy contracts and contracts for private chartering of Maritime Commission vessels. The policy intervention in the 1950s took the form of the Cargo Preference Law of 1954. This legislation, which was later incorporated into the Merchant Marine Act of 1936, provided that:

Whenever the United States shall procure, contract for, or otherwise obtain for its own account, or shall furnish to or for the account of any foreign nation without provision for reimbursement, any equipment, materials, or commodities, within or without the United States, or shall advance funds or credits or guarantee the convertibility of foreign currencies in connection with the furnishing of such equipment, materials, or commodities, the appropriate agency or agencies shall take such steps as may be necessary and practicable to assure that at least *50 per centum* of the gross tonnage of such equipment, materials or commodities . . . which may be transported on ocean vessels shall be transported on privately owned United States-flag commercial vessels, to the extent such vessels are available at fair and reasonable rates for United States-flag commercial vessels. . . .[25]

This legislation in effect extended the cargo preference requirement to all foreign aid shipments, although the 100 per cent requirement cited earlier for various government generated shipments was lowered to 50 per cent. The cargo preference requirement may be interpreted as a quota on imported shipping services related to a specific range of exportables, mostly Department of Agriculture and A.I.D. generated cargoes. Because only a limited range of potential exportables were covered by this requirement, it would not appear to have even approximated the optimum pattern of import taxes implied by our trade policy rule. We might add that this legislation also had no declared purpose of discriminating *among* foreign exporters of carriage services.

It should be emphasized that legislation has never been enacted specifically bringing commercial exports (for hard currencies) under any cargo preference requirement. This must be attributed either to the failure of policy makers fully to recognize the implications of the optimal trade policy conditions, or to political obstacles perhaps in the form of aggressive export interests who have seen the higher costs of domestically produced shipping services resulting from quotas or tariffs on such services as a hindrance to export expansion.

When the United States and the Soviet Union negotiated the massive 1963–1964 wheat transaction, however, there was extremely strong and vocal pressure from the maritime industry to impose cargo preference requirements on these shipments, even though these turned out to be commercial sales for gold and hard currencies. These interests urged the President to treat the wheat sales as if they were government-to-government transactions, thereby qualifying for the cargo preference requirements as prescribed by the 1954 law.[26] President Kennedy chose instead to operate under the broad discretionary authority allowed him under the Export Control Act of 1949 (as amended). As a result of this decision the export control regulations were amended, requiring, among other provisions, that 50 per cent of any commercial sale of wheat and wheat flour to the socialist countries of Eastern Europe (including the Soviet Union but excluding Yugoslavia and Poland) and 50 per cent of any commercial sale of feed grains (rice, barley, corn, rye, oats, grain sorghums and other cereal grains) to the Soviet Union be exported in United States-flag ocean carriers.[27]

In spite of the prevalent maritime industry pressures, the OEC waived the 50 per cent carriage requirement on several of the initial wheat shipments, because available U.S. shipping capacity could not be found. After the initial large transactions with the Soviet Union

> it became evident that strict application of the 50-50 requirement was not commercially feasible in the case of shipments of less than a full cargo. For this reason, since January 1965, Commerce has waived the 50-50 shipping requirement when a shipment constitutes less than a full cargo in the vessel in which it is to be carried and the balance of the cargo is destined for and will be off-loaded in a free world port. Contrary to the impression of some shippers, however, there is no requirement that part cargoes destined for Eastern Europe also be off-loaded in Western Europe.[28]

This extension of cargo preference requirements to wheat and feed grains exported to selected socialist countries represented only a small piecemeal change in accordance with the optimal policy condition applying to foreign trade, however (see expression (12), page 32), and cannot be said in general to have moved the United States any closer to the general optimum.[g] Moreover, the fact that the application of this requirement was heavily skewed towards particular commodities (wheat and feed grains) sold to a small group of countries (most of the socialist world) meant that the full "spillover" cost of this implicit tax on the import of shipping services was carried entirely by exporters concerned with a very small commodity-country subset. To the extent that U.S. exporters of wheat and feed grains to eastern Europe faced higher transport costs when forced to ship by American-flag carriers, they were at a competitive disadvantage in this particular foreign market. The strange blend of protectionist and national security arguments for this new cargo preference requirement were brought out most clearly in the 1969 congressional hearings concerning this provision (which debate will be summarized later in this chapter). In Chapter 8 some evidence concerning the trade restrictive effect of this measure will also be discussed.

---

[g] See our discussion of the theory of "second best" in Chapter 4.

The 1964 legislation limiting Eximbank participation in East-West trade should also be viewed in historical perspective. The utility considerations underlying the export credit support program of the Eximbank are basically two-fold: to promote foreign trade and to promote the development and reconstruction of certain foreign economies.[h] At its inception in 1934 and increasingly in the 1950s and 1960s the Eximbank has functioned as a promoter of foreign trade.[29] The basic utility consideration here is the notion of collective satisfaction from an increase in certain types of exports (particularly capital equipment) and imports. Both at the time of the Bank's establishment and recently, the absolute value of this collective utility parameter has probably been greater for exports than for imports. In other words, the need to stimulate domestic production and employment in the thirties, and the chronic balance of payments deficits in the last two decades, have undoubtedly led to a greater public concern for export expansion than for an increase in imports.

Basically the objective of promoting foreign trade is nondiscriminatory; that is, the jth market may be considered as the world ($j = 1$). It can be demonstrated that in this case the optimal trade policy rule is to employ nondiscriminatory lower taxes on foreign trade in the effected products, whether they be lower tariffs on imports or lower export taxes (or export subsidies) on sales abroad. One means of achieving this stimulus to expanded trade, of course, has been Eximbank credit support to importers and exporters, which in most cases lowers the effective cost of the transaction to these traders as well as in many cases being the crucial factor that makes the purchase or sale feasible.

In the late 1930s with respect to Latin America, in the immediate postwar period in connection with European reconstruction, and continuing up to the present, the Eximbank has also concentrated a great deal of its resources on credit support relating to exports to countries having major development or war recovery needs.[30] This undoubtedly reflects strong *positive* external effects in international consumption (positive collective utility parameter associated with y_{ij}^{k}, for the jth reconstructing or developing country), discussed before in the context of foreign assistance in general. As shown earlier, the implied optimal policies resulting from this consideration are lower export taxes or higher export subsidies on certain ith goods exported to targeted needy countries. Eximbank financing or other credit support is one method of reducing the effective cost to foreign purchasers of goods normally requiring costly financing schemes.

The net result of the combined influence of the positive collective utilities associated with certain types of foreign trade and the level of aggregate

---

[h] Export credit support includes export credit, guarantees, and participation with the FCIA in credit insurance.

consumption of particular countries, has been an enormous expansion in the role of Eximbank official credit support over the years. This particular technique has become generally acceptable among the Western industrialized nations, as each nation now has a similar official credit support program.[31] As it is primarily financial in nature, this type of export subsidy seems to have escaped the condemnation of international organizations, as contrasted with the GATT convention against explicit export subsidies. The unsuccessful attempt of the so-called "Berne Union" to establish a generally adhered-to maximum time period for long-term credit support, demonstrates the importance of government credit schemes as a competitive device in international commerce.

As we have seen, section 11 of the Export-Import Bank Act of 1945 exempts private exporters operating with Eximbank support from the prohibitions outlined in the Johnson Act. Also, the Eximbank itself, operating as an agency of the United States Government, is not subject to the Johnson Act provisions. Furthermore, "so long as an export *guarantee* or export *insurance* is within the range of common commercial practice, it is not considered 'assistance' and, therefore, is not prohibited by the Battle Act."[32] In spite of these provisions, Eximbank credit support for U.S. exports to the socialist countries was negligible prior to 1964.

Legislation specifically embodying restrictions on Eximbank support of exports to the East resulted from the interest of the Soviet Union and other socialist countries in the massive wheat purchases from the United States in 1963–1964. Initially it was feared that private credit would be insufficient to consummate these sales and that Eximbank support would probably be needed.[33] Following lengthy congressional debate as to whether Eximbank credit support to the socialist world was in the national interest, the following provision was incorporated in the Foreign Assistance and Related Agencies Appropriation Act of 1965 (actually enacted in 1964), Title III,[34] and in annual acts of this name in subsequent years:

> None of the funds made available because of the provisions of this title shall be used by the Export-Import Bank to either guarantee the payment of any obligation hereafter incurred by any Communist country . . . or any agency or national thereof, or in any other way to participate in the extension of credit to any such country, agency, or national, in connection with the purchase of any product by such country, agency, or national, *except* when the President determines that such guarantees would be in the *national interest* and reports each such determination to Congress within 30 days. . . .

This legislation essentially reflected the concern of Congress that in considering the emerging possibilities for large, Eximbank supported export transactions with the socialist countries, the Administration might ignore the basic utility considerations Congress had associated with increased consumption in the East. As we have seen, the basic collective utility consideration underlying enactment of the Export Control Act, the Battle Act, and other "containment" legislation consisted of severe dissatisfaction with eastern increases in y_{ij} and y_{hj} for a wide range of nonmilitary products as well as for all military goods. To the extent that Eximbank credit support aided the expansion of exports to the socialist world, and these exports were used to raise consumption levels for the target goods in these countries, such support was considered disadvantageous to U.S. national security. Thus the discriminating, higher export tax policy implied by the (y^k_{hj}, y^k_{ij}) consideration meant in this case a general prohibition of the export *subsidy* element implicit in Eximbank assistance.

It is noteworthy that Congress did not remove the President's discretion in regard to Eximbank activities in East-West trade. The Eximbank was permitted to engage in such transactions if the President determined "that such guarantees would be in the national interest" and reported such determinations to Congress. In spite of this discretionary feature, however, this statute still had a particularly discriminatory effect in practice. Eximbank in the following years limited its support of exports to the East to guarantees and credit insurance,[i] because the language of the foregoing legislation was not clear as to whether credit extension would also be allowed under the discretionary authority retained by the President.[35]

After passage of this legislation President Johnson issued four such determinations permitting Eximbank support of exports of all "peaceful" products and services to Bulgaria, Czechoslovakia, Hungary, Poland, Rumania, and Yugoslavia, and exports of agricultural products to the Soviet Union. Between 1964 and 1968 the Eximbank made use of its authority under these determinations with respect to all the foregoing countries except the Soviet Union.[36] Over this period, total Eximbank support to these nations was $145 million, of which $143.5 million was in the form of medium-term guarantees (six months to five years for Bulgaria, Czechoslovakia, Hungary, Poland, and Rumania; over five years for Yugoslavia), with the balance being composed of short- and medium-term FCIA insurance. Over $75 million of these guarantees supported exports to Yugoslavia alone.

It is interesting to note the relatively high level of discrimination evidenced by the Executive branch under its discretionary authority as permitted by the 1964 legislation. Potential export credit support was limited to agricultural products for the Soviet Union, and Yugoslavia was allowed much more favorable support terms than the other countries of Eastern Europe.[j] This pattern is in accord, of course, with our earlier assumption that the collective

---

[i] This insurance is actually provided by the FCIA in coordination with Eximbank.

[j] In addition, East Germany, which was not recognized as a soveriegn nation by the U.S., was ineligible for Eximbank support.

utility (or disutility) parameter associated with y_{ij}^k is in part a function of the degree of perceived polycentrism in Eastern Europe.

During this period the Johnson Administration also used its discretionary authority under the Export Control Act to selectively "decontrol" various exports to Rumania. This included eliminating the cargo preference requirement with respect to that country. As a result of these initiatives, which began in July 1964, Rumania was brought into the same favored position as Poland under the export control procedure. This liberalization was undertaken for the same reasons as the earlier actions in regard to Poland: a reward for Rumania's increasingly polycentric behavior within Comecon and as a possible encouragement to internal liberalization.[37]

Indeed, on a basis of polycentrism alone, the case could be made that Rumania should have received even more favorable treatment than Poland, as it had emerged as the principal obstructionist country within Comecon.[38] Further decontrolling of the Commodity Control List, applicable to all the socialist countries of Eastern Europe (including the Soviet Union), was undertaken in late 1966, when some 400 products were removed from the list requiring a validated license for export.[39]

The latent asymmetry between U.S. export and import policies toward East-West trade was activated by the discriminatory export liberalization for Rumania. As we have seen, a reduction of collective diseconomies arising from foreign consumption logically has the effect of also reducing the disutility experienced from foreign accumulation of foreign exchange to be used to finance increased imports of the affected commodities. This in fact was the rationale for the Eisenhower Administration also deciding to extend MFN to Poland after decontrolling a wide range of exports to that country. The Johnson Administration's desire to relax import barriers to Rumanian products after 1964 was frustrated, however, by the 1962–1963 legislation forbidding the President to extend MFN to any additional socialist countries.[40] The result was inconsistent treatment of Poland and Rumania as between exports and imports.

In response to this seemingly schizophrenic policy posture, the Johnson Administration introduced a new bill in Congress in early 1966 designed to return to the President full discretion regarding MFN. This bill, the proposed East-West Trade Relations Act of 1966, died in Congress. An identical bill was reintroduced in 1969 by several senators, but it never emerged from the Senate Committee on Finance. As we shall see in the next section, intensification of the war in Vietnam in the second half of the 1960s undoubtedly hampered serious consideration of this proposed legislation by Congress. Because of the enduring nature of the policy contradiction which the bill was designed to remedy, and the continuing importance of the MFN issue in developing a constructive East-West trade policy, excerpts from the bill are presented below. The stated purposes of the bill were:[41]

(a) To use peaceful trade and related contacts with Communist countries as a means of advancing the long-range interest of the United States in peace and freedom;

(b) To promote constructive relations with Communist countries, to contribute to international stability, and to provide a framework helpful to private United States firms conducting business relations with Communist state trading agencies by instituting regular government-government negotiations with individual Communist countries concerning commercial and other matters of mutual interest; and

(c) To increase peaceful trade and related contacts between the United States and Communist countries, and to expand markets for products of the United States in these countries by creating similar opportunities for the products of Communist countries to compete in United States markets on a nondiscriminatory basis.

The bill would have given the President the following authority:[42]

The President may make a commercial agreement with a Communist country providing most-favored-nation treatment to the products of that country whenever he determines that such agreement—

(a) will promote the purposes of this Act,
(b) is in the national interest, and
(c) will result in benefits to the United States equivalent to those provided by by the agreement to the other party.

The bill further listed some of the benefits that should be provided the United States by entering into such commercial agreements:[43]

1. Satisfactory arrangements for the protection of industrial rights and processes.

2. Satisfactory arrangements for the settlement of commercial differences and disputes.

3. Arrangements for the U.S. to establish or expand its trade promotion efforts in these countries.

4. Nondiscriminatory treatment of U.S. products in these foreign markets.

5. Settlement of financial and property claims, and so forth.

This proposed legislation would have limited such commercial agreements and associated MFN treatment to three years' effectiveness (renewable), and would not have authorized MFN treatment for the Asiatic socialist countries (People's Republic of China, North Korea, and North Vietnam), Cuba, or East Germany.[44]

Restraining Impact of Vietnam

Although the failure of the Johnson Administration's MFN bill to make its way through Congress probably reflected some of the same protectionist pressures which we suggested were active in 1951 and again in 1962 when restrictive East-West import legislation was enacted, more than anything else this bill was a casualty of the escalating Vietnam conflict. Although the bill did not foresee giving the President the discretion to extend MFN to North Vietnam, the socialist countries to which MFN might be given under this proposal were active supporters of the North Vietnamese, both in terms of political rhetoric and economic and military supplies. The majority of congressmen undoubtedly saw little difference between giving economic benefits to the belligerent in a "hot" war and extending such benefits to the belligerent's allies. At work here were the same national security variables that dictated the total embargo of North Korea and the People's Republic of China during the Korean War: severe diseconomies from belligerent consumption and earnings of foreign exchange.

It is doubtful that any members of Congress truly believed that continued withholding of MFN from most of the socialist world would really coerce any of these countries into limiting their aid to the North Vietnamese. Congressional intransigence in this matter was not an instrument of economic warfare, coldly used with the purpose of achieving a specific political result; on the contrary, it was primarily an emotional response to the continued assistance these nations were giving the "enemy" on the battlefield. Furthermore, it undoubtedly seemed to many to be a moral issue, as long as American soldiers were being killed on this battlefield. Indeed, the Administration was quite insistent in defending its motives regarding the proposed legislation, relying on the polycentric notion to explain its desire for passage of the bill.[45]

With respect to North Vietnam itself, the collective utility parameters associated with the (y^k_{hj}, y^k_{ij}) and (f^k_{hj}, f^k_{ij}) considerations were apparently prohibitively negative. The OEC had established a virtual embargo on exports to North Vietnam at least as early as 1961.[46] With the escalation of the war in 1964, the Foreign Assets Control Regulations, embargoing all commercial and financial relations, were applied to North Vietnam.[47] The total embargo of relations with North Korea and the P.R.C., which began in 1950, continued throughout this period. Presumably the proximity of these countries to North Vietnam, and their active assistance to the Hanoi regime, helped to perpetuate the prohibitive collective disutilities associated with U.S. dealings with them.

The active hostility to China persisted in spite of the most dramatic polycentric occurrence within the Communist world—the Sino-Soviet split in 1960. Indeed, the Chinese, who had relied extensively on Soviet trade (and, to a lesser extent, aid) in the fifties, were suddenly deprived of this economic support as the sixties opened, an interesting example of the use of offensive economic warfare by the Soviet Union.[48k] The persistent hostile rhetoric of the P.R.C. directed against the United States, together with continued political instability in Southeast Asia, undoubtedly overruled the polycentric consideration for most Americans in this period.

Under the press of the Vietnam War, Congress enacted several pieces of legislation which served to increase the restrictiveness of U.S. East-West trade policies. First, the Export Control Act was amended in 1965 to increase the penalties for violations of its provisions.[49] The amended legislation also continued to explicitly direct the President to restrict the export of goods which would make a significant contribution to the *economic* as well as military potential of nations threatening U.S. national security.

Second, Presidential discretion with respect to PL 480 sales of surplus agricultural commodities to the socialist countries was effectively removed by Congress in the Food for Peace Act of 1966 as it amends PL 480. Section 103 of the latter Act as amended now excluded "for the purposes of sales of agricultural commodities under Title I of this Act, any nation which sells or furnishes or permits ships or aircraft under its registry to transport to or from Cuba or North Vietnam . . . any equipment, materials, or commodities so long as they are governed by a communist regime . . . ," with certain exceptions in regard to countries dealing with Cuba. As a result, Poland and Yugoslavia, both of which traded with North Vietnam and Cuba, were now ineligible for PL 480 sales.[50]

Finally, Congress saw fit to remove from the President his discretion with respect to Eximbank credit support for exports to the East. It will be recalled from the last section that the Johnson Administration had differentiated quite extensively among the socialist countries in permitting Eximbank support. In October 1966 the President announced that the Eximbank was prepared to guarantee credits for the export of some $50 million worth of American machine tools, which FIAT of Italy required in connection with its construction of an enormous automobile plant in the Soviet Union. Congressional opposition to this proposal was strong. In August 1967 Congress amended the Export-Import Bank Act so as to prohibit the proposed Eximbank support, putting American suppliers at a disadvantage relative to foreign competitors.[51]

New restrictions were incorporated in PL 90–267, which was an amendment to Section 2(b) of the Export–Import Bank Act of 1945. This legislation,

[k] In one sense, Soviet withdrawal of technical assistance and reduction of trade with the P.R.C. represented a carrying through of the threat implicit in the offensive economic warfare consideration s_{ij}^k, defined as the relative dependence of the *j*th country on Home for supplies of the *i*th product (see Chapter 3).

enacted in March 1968, presumably reflected the same basic negative collective utility consideration associated with Communist consumption (y^k_{ij}) as was operative in the earlier denial of Presidential discretion with regard to the PL 480 program. PL 90–267 provided that:[52]

(2) The Bank in the exercise of its functions shall not guarantee, insure, or extend credit, or participate in any extension of credit—

(A) in connection with the purchase or lease of any product by a Communist country . . . or agency or national thereof; or

(B) in connection with the purchase or lease of any product by any other foreign country, or agency, or national thereof, if the product to be purchased or leased by such other country, agency or national is, to the knowledge of the Bank, principally for use in, or sale or lease to, a Communist country . . ., *except* that the prohibitions contained in this paragraph shall not apply in the case of any transaction which the President determines would be in the *national interest.*

Furthermore, this legislation provided that:

(3) The Bank shall not guarantee, insure, or extend credit, or participate in the extension of credit in connection with the purchase of any product, technical data, or other information by a national or agency of any nation—

(A) which engages in armed conflict, declared or otherwise, with armed forces of the United States; or

(B) which furnishes by direct governmental action (not including chartering, licensing or sales by non-wholly-owned business enterprises) goods, supplies, military assistance, or advisors to a nation described in subparagraph (A);

. . . nor shall the Bank guarantee, insure, or extend credit, or participate in the extension of credit in connection with the purchase by any nation (or national agency) of any product, technical data, or other information which is to be used principally by or in a nation described in subparagraph (A) or (B).

As a result of this legislation, there was to be an effective prohibition on all Eximbank support for exports to all Communist controlled countries except Yugoslavia. Paragraph (3) above allows for no Presidential discretion. Since all Communist controlled countries other than Yugoslavia provided direct governmental aid to North Vietnam, Eximbank support for these nations was prohibited. Provision (2) did allow Presidential discretion, however, and Yugoslavia continued to receive Eximbank credit support after 1968 under Presidential determinations that such support was in the national interest.

Subparagraph 2(B), quoted above, was designed to fulfill the transshipment requirement with respect to the subsidy element of Eximbank credit support. That is to say, even if the product or package of goods requiring Eximbank support of their export was not embargoed by the export control authorities for sale to the Communist countries, Congress still sought to deny these countries the possible benefits (in the form of a lower effective price) flowing from export subsidization to a transshipping country.

The restriction contained in subparagraph 3(B) was basically an offensive economic warfare measure directed at any third nation which chose to provide governmental assistance to North Vietnam. That Congress did not also require the Executive to impose stricter export controls on these countries probably stemmed from two factors: (1) the notion that while export *subsidies* should certainly be denied these nations (previously positive collective utilities associated with y_{ij} had diminished to zero), higher export *taxes* on trade with such countries were not warranted (the collective utility parameters associated with y_{ij} in these countries were not negative); and (2) possibly the practical infeasibility of passing such legislation at the time.

Pisar has noted that "it is under this congressional directive that reprisals were threatened against Sweden following that country's offer of $40 million in aid to North Vietnam in the fall of 1969. In concrete terms, the threat included a proposed denial of more than $200 million in EX–IM Bank credits for the purchase of American Boeing 747 aircraft by SAS (an airline which Sweden, Norway, and Denmark own in common)."[53] The final quoted excerpt from this legislation merely represented the congressional attempt to fulfill the transshipment requirement with respect to both North Vietnam and to third countries giving military or economic aid to North Vietnam.

PL 90–267 was unprecedented in that for the first time Congress was unwilling to tacitly leave to the President the responsibility for ensuring that the optimal conditions were met. Indeed, in this legislation Congress made quite explicit the kind of transshipment protection it expected the President to implement. Once again the basic asymmetry of policy making in trade policy was revealed. While the Executive had been left free to tailor its export control policies to the varied configurations of collective utility parameters which it perceived to be applicable to the socialist world, this discretion was now denied with respect to export subsidization policies. Furthermore, Congress saw fit, with respect to the latter, to spell out quite clearly what it expected from the Executive in the way of satisfying the more subtle requirements implicit in successfully launching economic warfare.

No doubt the "explicitness" of the subsidy feature of Eximbank credit support, as well as of the PL 480 program, is seen by Congress to require from it a closer degree of supervision than necessary in the case of export controls. In this sense, these programs resemble the setting of tariff rates implicit in the granting of MFN, as discussed in the last chapter. But this fact alone is hardly sufficient to explain the closer degree of congressional supervision over these policies as they relate to East-West trade. Congress has delegated vast discretionary authority to the President in these matters, such as the negotiation for reductions in trade barriers and credit terms on Eximbank support, in connection with U.S. trade policies toward the nonsocialist world.

Mounting Pressures for Change

In spite of the continuing war in Vietnam, the period since 1968 has been characterized by mounting pressures for a more liberalized U.S. East-West trade policy. On the one hand, there has appeared to be a growing readiness by both the East and West to move towards detente. Even China has begun to be slightly less belligerent towards the West, as it has turned from its own internal strife and become ever more preoccupied with its border disputes with the Soviet Union. In such an atmosphere the continued economic containment policy of the United States has seemed increasingly inappropriate.

On the other hand, there have been strong economic pressures, some arising out of the containment policy itself, which have caused a growing recognition of the trade-off between economic welfare and economic warfare, and a reassessment of U.S. policy making in this area. Also, many of the "reappraisals" of the old containment concept that underlay the earlier search for a new East-West trade policy by the Kennedy and Johnson Administrations have become ever more convincing in the light of the passage of time, the continuing, ineffectual war in Vietnam, and the inaction of the West in response to the Soviet-led invasion of Czechoslovakia in 1968. The new strategic notions of "peaceful coexistence," "internal liberalization," and "polycentrism" have by now become acceptable to a very broad range of Americans, although the polycentric concept has been tarnished somewhat by the August 1968 events in Czechoslovakia and the ensuing pronouncement of the "Brezhnev doctrine."

The reappraisals underlying these new strategic notions have already been discussed at some length earlier in this chapter, and this study is no place for an attempted analysis of the principal forces causing the political detente which has been evident in recent years. Consequently, we shall concern ourselves in the balance of this chapter with (1) noting the economic pressures that became quite important in the late sixties in influencing the continued liberalization of U.S. East-West trade policies, and (2) examining the actual liberalization measures which have been taken to date.

Perhaps the most important economic factor in the movement for East-West trade liberalization has been the increasing ability and willingness of American allies and other Western countries to trade with the socialist world. In spite of some liberalization measures in the early and mid sixties, the U.S. market share in the East continued to fall. In 1948, the year before the establishment of COCOM, the United States accounted for 21 per cent of total COCOM member exports to the socialist countries of Eastern Europe. By the 1957–1959 period this share in COCOM exports had fallen to seven per cent, and it further deteriorated to five per cent in the 1967–1969 period.

The loss in the position of the United States in the markets of the socialist countries of Asia was even more dramatic, however, because of the relatively high level of U.S.-Chinese trade before the Communist takeover and the virtual U.S. embargo on all economic relations with the P.R.C. and North Korea after 1950. The U.S. accounted for 75 per cent of total COCOM exports in 1948 to what was to become Communist Asia. U.S. trade with this area practically ceased after 1950 while the other nations' exports to this region grew at an annual average rate in excess of ten per cent throughout the fifties and sixties.[54]

Besides rendering the U.S. embargo policy less and less effective for a wide range of goods, this development presumably has also increased competition among Western exporters to the socialist countries in those U.S. goods which are permitted to be exported. This has resulted in ever growing competitive envy and frustration among those American export interests who wish to compete with other Western nations in the Eastern markets.[55] In terms of our model, this suggested diminished disutilities arising from socialist consumption (y_{ij}) for some subset of products, among the subset of Americans associated with the more aggressive U.S. export interests. Assuming that this effect was not offset by increased marginal disutilities for other individuals with respect to Eastern consumption of these products, the net result would have been diminished *collective* utility parameters associated with socialist consumption of these goods.

Private business displeasure with the severe unilateral U.S. export control policy had been considerable in the early sixties,[56] but it is possible that prior to the widespread public disillusionment with the Vietnam war, beginning in 1967–1968, most businessmen had been somethat inhibited about publicly urging the liberalization of these restrictions. The early and mid sixties were characterized as well by a domestic economic boom, and undoubtedly this had the effect of deflecting the attention of many companies away from possible new export markets. Furthermore, many private organizations, ranging from consumer groups boycotting Communist made merchandise, to dockworkers and the Young Americans for Freedom, undertook various programs of harassment in the early sixties designed to discourage American business from dealing with the socialist countries. This kind of harassment seemed to diminish, however, after the Johnson Administration issued strong denunciations of such private groups, which were trying to take foreign policymaking into their own hands.[57]

This competitive concern of U.S. exporters, particularly manufacturers of high technology products, was of course a major impetus for the congressional hearings on East-West trade in 1968 and 1969, and the introduction of legislation in 1969 aimed at liberalizing export controls and control procedures with respect to the socialist countries.[58] Their concern focused primarily on the uncertainty and administrative costs imposed on U.S. exporters by the export control procedures, and the general complaint that they were at a distinct disadvantage relative to their foreign competitors when it came to the export to socialist countries of those goods unilaterally controlled by the United States.[59]

The increased willingness and ability of other nonsocialist nations to trade with the target countries has consequently led domestic advocates of export liberalization to place growing emphasis on "foreign availability" as a criterion for control. On the one hand this reflects the quite obvious disadvantage of U.S. exporters with respect to those extra-COCOM controlled goods that are embargoed. On the other, this reflects the apparent reduction for many extra-COCOM controlled goods of product differentiation-by-source as a result of the significant technological gains by Western Europe and Japan over the past twenty years, as well as the greater supply elasticities for manufactured goods in these countries following postwar reconstruction. Outward supply shifts and reduced product differentiation-by-origin in technological goods has presumably increased the price elasticity of demand of the socialist nations for U.S. exports (see Appendix C on this question). With respect to those extra-COCOM controlled items not embargoed, this has made it more difficult for U.S. exporters competing in Eastern markets to pass on the costs of U.S. control procedures to their Eastern customers. Nonprice competitive considerations, such as inability quickly to consumate an export sale, are possibly even more important in putting U.S. exporters at a competitive disadvantage.[60]

A second economic factor influencing the liberalization movement has been the steadily worsening balance of payments position of the United States. Gradually, over the past twenty years, the perennial balance of payments problem has led to increasing concern within the United States for export expansion, and may have had the general effect, particularly in recent years, of diminishing the negative value for the collective utility parameter associated with socialist consumption of many nonmilitary goods. Thus, the disutility of exporting to these countries may have diminished in general. Indeed, the balance of payments argument for liberalization has often appeared in the public debate over this issue.[61] A third economic problem, domestic unemployment, has emerged in only the past two or three years as a strong argument for export liberalization to the Communist countries. Recent requests by exporters for validated export licenses have apparently often stressed the domestic job-creating effect of increased exports to the socialist world.[62]

The 1968–1969 congressional hearings on East-West trade had the effect of merging the "building bridges" strategy with grass roots business and economic pressure into a potent political force for liberalization. The result was the Export Administration Act of 1969, which represented an extension and yet a significant modification of the Export Control Act of 1949 (as amended). Many of the complaints by exporters and other advocates of liberalized trade which dominated the 1968–1969 hearings were reflected in the tone and policy declarations of the Export Administration Act. The highlights of the Act were:

(i) The following findings by Congress:[63]

...(2) The unrestricted export of materials, information and technology without regard to whether they make a significant contribution to the *military potential* of any other nation or nations may adversely affect the national security of the United States.

It should be noted that only "military potential" was referred to here, whereas in the superseded Export Control Act of 1949 (as amended in 1962), the corresponding reference was to "potential military and *economic* significance."

...(3) The *unwarranted restriction* of exports from the United States has *a serious adverse effect on our balance of payments.*

(4) The uncertainty of policy toward certain categories of exports has curtailed the efforts of American business in these categories to the detriment of the overall attempt *to improve the trade balance of United States.*

(ii) The following declarations of policy:[64]

...(1) It is the policy of the United States both (A) to encourage trade with all countries with which we have diplomatic or trading relations, except those countries with which such trade has been determined by the President to be against the national interest, and (B) to restrict the export of goods and technology which would make a significant contribution to the *military potential* of any nation or nations which would prove detrimental to the national security of the United States.

Again "military potential" replaced the notion of "military or economic potential." The new Act in effect incorporated the policy of selective export control within a policy framework that encourages international trade. This is a significant departure from the sole emphasis of the old Act on "control."

(iii) The policy of encouraging trade was to be implemented as follows:[65]

...(1) The Secretary of Commerce shall institute such organizational and procedural changes . . . as he determines are necessary to facilitate and effectuate the fullest implementation of the policy set forth in this Act with a view to promoting trade with all nations with which the United States is engaged in trade, including trade with (A) those countries or groups of countries with which other countries or groups of countries having defense treaty commitments with the United States have a significantly larger percentage of volume of trade than does the United States, and (B) other countries eligible for trade with the United States but not significantly engaged in trade with the United States. In addition, the Secretary shall review any list of articles, materials, or supplies, including technical data or other information, the exportation of which . . . was heretofore prohibited or curtailed with a view to making promptly such changes and revisions in such list as many be necessary or desirable in furtherance of the policy, purposes, and provisions of this Act. . . .

(2) The Secretary of Commerce shall use all practicable means available to him to keep the business sector of the Nation fully apprised of changes in export control policy and procedures instituted in comformity with this Act with a view to encouraging the widest possible trade.

(iv) Most significantly, with respect to the export of goods and technical data which would be controlled for "national security" reasons, availability abroad would have to be considered:[66]

. . . Rules and regulations may provide for denial of any request or application for authority to export . . . to any nation or combination of nations threatening the national security of the United States if the President determines that their export would prove detrimental to the national security of the United States, regardless of their availability from nations other than any nation or combination of nations threatening the national security of the United States; *but whenever export licenses are required on the ground that considerations of national security override considerations of foreign availability, the reasons for so doing shall be reported to the Congress* in the quarterly report following the decision to require such licenses on that ground to the extent considerations of national security and foreign policy permit. . . .

(v) The Executive must consult with private industry:[67]

. . . Consistent with considerations of national security, the President shall from time to time seek information and advice from various segments of private industry in connection with the making of these determinations . . . (with respect to which commodities shall be controlled).

(vi) A streamlining of procedures was to be undertaken.[68]

. . . Reporting, recordkeeping, and export documentation requirements shall be periodically reviewed and revised in the light of developments in the field of information technology. . . .

(vii) Finally, controlling agencies (principally the OEC) were required to keep license applicants informed as to reasons for approval delays or denials.[69]

In summary, while the Executive had been taking small steps toward liberalization of restrictions affecting the socialist countries of Eastern Europe, notably through the "decontrolling" process, this relaxation was not sufficient to satisfy the new political pressure for increased liberalization. This pressure focused on the Banking and Currency committees of the two houses of Congress which held hearings in 1968 and 1969 prior to the introduction of the several bills which served as a basis for the Export Administration Act of 1969. The discretionary application of these controls and their detailed implementation were left to the Executive, but passage of this Act reflected a fundamental change in Congress's view with respect to the intent and scope of general U.S. restrictions on exports to the socialist world.

As a result of this legislation the Office of Export Control has reported that it has liberalized export controls in a number of respects. The OEC has decontrolled an extensive list of nonmilitary goods for the socialist countries of Eastern Europe. Other liberalization actions have included the standardization of certain forms used in the licensing approval process, the raising of the maximum dollar exemption level for the filing of certain documents and licenses, and allowing high volume exporters to use monthly *summary* export declarations for exports to nonsocialist countries.[70]

Evidently the "polycentrism" notion has been accepted by the Nixon Administration, as well as by the three prior administrations. In May 1971 the Commodity Control List for Rumania was shortened, putting that country into a favored position with respect to U.S. export controls, even as against Poland.[71] This seemed to represent a belated recognition of the much greater degree of foreign policy independence shown by Rumania within Eastern Europe, relative to any of the other Comecon members.

Perhaps the most dramatic export control liberalization measure of this entire period, however, has been the move to open trade relations with the People's Republic of China. While the selective liberalizations in the past for Poland and Rumania may have been meant as "symbols" of American support and encouragement of these countries' foreign policy and/or internal reform initiatives, the expected political quid pro quos have seldom been clearly delineated, at least publicly. With respect to China, on the other hand, the Nixon Administration's evolving economic policy after 1968 seemed to play the role of a signalling device. The idea seems to have been to signal the Chinese, by progressively larger trade liberalization steps, that the United States wished to end the Cold War confrontation of some twenty years and to move towards a "normalization" of political and economic relations with the P.R.C.

Besides involving Big Power political considerations, the movement towards normalization also seemed to reflect a growing sentiment in the United States to terminate the embargo on relations with China. That is, the collective disutility parameters historically associated with consumption on the Chinese mainland (y_{ij}) seemed to be diminishing. The underlying motivations were probably reduced hostility because of the absence of direct fighting with the P.R.C. since 1953, and several of the factors that we have cited to explain diminished diseconomies with respect to Eastern European consumption—notably, the emphasis on U.S. export expansion; competitive envy of allied trade with China; clear evidence of polycentrism (the "Sino-Soviet split," which was brought into relief for most Americans by the Chinese-Russian border disputes beginning in 1969); and the several other strategic notions subsumed under the policy of "building bridges" to the Communist world.[72] Undoubtedly the vocal and very real material support given to North Vietnam by the P.R.C. tempered much of the pressure for liberalization, but with the withdrawal of U.S. combat forces from Vietnam, together with the growing realization that Mainland China would soon be admitted to the United Nations, support for a reopening of trade with the Chinese maintained its momentum.

Against this background, the U.S. began its policy of using trade liberalization as a signalling device in mid 1969, when certain restrictions were lifted on travelling to Mainland China and on bringing back small quantities of Chinese goods. In December 1969, amendments to the Foreign Assets Control Regulations included authorization for U.S. controlled firms and banks located abroad to engage in trade and financial transactions with the People's Republic of China provided that (1) the merchandise was not of U.S. origin and (2) the merchandise was not included on the COCOM list or prohibited by other agencies of the government.[73] Aside from serving as another sign to Mainland China that U.S. policy makers were willing to consider a move towards normalization of political-economic relations between the two countries, this change in regulations also helped to smooth some of the extra-territoriality problems which had arisen between the United States and its COCOM partners.

In April 1971 President Nixon announced further liberalization measures with respect to Communist China. These included:[74]

1. The drafting of a list of "nonstrategic" goods which U.S. companies would be able to export *directly* to Mainland China on a general license basis.

2. Authorization for U.S. companies to sell fuel to ships or planes bound to or from Mainland China, except for Chinese owned or Chinese chartered carriers bound to or from North Korea, North Vietnam, or Cuba.

3. Authorization for American carriers to haul Chinese cargo between nonChinese ports, and for U.S. owned carriers operating under the flag of another nation to call at Chinese ports.

The list of "uncontrolled" exports for China was published in June 1971. While controls on this trade were still stiffer than for the socialist countries of Eastern Europe, the OEC made it clear that it would at least consider applications for validated licenses.[75] Reflecting diminished disutilities associated with Chinese foreign exchange earnings (f^k_{hj}, f^k_{ij}), which consideration, as we have seen, is logically tied to international diseconomies in consumption, the embargo on imports from China was also totally lifted in June 1971.[76] Finally, just before his visit to Peking in February 1972, President Nixon authorized the OEC to further decontrol the China list to put it on an equivalent basis with the controls applicable to the Soviet Union and most of the other socialist countries of Eastern Europe.[77]

At the same time that Congress was reviewing the premises upon which general controls were imposed on U.S. exports to the East, the 50 per cent "cargo preference" requirements on this trade were also coming under increasing public attack. The spillover effect of the cargo preference provision onto exporters of agricultural commodities finally received specific attention in Congress in 1969, when legislation relating to general export restrictions was being formulated. One of the provisions of the proposed Export Expansion and Regulation Act of 1969, a precursor of the Export Administration Act of 1969, proposed taking away from the President some of his discretion with respect to cargo preference requirements. Section 4(f) of this bill, referring to the export control authority conferred upon the Executive, provided that:[78]

> The authority conferred . . . shall not be exercised with respect to any agricultural commodity . . . during any period for which the supply of such commodity is determined by the Sectetary of Agriculture to be in excess of the requirements of the domestic economy, except to the extent required to effectuate the policies . . . relating to foreign policy and national security.

Clearly the sponsors of this legislation chose to see the 1963 cargo preference requirements as protectionist rather than national security inspired. At the hearings relating to section 4(f), enactment was supported by various agricultural and related interests, such as the American Farm Bureau Federation, National Association of Wheat Growers, National Corn Growers Association, the Grain Sorghum Producers Association and the Chicago Board of Trade.[79] Opposition to this section came from the AFL-CIO Maritime Trade Department and the Seafarers International Union. The spokesman for the latter group argued that since feed grains and wheat are subsidized, the Maritime industry should likewise be subsidized for their shipment abroad. His basic emphasis, however, was on the contribution of seapower to "national power."[80] Thus we see an intermingling of the two considerations underlying the collective good $m_{ij}^{k} = \frac{z_{ij}}{X_i}$; the protectionist and national security objectives.

Administration spokesmen were also against legislation removing the cargo preference requirement. Three basic reasons were cited for their opposition: (1) removal of the requirement (which was admitted to be restrictive with respect to wheat and feed grain exports) would not *necessarily* increase U.S. exports of these commodities to the target nations, since the demand for these products in such countries is also a function of erratic harvests, bilateral clearing arrangements, and other considerations; (2) the strong opposition of the maritime industry to such legislation; and (3) the feeling that rejecting the maritime industry's position on this point would limit the President's flexibility in arranging deals in the future similar to the massive 1963–1964 transactions with the Soviet Union. In other words, maritime opposition to future sales could be expected to be even stiffer if the President was denied the discretion to apply cargo preference requirements to such transactions.[81]

Because of the strength of the opposition, section 4(f) or a similar provision was not included in the final legislation emerging from the Senate Committee on Banking and Currency on the question of export control liberalization. Instead the Committee merely urged the President, in its report on the bill, to review and remove the cargo preference provision from the export control regulations.[82] In June 1971 President Nixon repealed the cargo preference requirement with respect to exports to all socialist countries. Significantly, this was followed five months later by an agreement with the Soviet Union whereby U.S. grain producers would sell to the U.S.S.R. $136 million of corn, barley, and oats between November 1971 and June 1972—easily the largest such transaction since the massive 1963–1964 wheat shipments to the Soviet Union, which had triggered the cargo preference regulations in the first place.

Announcement of this agreement was accompanied by disclosure that the Administration had also obtained the agreement of the maritime unions to load these grain shipments regardless of the proportion ultimately going by U.S.-flag carriers.[83] While there is little evidence that the disutility connected with the protectionist-national security consideration m_{ij}^{k} had diminished in recent years, this represented a radical change in the Administration's position on cargo preference. Presumably the export expansion and foreign policy motivations leading to diminished collective disutilities connected with socialist consumption of agricultural goods in surplus in the U.S. more than offset these protectionist considerations in the President's deliberations on this issue. Nevertheless, the protectionist consideration of the U.S. maritime industry has continued to influence U.S. grain exports to the Soviet Union. The $750 million grain deal announced in July 1972 provided that one-third of these shipments were to be made on U.S. and Soviet ships, respectively. Because of the Soviet Union's extremely inelastic demand for grain at this time, they were willing to pay premium rates for the uncompetitive American ships.[84]

The same business and economic pressures which forced the general export control and cargo preference liberalizations of recent years also led to growing congressional dissatisfaction with the prohibition on Eximbank support for exports to the East that had been legislated in 1968. There was increased awareness in Congress that this effective ban on Eximbank support was inconsistent with the declared policy of expanded trade in nonstrategic items expressed in the Export Administration Act of 1969.[85] The Nixon Administration did not actively support changing the 1968 legislation, although it did suggest that should discretion in regard to Eximbank support be returned to the President, it would be utilized "only for Rumania under present circumstances."[86] This of course was in line with the more favorable treatment now accorded Rumania under the export control regulations.

In January 1971 Senator Mondale introduced legislation designed to make the U.S. credit support program more competitive. Among his proposals was a return to the President of basically the same discretionary authority prescribed under the original 1964 legislation regarding Eximbank support of East-West trade. Presidential discretion was to be disallowed only with respect to the use of Eximbank credit support for exports made either directly or indirectly (through third countries) to "any nation which engages in armed conflict, declared or otherwise, with the armed forces of the United States."[87]

This amendment was incorporated in the Export Expansion Finance Act of 1971, which was enacted into law in August 1971.[88] In effect the amendment prohibited Eximbank support only for exports to North Vietnam (which exports are prohibited anyway by the Foreign Assets Control Regulations), and for exports to other countries intending to reexport the supported goods to North Vietnam. Other than this, there were now no restrictions on Eximbank support for exports to the socialist countries, except that the President would be required to make the determination that such transactions would be in the "national interest."[1] Furthermore, the sanctions applying to third countries giving aid to North Vietnam were eliminated. Under the new discretionary authority given him by this legislation, President Nixon in December 1971 authorized the Eximbank to extend export credits to Rumania. The recent trade agreements with Poland and the Soviet Union also provide for the eligibility of these two countries for Eximbank support.[89]

We have at several points in this book pointed out the logical link between international external effects in consumption (the y_{ij}^k consideration) and the collective good aspect of foreign earnings of foreign exchange (the f_{hj}^k, f_{ij}^k consideration). This link should be particularly strong in East-West trade, because of the necessity of the socialist countries to approximate bilateral balancing of their foreign trade in the absence of convertible Eastern currencies. In other words, their capacity to absorb exports from each of the Western countries is vitally dependent upon their own ability to generate exports to each of these countries. While extension of credits by the West can

[1] In other words section 2(b) (2) of the Export-Import Act of 1945 (as amended) would still apply, *supra*, page 98.

relax this foreign exchange constraint, this, like most credit mechanisms, can be safely used only as a "bridging" device, and in the long term the ability to repay these credits is again a function of the East's own export capabilities.

Yet despite the various liberalization initiatives taken by the United States in the past four years with respect to exports to the East, the basic import barriers have persisted. But not only have they persisted, they have actually become relatively more restrictive. This is because while the old "Column Two" tariff rates have continued to apply to imports from those socialist countries to which MFN is denied, most of the rest of the world has benefitted from a general reduction in U.S. tariff rates as a result of the Kennedy Round negotiations.

The failure of import liberalization to proceed along with export liberalization is not too surprising when we recall some of the recent economic forces which have promoted the latter. Chronic U.S. balance of deficits would not tend towards diminished disutilities in connection with (f_{hj}^k, f_{ij}^k). On the contrary, balance of payments problems usually lead to a common desire to restrict, rather than expand, imports. Furthermore, while a falling U.S. export share in the socialist markets has a direct effect upon the utility functions of the exporter subset of Americans, no comparable group is affected in such a way as to revise downward its collective disutility arising from the dollar earnings of the socialist nations in the U.S. market. The export oriented industries have generally failed to recognize, or at least to publicize, the crucial linkage between the ability of the Eastern countries to earn hard currencies and their ability to increase the level of their imports from the West.[90] Academic and other experts on East-West trade, however, have increasingly focused their attention on this linkage.[91]

Moreover, one would expect no great consumer pressure for liberalization of these import barriers until socialist exports become well known for their quality and other competitive features. As has often been pointed out, a wide range of the export products of these countries would probably find little or no market in the United States.[92] Even if socialist made products were more competitive, the likelihood of strong, cohesive *consumer* pressure for their import is small.

Finally, protectionist sentiment among many U.S. industries has continued to strengthen in recent years. While there is little recent evidence of protectionist inspired political activity aimed at maintaining U.S. restrictions on socialist imports, the strongly anti-import mood among many labor and business groups in general (and often the Administration) would tend to discourage efforts by trade-biased congressmen to press this issue.[93] In general, we may therefore conclude that the forces causing diminished disutilities for a broad subset of products consumed in the Eastern countries have not worked to cause similar changes in the collective utility parameters associated with socialist earnings of foreign exchange.

It will be recalled that the Johnson Administration introduced legislation in 1966 designed to return to the President his discretion with respect to granting MFN to socialist countries. This initiative died in Congress as did an identical bill introduced in 1969. The failure of the later proposal to be enacted has been attributed to the objections by some congressmen that the proposed concessions to be made and received in the commercial agreements were not specific enough (in other words, the President would be allowed too much discretion under this bill), and to the general objections by many to such a dramatic bid for rapprochement with the East.[94] Clearly another factor was the absence of strong commercial interests encouraging import liberalization in the same way that aggressive export industries successfully pushed export liberalization in the 1969 Congress.

Congressional advocates of a more liberal East-West import policy have persisted, however, in their efforts. A new bill was introduced in the Senate in September 1971 that would give the President authority to grant MFN to any of the socialist countries.[95] Recently a bill which would provide MFN for Rumania was introduced in the House. The Nixon Administration, which had previously not pushed the MFN issue, began to lend its active support to legislation designed to permit the granting of MFN treatment to Rumania.[96] Finally, as a direct result of the 1972 U.S.-Soviet trade agreement, the Administration was expected to introduce MFN legislation as one of the first orders of business when Congress reconvened in January, 1973.[97] Indeed, the American public finally seems to be willing to accept the important linkage of exports and imports in East-West trade. The basic question would seem to be *when* rather than *whether* the President will regain his discretion with respect to making MFN available to the other socialist countries.[m]

In summary, the years since 1968 have seen an array of initiatives taken with regard to liberalization of U.S. East-West trade policy. The schizophrenic appearance of this policy continues, however, with the United States presenting an increasingly liberal face to the East in respect of exports, but continuing to discriminate against imports from most Communist countries. With the exception of Poland, all the socialist countries are still denied MFN treatment. North Korea and North Vietnam are still subject to a total embargo on trading relations. The People's Republic of China, the Soviet Union, and the other socialist countries of Eastern Europe (excepting Poland and Rumania) are now treated equally with respect to export controls. These controls are still considerably more severe than those imposed on trade with

---

[m] In late 1972 and early 1973 there was considerable support in Congress for making the granting of MFN (and in fact other forms of trade liberalization, including Eximbank support) to the Eastern countries, particularly the Soviet Union, contingent upon their eliminating the high exit fees for emigrants. The ideological-moral stance on this issue, which confronted little direct domestic *economic* pressure for import liberalization, is in striking contrast to the emphasis on the economic benefits of export liberalization.

the rest of the world. Poland and Rumania receive preferential treatment, with Rumania being subject to the most liberal system of controls. Eximbank credit support is now effectively available for all the socialist countries except North Vietnam, should the President determine that such assistance is in the national interest. A determination along these lines has already been made with respect to Rumania, and Eximbank support seems also to be forthcoming for Poland, the Soviet Union, and other socialist countries. Under the provisions of the Johnson Act, the export of private capital not tied to "customary commercial transactions" is still prohibited to most of the socialist countries. Recently, however, the Government's Overseas Private Investment Corporation (OPIC) has received general authorization to guarantee private investments that might be made in Rumania.

Throughout the past decade there has been increasing recognition in the United States of the fundamental trade-off between economic welfare and economic warfare pursued in the name of national security. Indeed, it is likely that only because of the increased competitive envy of U.S. exporters in the sixties, together with the worsening U.S. balance of payments and domestic unemployment situation late in the decade, was it possible for the advocates of the "building bridges" strategy to actually muster the political strength to push through the new trade liberalization measures of 1969–1972.

Just what the economic gains from expanded U.S. trade with the East might amount to is the subject of the next chapter. In the final chapter we will be discussing the East-West trade policy choices facing the United States for the balance of the 1970s, as seen in the perspective of our optimal trade policy model and the lessons that can be learned from past U.S. East-West trade policy.

8 U.S. East-West Trade Potential

Trade between the socialist countries of Eastern Europe and Asia and the Western industrialized countries[a] has never represented a significant portion of world trade. In the late sixties East-West trade amounted to less than three per cent of total world trade turnover.[1] Even before the war, trade between these two regions was relatively insignificant, representing a little over six per cent of world trade in 1938.[2] Nevertheless, the disparity between these two figures suggests that there may yet be considerable untapped potential in East-West commerce. With total world trade currently exceeding $300 billion, a return to the prewar East-West trade share would mean a trade increase of over $10 billion.

But it is not at all certain that this higher prewar trade proportion shall ever be achieved. The Eastern European countries have undertaken a massive realignment in their trading relations since the war, and the gradual evolution of Comecon as an integrating force may perpetuate the high proportion of intraComecon trade, which currently approximates 60 per cent of total Eastern European turnover.[3] Furthermore, expansion of Eastern European trade with Western Europe may well be limited in the future by the heavy reliance of the East Europeans on exports of raw materials, fuels and semimanufactures, which are subject to relatively low income elasticities of demand in Western Europe. Relatively slow growth of Eastern exports could effectively be a severe foreign exchange constraint on these countries, which would restrict their ability to rapidly expand their imports from the West.[4] Longer term prospects for trade with the socialist countries of Asia are even less certain.

The socialist countries are presently relatively negligible trading partners for the United States. In the 1967–1969 period, East-West trade amounted to only 0.6 per cent of total U.S. turnover. The United States' NATO partners, on the other hand, transacted 4.3 per cent of their combined foreign trade with the Eastern countries in this period.[5] Contrary to what is often believed, East-West trade has not always been so relatively unimportant for the United States. In 1938, U.S. exports to the socialist countries represented six per cent of total U.S. exports. In the same year, exports to the East accounted for 9.4 per cent of total exports of the other COCOM member nations.[6]

Measuring the actual restrictive effect of even the most conventional trade barriers is always a fairly uncertain exercise; estimating the impact of East-

[a] Basically O.E.C.D. members together with several other small European nations.

West trade policies is particularly fraught with uncertainty. As Adler-Karlsson has demonstrated, it is extremely difficult to separate out the actual effects of the postwar embargo policy from the general trade dampening effects of the Cold War, and the internal supply constraints and early autarkical trade policies followed by the eastern countries.[7] What is clear is that the level of East-West trade in 1952–1953 was considerably less than had been projected by the Organization for European Economic Cooperation (OEEC) in late 1948.[8] The changing fortunes of East-West trade after imposition of the strategic embargo are portrayed in Table 8-1.

Table 8-1. Total Trade with the Socialist Countries (U.S. and Other COCOM Countries)

Trade with Socialist Countries of Eastern Europe	1948	1952	(1957/59)	(1967/69)	Average Annual Growth Rates	
		(in $ millions)			(1948–1957/59)	(1957/59–1967/69)
Exports						
U.S.	123	1	95	220	Negative	8.7%
Other COCOM	453	519	1,295	4,064	11.1%	12.1%
Total	576	520	1,390	4,284		
Imports						
U.S.	113	40	68	190	Negative	10.8%
Other COCOM	697	655	1,456	4,346	7.7%	11.5%
Total	810	695	1,524	4,536		
Trade with China						
Exports						
U.S.	273	+	+	+	Negative	—
Other COCOM	91	26	331	973	13.8%	11.4%
Total	364	26	331	973		
Imports						
U.S.	120	+	+	+	Negative	Negative
Other COCOM	84	88	213	656	9.7%	11.9%
Total	204	88	213	656		

+ Negligible.

Source: Compiled from *Battle Act Report*, U.S. Department of State, (Washington D.C.), various issues.

Between 1948, the year before the establishment of COCOM, and 1952 total COCOM exports to Eastern Europe fell from $576 million to $520 million. Over the same period, COCOM imports from Eastern Europe also declined, from $810 million in 1948 to $695 million in 1952. Trade with China declined even more dramatically in this period. Total COCOM exports to the P.R.C. fell from $364 million in 1948 to $26 million in 1952; imports from China also fell sharply, from $204 million in 1948 to $88 million in 1952. While the degree to which the embargo policy itself was responsible for the downward spiral in trade volume after 1948 cannot be precisely calculated, undoubtedly it played an important role. Adler-Karlsson, who has studied this period quite extensively, concludes that there is "a not insignificant probability that the embargo policy was a main explaining factor behind the total trade development."[9]

The relative restrictiveness of the U.S. embargo policy, as exemplified by the U.S. "COCOM differential" and perhaps stiffer U.S. enforcement procedures, is reflected in the relative deterioration of the U.S. East-West trade share among the COCOM allies throughout the first twenty years of the embargo policy. As Table 8-1 shows, although the U.S. had virtually embargoed all exports to the socialist countries by 1952, exports of the other COCOM countries to Eastern Europe actually rose between 1948 and 1952. The relative early success of the China embargo, however, is demonstrated by the fact that "other COCOM" exports to this country declined by over 70 per cent during this period.[b]

As we know, the COCOM embargo list began to wither away in 1954, and the Eastern countries also turned away somewhat from their autarky policy. Apparently the "other COCOM" countries responded quite strongly to these developments, as their exports to Eastern Europe climbed to almost three times the 1948 level by 1957–1959, and exports to China to over three times the 1948 level by the later period. As Adler-Karlsson has concluded, "after 1953–1954 in most groups, and a few years later in a couple of groups, East-West trade seems to regain not only the loss of the early 1950s, but also the nonrealized trade expansion."[10]

Nevertheless, while the COCOM allies trade with the East grew at an average annual rate approximating ten per cent during the first ten years of the cooperative embargo, U.S. trade, although increasing with Eastern Europe after 1952, remained below the 1948 levels. The relative U.S. position continued to deteriorate over the next decade, in spite of some "decontrolling" in favor of Poland after 1957 and Rumania beginning in 1964, and general decontrolling of its extra-COCOM list in 1966. As can be seen from Table 8-1, while "other COCOM" exports to Eastern Europe rose at an average annual

[b] Interestingly enough, the COCOM "China differential" was not established until late 1952.

rate of 12.1 per cent between 1957–1959 and 1967–1969, U.S. exports to this area grew by only 8.7 per cent in the same period. The average annual growth rate of other COCOM members' trade with the P.R.C. exceeded 11 per cent in this decade, while the U.S. continued to impose a virtual embargo on all trade with the Chinese.

Despite such evidence that the U.S. has unilaterally deprived itself of trading opportunities in the East, which in many cases have merely been snapped up by its Western competitors, many have remained unconvinced that the removal of the most severe U.S. trade restrictions will really lead to a significant expansion in U.S. East-West trade. It is often argued that many other obstacles remain to expanded U.S. participation in East-West trade, giving the explicit trade policy barriers only marginal meaning. These additional barriers may be classified into three broad types: structural, ideological, and policy obstacles.[11]

The structural obstacles are perhaps most often mentioned, and are the most persuasive. Such barriers would include: (1) the inconvertibility of socialist currencies, resulting in the need for these countries to more or less bilaterally balance their trade with individual Western nations; (2) the relative lack of historic trading ties between the United States and the socialist world; (3) the greater geographical distance between most of the Eastern countries and the U.S., which means in most cases higher transport costs; and (4) the alleged uncompetitive nature of socialist exports in the U.S. market.

The ideological obstacle often cited refers to the alleged unwillingness of U.S. businessmen to trade with the Communists. The recent junkets of dozens of American business leaders to Moscow and other Eastern capitals would seem to belie the importance of this barrier to trade, although in the past it may have constituted a significant trade restricting factor. Finally, the principal policy obstacle aside from the various explicit trade restrictive policies mentioned in the previous three chapters would seem to be the lack of U.S. bilateral trade agreements with the socialist countries.

Undoubtedly many of these obstacles have and will continue to restrict U.S. East-West trade to lower levels than it might otherwise attain. It is also quite possible that several of the foregoing "structural" barriers in particular will keep U.S. trade with the East from ever being as important to the United States as East-West trade is to many of the Western European nations and Japan. We have seen, however, that U.S. trade with the East in the pre-war period, while representing only six per cent of total U.S. trade at that time, was relatively far more important to the United States than in recent years. Indeed, if U.S. exports to the Eastern countries in 1970 had also represented six per cent of total U.S. exports, this trade would have amounted to some \$2.6 billion, as compared with actual U.S. exports to the East in 1970 of \$354 million. Even if only the pre-COCOM ratio were achieved (3.2 per cent in 1948), 1970 exports to the socialist world would have totalled \$1.4 billion.

As we shall see, the few published empirical studies on this subject suggest that the various existing restrictions and recently removed barriers to U.S. East-West trade have had a significant inhibiting effect on this commerce. The potential for expanded U.S. trade with the East therefore looks quite bright, provided the recent liberalization spirit continues.

Until very recently, estimates of likely U.S. East-West trade expansion arising from policy liberalization have been rare. At the 1969 Senate hearings on East-West trade, Michael Blumenthal testified that "if there were a liberalization of East-West trade, then over a period of time—probably between five and ten years—the United States should expect that its share of these countries would approximate roughly our share of world trade, and that would be about five times as much as it is at the present time."[12] Based on U.S. exports to the socialist countries of $217 million in 1968, this would indicate annual exports in the second half of the seventies of approximately $1.0 billion. Another, shorter term estimate was made by Samuel Pisar, a noted proponent of U.S. East-West trade liberalization, in his 1970 book, *Coexistence and Commerce*: "If political tension were lessened, active promotional efforts undertaken, and artificial barriers abolished, the likely annual volume of U.S. exports to the Eastern region *in the early seventies* might reach $500 million."[13]

Several studies have also been made of the apparent restrictive effect of various U.S. trade restrictions on particular product groups. Evidence of the restrictive effect of unilateral U.S. export controls at the level of the individual firm was offered before the 1969 hearings. The Hewlett-Packard Co., a major designer and manufacturer of electronic equipment and instrumentation, determined that in 1968, 44 per cent of its worldwide sales were in products on the COCOM list. But more significant, an *additional* 53 per cent of its worldwide sales were made up of products that would have been subject to extra-COCOM U.S. controls had the company attempted to export these products to the socialist world. In every case investigated, Hewlett-Packard found that competitive suppliers in other Western countries could have supplied these extra-COCOM products to the East.[14] Thus not only were the unilateral U.S. controls ineffective in denying the Communist countries these goods, but these sales were being lost, unnecessarily, to competing foreign suppliers.

This same company also submitted a statement to the 1971 hearings dealing with liberalization of Eximbank activities, which sought to measure the restrictive impact of unilateral U.S. export controls, continued denial of MFN treatment to most Eastern imports, and the denial of Eximbank credit support for exports to the East. Hewlett-Packard estimated that the U.S. share of the Eastern European export market for "other electric measuring and controlling instruments" might "double in fairly short order, going from the present 7.5% to, say, 15%" were these restrictions to be lifted. The company's spokesman went on to suggest that "a tripling of the 1969 U.S. market share from 7.5% to 20–23% might be more nearly appropriate," given the "great needs for basic instrumentation that presently exist in Eastern Europe." He concluded "that most U.S. firms would aggressively exploit increased freedom to trade with Eastern Europe and that an increase in U.S. exports from the present $350 million to, say, $1 billion might be quite realistic."[15]

Evidence concerning the probable restrictive effect of the U.S. unilateral export controls on machinery exports has been developed by John M. Montias.[16] Utilizing comparative East-West trade statistics for 1928 and 1969, Montias has shown that the United States share in the export markets of Eastern Europe has fallen quite sharply since the early period, particularly with respect to exports of machinery. He has calculated that if the U.S. had had the same relative position in the Eastern European market in 1969 as it had in 1928, these exports alone would have been some $550 million greater than actually recorded in the later year. While Montias attributes much of this deterioration to some of the "structural" factors we have mentioned, he concludes that the major obstacle to U.S. machinery exports has been the unilateral controls.

Table 8-2 summarizes data submitted by N. R. Danielian to the 1969 East-West trade hearings, concerning the restrictive effect of U.S. policies on exports of wheat to the socialist countries.[17] It will be recalled that until just recently a 50 per cent cargo preference requirement applied to sales of wheat to most of the Eastern countries, as well as to exports of various feed

Table 8-2. Western Exports of Wheat to the Socialist Countries and Yugoslavia, 1960–1968

Crop Year	Western Wheat Exports to All Socialist Countries (millions of bushels)	U.S. Share of Exports to the Socialist Countries of Eastern Europe and Cuba (per cent)	U.S. Share of Wheat Exports to Yugoslavia (per cent)
1960–61	164	64	88
1961–62	265	32	98
1962–63	292	32	98
1963–64	699	24	58
1964–65	466	2	98
1965–66	765	—	100
1966–67	405	3	100
1967–68	261	2	100

Source: Calculated from data provided in the testimony of Dr. N. R. Danielian, President, International Economic Policy Association, before *Hearings on the Export Expansion and Regulation Act*, U.S. Congress, Senate, Committee on Banking and Currency, 91st Congress, 1st Session (Washington, D.C., 1969).

grains to the Soviet Union. In addition, since 1966, PL 480 sales of surplus agricultural commodities have been denied to all the socialist countries.

As Table 8-2 shows, Western exports of wheat to the Communist countries vary significantly from year to year, primarily because of erratic harvest results in the East. The U.S. share in these exports had declined throughout the 1960s, but the drop in 1964, after the massive U.S.-Soviet wheat sale and the introduction of the cargo preference requirement, was particularly significant. Throughout the later sixties and until the massive U.S.-Soviet grain transaction negotiated in 1972, U.S. wheat sales to the East were negligible. That the cargo preference requirement was probably a more restrictive influence than the ban on PL 480 sales is shown by the maintenance by the U.S. of its domination of the Yugoslav wheat export market, in spite of the fact that Yugoslavia was also subject to the 1966 PL 480 prohibition.

While they are helpful indicators of the latent potential of East-West trade for the United States, the varying time horizons of many of the foregoing studies and estimates, together with some uncertainty as to precisely what their authors were assuming with respect to the elimination of various trade barriers, make it difficult to paste the various pieces together into a summary measure of trade potential. In several recent studies, the author has attempted to take a more or less unified view of U.S. East-West trade potential, but only with respect to the socialist countries of Eastern Europe.

In one study, we made a rough comparison of the U.S. share of the Western industrialized nations' exports to Eastern Europe, both for U.S. unilaterally controlled exports on the one hand, and multilaterally (COCOM) controlled or uncontrolled products on the other.[18] The results are summarized in Table 8-3. As the Table indicates, the absolute market share shortfall in Eastern Europe experienced by the United States with respect to the unilaterally controlled products is over twice the shortfall for all other goods sold to the East. Indeed, this study concluded that in 1968 the U.S.

Table 8-3. Percentage U.S. Share of Western Industrialized Countries' Export Markets, 1968

Export Market	Unilaterally Controlled Products	Uncontrolled or COCOM Controlled Products
Rest of World	24	16
Socialist Countries of Eastern Europe	3	6
Market-Share Shortfall	21	10

lost over $300 million in exports to Eastern Europe as a result of the unilateral controls. This compared with actual 1968 U.S. exports to that region of $217 million. Furthermore, under the assumption that the ten per cent shortfall for the COCOM-controlled and uncontrolled products reflected the various structural, ideological, and other policy factors mentioned previously, we concluded that the inhibiting effect of the unilateral export controls was roughly equal to the combined restrictive effect of the structural and other indirect barriers to East-West trade.

A second study by the author sought to measure the restrictive effect of the three principal barriers to U.S. East-West trade as they existed in early 1971: unilateral export controls, prohibition on Eximbank credit support, and denial of MFN treatment to the imports of most socialist nations. Again, this study was confined solely to the socialist countries of Eastern Europe.[19] Table 8-4 portrays the principal conclusions of this study.

Table 8-4. Estimates of Expansion in U.S. Trade with the Socialist Countries of Eastern Europe After Trade Liberalization (in $ millions)

	1968		1975		
			U.S. Exports		
	U.S. Exports	U.S. Imports	Conservative Assumption*	Extrapolated Growth Rates†	U.S. Imports
Before Liberalization (1968: Actual Trade Volume)	217	198	320	523	457
1 Elimination of Unilateral Export Controls	+342	—	+585	+971	—
2 Elimination of Ban on Eximbank Support	+48	—	+85	+141	—
3 (1) and (2)‡	+589	—	+1,000	+1,712	—
4 Granting of MFN	—	+220	—	—	+473

* 1968 OECD exports to Eastern Europe in each two-digit SITC division were assumed to grow at an average annual rate equal to *one-half* the average annual growth rate for exports to Eastern Europe in that division over the 1962/64–1967/69 period.

† 1968 OECD exports to Eastern Europe in each two-digit SITC division were simply extrapolated at the historic growth rate.

‡ The impact on trade volumes of alternative (3) would be more than the simple sum of the impact for alternatives (1) and (2) separately. For explanation see Source, below.

Source: Thomas A. Wolf, "The Quantitative Impact of Liberalization of United States Unilateral Restrictions on Trade with the Socialist Countries of Eastern Europe," *External Research Study*, XR/RECS-3, U.S. Department of State (Washington, D.C., 1972).

Each of the trade liberalization "combinations" in Table 8-4 assumes that the relevant restriction would be completely eliminated. In other words, alternative number 3 means that the U.S. Commodity Control List is reduced to the COCOM list, and that the Eximbank is subject to no political limitations on its activities in East-West trade. Alternative number 4 assumes that MFN treatment is granted to the imports of all the socialist countries of Eastern Europe. Moreover, the implicit assumption is that the full static effect of eliminating each of these restrictions would be realized by 1975 (or would have been realized by 1968).

Under these extreme assumptions, one could conclude that U.S. exports to Eastern Europe (including the Soviet Union) might rise to between $1,320 and $2,235 million by 1975, while imports from that area might climb to over $900 million. In any case, the Eastern European countries could expect to run a sizable trade deficit with the United States. The study goes on to indicate that the product groups most likely to benefit from the relaxation of export controls (and this would include the cargo preference requirement), as well as from a more active Eximbank, would be machinery and transport equipment, certain chemicals and chemical-based products such as plastics, and wheat and feed grains. Indeed these results have been somewhat validated by the trend of U.S.-Soviet trade negotiations in the past two years, which have resulted in vast approvals of export licenses for the sale of plant and equipment and associated technology in connection with the Kama River truck factory and other projects, as well as the massive U.S.-Soviet wheat sales announced in July 1972.

The estimates for U.S. export potential in 1975 of course reflect the particular U.S. export shares in both the world and Eastern Europe markets in 1968, and the commodity composition of East-West trade prevailing in that year. The import projections are also based upon the commodity-country structure of U.S. imports from Eastern Europe in the base year, 1968. Consequently, to the extent that there are forces serving to change the fundamental structure of East-West trade, and in particular Soviet trading propensities, these export and import estimates may turn out to be unduly conservative. Indeed, as we shall discuss a little later, significant changes seem to be occurring with respect to Soviet trade propensities, which have accounted for much of the recent escalation of expectations regarding the U.S.-Soviet trade potential.

Should the United States extend MFN treatment to additional socialist countries, U.S. imports from these nations should rise for two reasons. First, there would be substitution of lower cost socialist products for higher cost importing-competing goods produced in the United States. Second, lower cost Eastern products should substitute in U.S. consumption for higher cost imports from other countries which have heretofore been favored by U.S. discrimination against socialist imports. In most cases, the differences between the "Column 2" rates applicable to most of the socialist countries and the more favorable "Column 1" rates are quite large. In this same study we roughly calculated that for 55 two-digit SITC product groups examined, the ratio of average Column 2 to Column 1 tariff rates exceeds 2:1 for 38 groups, and is greater than 3:1 for 14 of these product categories.[20]

Although these tariff differentials are quite large, it is not at all evident that the socialist countries have the productive capacities, product quality, or marketing skills to fully exploit the new export opportunities in the American market created through U.S. extension of most-favored-nation treatment. As mentioned, this is a favorite argument of those who are skeptical about any significant expansion of East-West trade. Evidence concerning Poland, which, it will be recalled, was granted MFN in late 1960, should temper the enthusiasm of anyone who envisions large-scale penetration of socialist imports into the U.S. market. Although Polish exports to the United States have more than tripled since the period before MFN was granted, from an annual average of $31.6 million in the 1956–1960 period to $101 million in 1969–1971, the growth of the other Eastern European exports to the U.S. has practically kept pace. Poland accounted for 45.2 per cent of U.S. imports from Eastern Europe in 1956–1960, and 46.5 per cent in the later period.[21] In other words, Poland was not able to significantly increase its share of the U.S. market, even though it had been receiving MFN treatment for a decade.

The import projections summarized in Table 8-4 are even more tentative than the export estimates, primarily because of the relative crudity of some of the underlying assumptions. Nevertheless, even if the import figures should really be higher than indicated, it is likely that the separate estimation process used in the study for exports and imports would still generate a significant export surplus for the United States. Since the Eastern countries are expected to continue to rely on approximate bilateral balancing in their foreign trade, these estimates would then suggest that the limited socialist export potential in the short run may seriously restrict U.S. exports to this region, perhaps considerably below the more optimistic Table 8-4 level.

This conclusion should be qualified, however, in at least two respects. First, now that Congress has returned to the President his discretion regarding Eximbank credit support, a large part of the Eastern trade deficit could be financed on credit. There is an upper limit, of course, to the trade debt with which the socialist countries could afford to burden themselves. Second, to the extent that U.S. exports of technology and plant and equipment are used by the Eastern countries to augment their own export oriented productive capacities, U.S. credits associated with such exports could be repaid by sale abroad of the output of Eastern mines and factories. This indeed appears to be the rationale underlying the recently announced contracts under which U.S. firms would supply $65 million worth of ore mining, oil drilling, and other equipment and technology to the Soviets in return for nonferrous metal production valued at $60 million.[22] Negotiations have also been proceeding with respect to Soviet sales of over $40 billion worth of liquified natural gas (over a period of 25 years) as payment for U.S. (and U.S.-Japanese) construction of pipelines, liquefaction plants and special ships for transporting this fuel to Western markets.[23] The Occidental Petroleum-Soviet agreement, which includes such areas as oil, natural gas, agricultural fertilizers, and chemicals, undoubtedly is intended to incorporate this type of "payment in kind" arrangement.[24]

The scope and magnitude of these and other proposed Soviet-U.S. transactions indeed suggest that a fundamental discontinuity may come to characterize U.S. East-West trade in the seventies, which to be sure could hardly have been forecast prior to 1970 or 1971. This discontinuity is likely to be reflected both in the magnitude of trade with the East—particularly with the Soviet Union—as well as in the structure of trade. We are beginning to see that trade projections based upon extrapolating the commodity structure of trade of the late sixties may be greatly misleading.

This would appear to be the result of the happy conjunction of two trends: (1) the increasing recognition in the U.S. of the trade-off between economic welfare and economic warfare considerations, and the resulting acceleration of liberalization of the old "containment" oriented barriers to trade; and (2) a fundamental shift in the trade propensities of the Soviet Union, which now recognizes that only with Western—notably American and perhaps Japanese—assistance can it even begin to fully exploit its natural resource endowment.

An important aspect of this discontinuity is the apparent emergence of the Soviet Union as the preponderant U.S. trading partner in Eastern Europe. In the 1969–1971 period the U.S.S.R. accounted for 39.1 per cent of U.S. exports to Eastern Europe, and only 27.7 per cent of U.S. imports from that region.[25] Based on recent trade figures and announcements, the relative importance of the Soviet Union in this trade will probably increase dramatically. This is not to imply, however, that the other Eastern European countries are likely to become less economically dependent upon the Soviet Union. It is not at all clear that the Soviets would allow this to happen. Nevertheless, this does suggest that henceforth the Soviet Union should be treated separately in any attempts to project future U.S. East-West trade. Interestingly enough, the present discussions concerning U.S.-Soviet cooperation in exploiting the latter's natural resources also suggest that the very factor which may tend to restrict the growth of intraEuropean East-West trade—the heavy preponderance of raw materials and semimanufactures in the westward flow—may have the effect, in the U.S.-Soviet case, of generating quite rapid trade expansion.

Indeed, the more optimistic export growth estimates in Table 8-4 may not turn out to be so wildly unrealistic. Compared to actual U.S. exports to Eastern Europe in 1968 of $217 million, U.S. exports to this region rose to $249 million in 1969, $354 million in 1970, and $384 million in 1971.[26] In 1972 U.S. exports to Eastern Europe may reach $600 million,[c] before taking into account the massive grain transaction negotiated with the Soviet Union.[27] It has been estimated that grain sales to the U.S.S.R. in the year ending August 1973 may amount to $1 billion.[28]

Further trade increases would appear to be in the offing, as the Office of Export Control has approved over $1 billion worth of export licenses in connection with the Soviet Kama River truck project. Consummation of the proposal liquified natural gas transactions would mean an expenditure of some $10 billion for pipelines, liquefaction plants, and tankers, and annual U.S. imports of LNG exceeding $1 billion.[29] Nixon Administration estimates of Soviet-U.S. trade potential differ, ranging from total turnover of $2 billion in 1975 to $10 billion by 1980.[30] The range of these estimates is merely a symptom of the fundamental discontinuity now appearing in U.S. East-West trade, particularly with the Soviet Union.

In passing, we should note that liberalization of U.S. export controls will affect many foreign-based companies as well, including both subsidiaries of U.S. firms and other foreign enterprises presently subject to certain of the U.S. transshipment regulations. Undoubtedly the severity of the U.S. unilateral controls has encouraged some use of foreign based companies in order to trade with the East. Little evidence exists, however, as to the extent of such trade diversion. While relaxation of U.S. controls might induce some firms to shift their export base back to the United States, it is also possible that much of the vast U.S. export potential now being discussed might well be captured instead by overseas subsidiaries of U.S. companies, particularly if the socialist countries are not able to significantly expand their exports to the United States, as would be required for bilateral balancing.

Practically the entire discussion so far has been concerned with the potential for U.S. trade expansion with the socialist countries of Eastern Europe. The People's Republic of China and the other socialist countries of Asia have been ignored because of the dearth of evidence concerning trade prospects with these countries. The total absence of trade with most of this area for over twenty years gives practically no base for projections. Most likely the absolute growth of U.S. trade with these countries will be quite small for the balance of this decade in relation to the expansion of U.S. trade with Eastern Europe. In terms of percentage growth, of course, this trade should expand astronomically. Some perspective on this question has been offered by Robert F. Dernberger, who has suggested a "most plausible" estimate of U.S.-Chinese trade in 1980 ranging from balanced trade at $25

---

[c] Of which about $250 million would be to the Soviet Union.

million both ways to total turnover of some $525 million, with the U.S. in the latter case having a trade surplus of perhaps $125 million.[31] As he points out, U.S. exports to the P.R.C. will probably be limited primarily by the desire and the ability of the Chinese to export to the American market.

In summary, the prospects for U.S. East-West trade seem more favorable now than at any time in the postwar era. Recent U.S. trade with the East, in relation to total U.S. foreign trade, is still insignificant when compared to prewar trade with this area. The few studies on the restrictive effect of recently removed or existing U.S. East-West trade barriers are unanimous in concluding that these policies have had a significant trade inhibiting impact. There is wide divergence of opinion, however, as to just how large an expansion in U.S. East-West trade is likely.

The new spirit of East-West trade liberalization in the United States, in conjunction with the development of enormous new industrial projects and plans for massive natural resource exploitation in the Soviet Union, seems likely to lead to a tremendous expansion in U.S.-Soviet commerce. Trade with the rest of Eastern Europe and China should also grow rapidly, but probably not so dramatically. Undoubtedly a continued movement towards detente between East and West will remain a fundamental precondition for greatly expanded U.S. trade with the socialist world.

9 Alternative Trade Policies for the 1970

Over the past decade, the American public and U.S. East-West trade policy makers have increasingly come to recognize the fundamental trade-off between economic welfare and the pursuit of economic warfare. Furthermore, there has developed a growing awareness that the particular mode of economic warfare utilized in the postwar period has been, in many respects, ineffective in achieving the desired national security objectives. In the first section of the chapter we shall summarize this growing disenchantment with postwar U.S. East-West trade policies, drawing on the conceptual framework of Part I and our earlier discussion of U.S. policies and their restrictive effect on trade.

Certain other lessons may be learned from our analysis of past U.S. East-West trade policies. It is not at all clear, however, that the American public or even many policy makers are fully aware of some of the implications of the successes and failures of past policies. The second section of this chapter attempts to explore what these implications are for future U.S. East-West trade policy making. Finally, drawing on the conceptual structure we have developed, as well as on the various lessons to be learned from past policy making, we shall discuss in some detail in the last part of this chapter the basic East-West trade policy options available to the United States for the balance of the 1970s.

Recognition of the Trade-Off

We have seen in Chapters 2 and 3 that economic warfare implies a departure from a policy designed to maximize a nation's *economic welfare*; regardless of whether or not this economic warfare is successful in terms of somehow enhancing the nation's national security. The pursuit of national security can be seen as sacrificing current consumption in return for reducing the uncertainty involved with future consumption. Continued sacrifice of current consumption over, say, a twenty- or twenty-five-year period, will presumably only be acceptable to a nation's citizenry if they perceive that both a clear threat to the nation's security persists, and that the particular mode of economic and/or military warfare employed seems to be achieving the intended results. If either or both of these conditions are not satisfied, public support for continued sacrifice of current economic welfare is bound to diminish.

This economic welfare-warfare trade-off has only gradually come to be recognized by the vast majority of the American public and their leaders.

That its recognition was so long in coming can be best explained by the tremendous emotionalism associated with the postwar "containment" policy, the insufficient empirical evidence as to the effects of this policy, and the inadequate public discussion of the pros and cons of launching a massive economic warfare offensive against the East. That awareness of the trade-off has finally become widespread is due to growing doubts concerning the general effectiveness of the economic warfare offensive, as well as increasing recognition of the heavy economic costs of this policy to the United States, particularly as borne by certain powerful interest groups.

There are many reasons for the general lack of effectiveness of the postwar economic containment policy. First of all, the United States never really conducted "maximum" offensive economic warfare against the socialist countries. As we have seen in Part I, such a maximal policy would include: (1) a complete export embargo on all military and nonmilitary goods[a] (the y_{hj}, y_{ij} consideration); (2) "dumping" certain products on third markets so as to depress the Communist countries' terms of trade and to reduce their foreign exchange earnings (the s_{ij} collective good); and (3) an embargo on all imports from these countries (the f_{hj}, f_{ij} consideration). While the United States pursued something close to a virtual export embargo of the socialist world in the early fifties, there is no evidnece of purposeful dumping, and denial of MFN treatment to these countries was an illogical "second best" approximation to a complete embargo on imports from the East.[b]

Furthermore, the United States could never persuade its COCOM allies to embargo as broad a list of products to the East as the U.S. itself embargoed. As was discussed in Chapter 5, this inability to satisfy the isolation requirement may not have been too serious a problem as long as the other COCOM countries were primarily concerned with meeting pent-up post war domestic demand and were still in the process of reconstructing their productive capacities. Yet despite such constraints to exporting, we have seen that "other COCOM" exports to the East actually increased between 1948 and 1952, while U.S. exports to this region diminished to a trickle. Moreover, even the less rigorous transshipment requirement was apparently very difficult to satisfy in the early years of the cooperative embargo, because the United States never was able to achieve complete backing from its allies for its severe embargo policy.

While postwar recovery of the Western European and Japanese economies was a primary objective of the United States in its policy of "containing"

---

[a] The important practical problems of distinguishing, on the margin, between military and nonmilitary goods have of course been ignored in this study.

[b] There is, however, some evidence that the U.S. may have pursued a policy of preemptive buying abroad of "strategic" commodities in the early period of the economic containment policy.[1]

communism, it proved in fact to work against the companion policy of economic containment. The stronger these economies became, and the less dependent on U.S. aid, the greater their ability and willingness to export "strategic" goods to the East and the fewer sanctions (threats to cut off foreign aid) the U.S. had to keep them in line. We have seen that after 1953 the other COCOM countries forced a continual shortening of the cooperative embargo list. At the same time, the United States "extra-COCOM" control list grew in length because of the U.S. refusal to go along with this multilateral embargo policy. While still effectively raising the costs to the socialist countries of a wide range of products, the extra-COCOM list failed to deprive the East of many of these goods.

Even if the U.S. had succeeded in satisfying the isolation and transshipment requirements for all goods on the U.S. control list, it is not at all clear that a maximum embargo policy really would have brought the socialist regimes, and particularly the Soviet Union, "to their knees." It seems likely that the policy makers who framed the massive U.S. economic warfare offensive in the early postwar period made two serious underestimations. First, they appeared to underestimate the internal resources (economic, political, ideological) of the socialist "bloc." Indeed, the larger a country or region is in terms of population and natural resources, the more ideologically unified, the more paranoic it is with respect to the outside world, probably the less it will prove vulnerable to severe economic bottlenecks brought on by offensive economic warfare launched by the rest of the world. Furthermore, as we have seen, the appearance of a U.S.-led "Western" economic alliance in the late forties and early fifties undoubtedly spurred the Eastern countries to greater cooperation, and played into the hands of the Soviets, who wanted to consolidate their hegemony over this area.

A second mistake was to underestimate the resilience of the various Communist regimes in the face of economic adversity. A basic assumption underlying the economic containment policy seems to have been the vulnerability of these regimes to internal unrest arising from domestic economic deprivation. Ironically, this assumption failed to take into account the very absence of democracy in these systems and the ability of totalitarian regimes to crush dissent, which features lay at the root of the Western moral-ideological opposition to communism.

Over the past twenty years the rising economic costs of the near-maximal U.S. economic warfare policy also have gradually come to be realized by a broad segment of the American public. As we have seen, however, it appears to have been only the severe worsening of the U.S. balance of payments situation in the late sixties, combined with increased pressure from specific American export interests, which have brought this awareness of the economic costs home to the public and U.S. policy makers. Undoubtedly the domestic unemployment problem since 1970 has also helped to dramatize the costs arising from artificial barriers to export. As discussed in Chapter 7, these mounting economic pressures for a change in policies affected only the public debate over export controls and Eximbank activities in East-West trade. Little pressure came to be felt on the import side because the economic costs (in the form of higher domestic prices) arising from import barriers erected because of the (f^k_{hj}, f^k_{ij}) consideration were dispersed over most of the domestic economy. Generally speaking, the only strong, well defined economic groups affected by import barriers were domestic import-competing producers, who were certainly not likely to press for a reduction in such barriers so as to increase their competition.

As a result of United States inability to enforce Western compliance with the full scope of its own embargo list, and particularly after the COCOM list itself began to wither away after 1953, the competitive position of American exporters in Eastern markets sharply deteriorated. Not only were U.S. companies missing out on export opportunities in the socialist world, they were losing this business in many cases to Western competitors. In Chapter 8 we summarized some of the evidence as to just how large these losses were, which also indicates in approximate terms the latent U.S. export potential in the East, to the extent that Western competitors have not already established exclusive footholds in certain Eastern markets.

We saw that in purely static terms, based upon the structure of trade and U.S. market shares in the late sixties, this export potential is significant—if not in relation to total U.S. foreign trade, certainly in the perspective of the existing level of trade with the East. We also observed that to the extent a fundamental discontinuity has come to characterize the Soviet Union's western trading propensities, the prospects for greatly expanded U.S.-Soviet trade are quite bright.

It is therefore the growing awareness of the missed opportunities in trade, and the fear of possibly permanently losing such opportunities to Western competitors, which has had a significant impact on the recognition by Congress and recent administrations of the large, and growing, economic costs of the massive economic warfare offensive against the Communist world. Taken together with the growing realization of the ineffectiveness of the economic containment policy, and in fact even the inappropriateness of such a containment policy, the American public and policy makers have been led to a fundamental reevaluation of U.S. East-West trade policy.

Other Lessons

In Chapter 7 we discussed at some length the new strategy of "building bridges," which grew out of the reappraisal of the old containment policy. This new strategy, which represented a rejection of the massive economic warfare approach, included the notions of "peaceful coexistence," "polycentrism," and "internal liberalization" as objectives of U.S. foreign economic policy. We observed, however, that while it was a rejection of the economic containment approach, the building bridges strategy was based on the same essential premise—that trade policy instruments could be utilized to achieve political goals.

In turning away from the containment policy, U.S. policy makers were implicitly renouncing the negative (y^k_{hj}, y^k_{ij}) consideration except with respect to a more narrowly defined subset of "strategic" products. As we have shown, this also logically implies renunciation of the negative (f^k_{hj}, f^k_{ij}) national security consideration. Yet building bridges also has offensive economic warfare connotations, although they are somewhat more subtle than the various national security considerations discussed in Part I. Building bridges suggests increased economic interdependence between East and West, and the notion that increased Eastern dependence upon economic relations with the West will naturally lead to desirable changes in the economic systems of the socialist countries and eventually, to favorable political changes.

A policy of "peaceful coexistence," accompanied by increased trade and contacts between the two regions, is thought to increase the interests of both sides in encouraging the growth of trade, and to maximize the possibilities for increased personal freedom within the Communist societies. Expanded trade with the Eastern countries is also presumed to increase the concern of the socialist regimes for the consumers in these countries, and to induce "internal liberalization," initially with respect to economic decision making, and ultimately (and, it would seem, inevitably), in the political sphere. This policy suggests as well that selective use of trade concessions would likewise be used to "encourage independence from Soviet domination and a rebuilding of historical ties with the West."[2]

The building bridges strategy is quite appealing, for it combines the positive, liberal notion of freer trade with the possibility of using expanded trade as an instrument to achieve national security-related political ends. Empirical validation of the building bridges theory, however, would be difficult. There also appears to be considerable disagreement among policy makers, and among experienced academic observers, as to the wisdom of such an overall strategy. The detractors are typically not against an expansion of trade relations. Rather, they believe that the granting of economic concessions in return for expected direct or even indirect political quid pro quos is bound to be a frustrating exercise. Better, they argue, to limit U.S. objectives to the economic sphere and avoid disappointment. George Kennan, for example, has observed: "To demand political concessions as a quid pro quo for normal commercial transactions is, after all, only another way of renouncing trade altogether; for Communist governments will never yield to overt demands of this nature."[3]

The notion of encouraging internal reform and liberalization through trade policy is criticized by John M. Montias: "For one thing, enormous bureaucratic inertia has to be overcome in our organs of government before any such measures can be undertaken. By the time they are taken, the chances are that the political advantage will have vanished."[4] Montias goes on to note that the use of trade policy in this manner may not yield any enduring advantage. He cites the case of Poland, which was granted favorable export control treatment and PL 480 aid not long after the accession of the Gomulka regime in 1956, and later was granted MFN in the hopes that the new regime would undertake widespread internal reforms and adopt a more independent foreign policy line. Yet as he noted, Poland, since that time, "tightened up its political and economic system" and became "one of the more centralized states in Eastern Europe, one of those least engaged in economic or political reforms." Furthermore, the Polish workers' riots of December 1970 and subsequent economic reforms can hardly be traced to the United States's relatively more liberal East-West trade policies toward that country.

To be sure, the building bridges strategy is no longer shown the respect it received in the famed "Miller Report" of 1965 or in various official pronouncements of the Kennedy and Johnson administrations. As Stanislaw Wasowski has observed:[5]

> The policy of bridge building has changed as a result of the Soviet invasion of Czechoslovakia. The United States, instead of providing initiatives, is more likely to see its role as that of a judicious and selective respondent to needs and overtures coming from Eastern Europe. Instead of placing political *rapprochement* near the top of the list of desired achievements, the United States should rather expect it to emerge as a result of a long-term process of introducing rationality and efficiency into the social and economic structure in Eastern Europe. This new bridge building approach may require more patience than did its preinvasion version, but, like the latter, it would use as an important base the developments in Eastern Europe that provide political opportunities pointing toward *détente*.

If we can abstract one lesson from the use of trade liberalization as a political instrument in East-West relations, it is that Americans should be extremely skeptical of the attempt to bargain economic concessions to the East in return for explicit or implicit political quid pro quos.[6]

Another conclusion emerging from our discussion of postwar U.S. East-West trade policy is that trade restrictions, once imposed, are usually extremely difficult to remove. As Allen and Walter have demonstrated, this phenomenon is not limited to East-West trade policies.[7] Nevertheless, several characteristics somewhat unique to East-West trade policy making have made U.S. restrictions on this trade particularly resistant to change. One reason, of course, has been the high degree of emotionalism surrounding the question of "trading with the Communists." Indeed, national security is one of the few topics that can be expected to elicit a strong emotional response from practically all segments of the community. Also, we have seen that Congress chose to remove from the President his discretion with respect to MFN in 1962 and PL 480 aid in 1966, and denied him discretion concerning the role of the Eximbank in East-West trade between 1968 and 1971. By its nature the Congress is less flexible than the Executive, and, as we have observed, this has resulted in a curious asymmetry between U.S. export control policies on the one hand and MFN, PL 480, and (for four years) Eximbank policies on the other.

Finally, the imposition of *implicit* taxes on foreign trade, in the form of controls rather than explicit tariff or export tax rates, leaves the way open for considerable bureaucratic inertia. Thus even though the Executive has had continued discretion over export controls since the beginning of World War II, it is not at all clear that this discretion, and the range of decision making that it implies, has been utilized in a highly discriminating fashion. Indeed, much of the testimony from businessmen and others at the 1968 and 1969 hearings on East-West trade suggested that the successive administrations had been overly conservative in interpreting their mandate provided by the Export Control Act.[8] In a national security context this is of course understandable, since the last thing public officials want to do is to encourage complaints that they are "soft on communism," or on any other perceived threats to national security.

A second lesson our analysis thus suggests is that Americans should be wary of imposing new restrictions on foreign trade, particularly in a national security context. If new trade barriers are believed necessary, after all, considerable attention should still be given as to who shall exercise discretion over their application. Experience has shown that with regard to East-West trade, an optimal course would have been to leave this discretion with the President for all such policies, with Congress spelling out in the basic authorizing legislation the general guidelines that the Executive should follow. Only in this way can the risks of a schizophrenic East-West trade policy be *reduced.* These risks cannot be eliminated, of course, since the Executive may still not choose to follow the kind of "logical" policy making process implied in our model.

Another striking characteristic of postwar U.S. East-West trade policy making has been the general lack of sophistication of the political debate surrounding this issue. In the language of our welfare maximization model, there has been inadequate conceptual and empirical "feedback" to individual American utility functions. Throughout this study we have continually attempted to ferret out the fundamental utility considerations motivating U.S. policies towards East-West trade. Usually we have merely reported these apparent preferences; we have not attempted to question whether they were good or bad, rational or irrational. What we have done in several cases, however, has been to analyze the consistency of certain utility considerations with one another, and in particular, to point out situations in which apparent unchanged utility parameters seemed to have become increasingly out of tune with changing economic and political realities.

It will be recalled from Chapter 4 that we have been assuming that there have not been unreasonably long lags in the political process regarding East-West trade matters. That is to say, we have been assuming that both Congress and the successive administrations have been reasonably responsive to popular demands for changes in policy. In the view of currently fashionable criticism that "the system" does not work, this may be a very heroic assumption indeed. Nevertheless, there is very little evidence that U.S. East-West trade policy makers have been seriously out of touch with the majority of their constituents. If our assumption on this point is valid, the analysis of the previous chapters suggests that the collective utility parameters underlying the U.S. offensive economic warfare policy remained relatively unchanged over a very long period. After the mid 1950s these utility considerations fossilized in the face of some quite fundamental changes in the economic and political spheres, including the loss of U.S. market share in the East because of the withering away of the cooperative embargo policy, the deteriorating U.S. balance of payments, the Sino-Soviet split of 1960, and what should have been a gradual recognition that near-maximal offensive economic warfare just was not accomplishing the political goals it was presumably meant to achieve.

The fossilization of U.S. East-West trade policy, and the inability or refusal to reevaluate the "optimality" of these policies once the assumptions underlying them proved to be erroneous, is basically attributable to the low quality of information and public debate on this issue. On the one hand, there is little evidence that very much rigorous empirical research had been undertaken in the United States until the very late sixties and early seventies on the economic costs of the offensive economic warfare policy. These costs include not only the loss of exports and higher domestic prices for consumers arising from import barriers, but also the administrative costs of the entire governmental machinery responsible for this program.[9] On the other hand, before the mid to late sixties, there seems to have been little reasoned discussion in the public forums, and insufficient Presidential leadership, concerning the effect that U.S. policy was having on the Communist world (as well as the effect on the U.S. allies, such as the extraterritoriality problem) and the implications of this for U.S. policy.

Furthermore, although there were some exceptions, there was really little attempt to relate the question of the economic costs of continued massive economic warfare to the question of the most *appropriate* national security policy. Only in the late sixties, when the advocates of the bridge building approach and the export interests suffering from the unilateral export controls and Eximbank ban in a sense joined hands and made common cause with public officials concerned with balance of payments problems, was the fundamental economic warfare-welfare trade-off brought home to a large part of the public and U.S. East-West trade policy makers.

Consequently, a further lesson to be learned from past East-West trade policy making is that because of the emotionalism surrounding "national security" questions, more than usual care must be taken to preserve the awareness of the basic trade-off between national security inspired economic warfare and short-run economic welfare considerations. This means that the flow of information and research on the effects of policies undertaken in the name of national security should be maintained, and indeed increased, so as to keep the trade-off before the eyes of the public, thereby encouraging continual reevaluation of these policies.

Finally, our examination of various national security inspired restrictions on imports has suggested the natural attractiveness of national security arguments to domestic protectionist interests. As demonstrated in Chapter 3, certain variants of the m_{ij}^k collective good (relative dependence on imports), have the same policy implications as the clearly national security motivated (f_{hj}^k, f_{ij}^k) consideration (the foreign exchange earnings of a particular foreign country or region). The trade policy implication is to impose discriminatory, higher tariffs or quotas on the relevant imports, and if the m_{ij}^k consideration involves the notion of *relative* dependence on foreign suppliers, this intervention in foreign trade should optimally be accompanied by subsidization of domestic producers.

In the course of our analysis of the cargo preference requirements applying to U.S. exports of certain feed grains to the East, we observed the intermingling of protectionist and national security considerations, which have long been used to justify both subsidization and protection of the U.S. shipping trade. Because the price of shipping services is an important transport cost for certain products, government intervention, which artificially raises shipping costs, also has direct spillover effects on these other products. In the case of U.S. exports of feed grains to the socialist world, the cargo preference provision apparently had a significant restrictive impact, until this requirement was eliminated by Presidential discretion in 1971. Just as in the case of the U.S. oil import quota program[c] (which up to now has not involved East-West trade considerations), the cargo preference development suggests two lessons that should be kept in mind when formulating trade policies based on the m_{ij}^k consideration: (1) it is quite easy for protectionist wolves to wrap their arguments in national security clothing—such arguments should be chal-

---

[c] The treatment of crude oil in the U.S. is in general accordance with the optimal policy rules suggested by the m_{ij}^k collective good: (1) a quota on imports, and (2) subsidization of domestic production (exploration) through the oil depletion allowance.

lenged and the reasoning made perfectly clear; and (2) combined subsidy-tariff protection of domestic industry can be unexpectedly costly if the spillover effect of such programs is heavily skewed towards certain other products that have a particular economic importance to the domestic economy, whether in terms of domestic consumption or the ability to compete on foreign export markets. Consequently, U.S. policy makers have a responsibility to the public to be highly discriminating when evaluating the need for national security inspired barriers to foreign trade.

Alternative Strategies for the 1970s

Drawing on the conceptual framework developed in Part I, together with our analysis of past U.S. East-West trade policy making and the apparent potential for expanded trade, we can now evaluate the broad strategic options facing the United States in formulating East-West trade and investment policies in the seventies. There are at least five basic strategic approaches, and we shall deal with each of them in turn.

First, the United States could decide simply to maintain the diminished, yet still imposing, battery of offensive economic warfare weapons that grew out of the early postwar economic containment policy. Such a policy would be illogical, given the various political and economic factors that we have shown inhibit the effectiveness of massive offensive economic warfare against the East. The United States historically has been unable to gain the full cooperation of the other Western countries in such a policy, and there is nothing to suggest that this would be possible now. This, of course, would be even more true for a policy of maximum economic warfare, which even the U.S. has never been willing to wage against the socialist countries of Eastern Europe.

Not only would such a policy be virtually impossible to implement successfully; the vast majority of Americans have undoubtedly ceased to experience extreme diseconomies from socialist consumption of a very wide range of nonmilitary products. This is true for Chinese consumption as well as for consumption in Eastern Europe. Furthermore, even if the Cold War were to revive with all the intensity of the 1948–1950 period, it is doubtful whether such a massive economic warfare offensive would be desirable. Most of the Communist countries are considerably better off economically now than they were in the immediate postwar period, and hence even less susceptible to the pressures created by outside embargo than they were then. The more cohesive any new "Western economic alliance" against the East, the more likely would Soviet hegemony over Eastern Europe be strengthened and the Sino-Soviet split be reconciled. An intense Cold War situation might well suggest some lengthening of the COCOM embargo list, however, and a strengthening of enforcement procedures.

The only conceivable situation suggesting maximal economic warfare might be a major "hot" war with the Eastern countries, were there indeed sufficient time to put the total embargo machinery into operation. On moral as well as practical grounds, a total embargo on economic relations with a belligerent in a hot war would seem to be defensible, and the U.S. embargo on North Vietnam would be an example of such a policy. But as the temporary prohibition on Eximbank activities in East-West trade between 1968 and 1971 demonstrated, and as the U.S. Cuban policy has shown, it is very difficult to pressure third countries into ceasing trade and aid-giving to the socialist countries, even if they are active belligerents. Furthermore, the movement for repeal of the Eximbank ban showed that for balance of payments reasons and because of the interests of important U.S. exporters, such attempts to coerce third countries (whether they be socialist or not) into boycotting the "enemy" involve prohibitively high economic costs for the United States.

A second East-West trade strategy would involve the conscious swapping of economic concessions by the U.S. in return for explicit or implicit political quid pro quos by some or all of the Eastern countries. The building bridges approach, for example, would seem to be based on a notion of at least indirect political quid pro quos following from the active use by the United States of trade as an "instrument" of foreign policy. While one cannot disagree with the notion that trade *can* be used as an instrument of policy, it is the argument of this book that policy makers must be highly discriminating in following such a strategy.

We have already discussed the dubious results of the more liberal treatment of Poland dating from 1957. Similarly, it is not at all clear that preferential treatment of Rumania, which began in 1964 and has been accelerated by the Nixon Administration, has really had an effect on the degree of Rumanian "polycentrism" or the extent of internal reform in that country. Indeed, the Rumanians operate one of the more centralized Eastern European regimes, and Hungary, which has been boldly experimenting with economic decentralization since 1968, has never received favored trade policy treatment from the United States. The particular foreign policy course taken by Rumania in the past few years probably has had more to do with its opposition to some of the Comecon integration proposals, and its general relationship with the Soviet Union, than it has to marginal changes in U.S. commercial policy toward that country.

It is also doubtful that the Soviet Union is prepared to allow any of the other Eastern European countries to swap political concessions of some sort for economic favors from the United States. As Wasowski observed in the excerpt quoted above, the Brezhnev Doctrine should serve to temper the expectations of Americans in this respect. Bridge building may still be a sound policy, but only if interpreted in *very* gradualist terms, and this implies very low expectations indeed concerning political quid pro quos. Despite Kennan's observations to the contrary, it might just be possible that the Soviet Union might be a willing partner for a swap of economic for political concessions. This of course would depend upon the relative value it attributed to these concessions, and the extent to which questions of prestige and total political power were not involved.

Recent experience suggests, however, that the potential for bargaining economic for supposed political concessions from the Soviet Union may be limited by domestic political considerations. In negotiating the massive grain sale to the Soviet Union in 1972, the Nixon Administration may or may not have had in mind a specific a political quid pro quo from the Soviets. Nevertheless, it is clear that the Administration's thinking was strongly influenced by a positive y_{ij}^k consideration for the USSR with respect to wheat and other grains, in contrast to the diseconomies associated with most Soviet Union consumption throughout the postwar period. The subsidy implication of a positive external effect constituted the very problem, for a large segment of the American public. Because of the massive size of the grain sales (roughly one-fourth of annual U.S. wheat production was involved) the domestic price of wheat skyrocketed while the export price to the Soviets was roughly maintained. Widespread public criticism of the sale followed, presumably because the Administration's positive marginal utility attached to Soviet wheat consumption was not generally shared in the United States.[10] The Administration had not clearly demonstrated the "political" benefits expected to accrue from the wheat sale (which helped to offset a critical harvest failure in the Soviet Union), nor were humanitarian reasons offered as the rationale. If, indeed, political pro quos were involved, it is understandable that they could not be advertised by the President. This only points to the difficulty in pursuing political objectives (in a democracy) in the commercial policy sphere which have dramatic domestic effects, if unsupported by an easily comprehensible ideological or national security consideration. Once again, the fundamental trade-off between national security inspired trade policy actions and short-run economic welfare is apparent.[d]

Still another approach to East-West trade would be to insist upon a *mutual* reduction in trade barriers, or, more generally, swapping economic concessions for economic concessions. Assuming that U.S. national security is not damaged by the economic concessions granted, this is obviously a mutually beneficial strategy. Certain trade barriers would seem to be more appropriate to this approach, however, than others. With respect to the extra-COCOM export control list, the refusal to export certain products may be more

[d] The prospect of importing relatively high-cost Soviet natural gas has likewise generated considerable public criticism.

economically damaging to the U.S. than to the "deprived" eastern country, which may be able to obtain reasonable facsimiles from other western nations. This suggests Peter Wiles's notion of the "principle of relative gain": "It is not irrational to do the enemy absolute good, provided we do ourselves more good."[11] Consequently, there is little reason to "decontrol" exports only on a basis of mutual economic concessions.

On the other hand, the granting of MFN treatment to imports from additional socialist countries should be carried out only under the aegis of a formal or informal trade agreement. The provisions of the ill-fated East-West Trade Relations Act, first introduced into Congress in 1966, indicate the type of framework under which MFN should be given to the socialist world (see Chapter 7, pp. 94–95). As our analysis of U.S. policies has demonstrated, there is no question but that the President should be returned his discretion for granting MFN to these countries. Only in this way can the fundamental linkage between the (y^k_{ij}, y^k_{hj}) and (f^k_{hj}, f^k_{ij}) national security considerations be adequately taken into account, and the policy schizophrenia which has characterized U.S. East-West policy making since the early sixties be eliminated.

There are numerous precedents for reducing trade barriers within the framework of formal bilateral or multilateral agreements. The Reciprocal Trade Agreements negotiations dating from 1934, and the multilateral negotiations conducted under the aegis of the GATT since 1947, are ample testimony to the wisdom of this procedure. Furthermore, the accession of Poland and Rumania to the GATT, as well as the recent GATT negotiations with Hungary, reflect a long series of discussions aimed at assuring market access on both sides. Throughout the postwar period other Western countries have negotiated mutual market access with the socialist countries within the framework of formal bilateral agreements. This approach has often been criticized in the United States, as it seems to strike at the native American determination to minimize government intervention in business affairs, and comes up against the historical unfamiliarity with—and often active dislike for—formal governmental bilateral trade agreements involving more than just "impersonal" tariff rates. These traditional American propensities are obviously undergoing change. The United States now has agreements with various foreign governments to "voluntarily" restrict their exports to the American market of steel, textiles and footwear. In addition, the Government increasingly is playing an active role in promoting the export of goods and capital, through the enlargement of the lending authority of the Eximbank, the establishment of the Domestic International Sales Corporation (DISC) scheme, as well as the creation of the Overseas Private Investment Corporation (OPIC) to guarantee and insure direct foreign investments of U.S. companies. The new trade agreement with the Soviet Union, with the stress on the interdependence of U.S. Eximbank credit support, MFN, Soviet payment of World War II lend-lease debts, and other commercial policy considerations, also reflects a new willingness on the part of U.S. policy makers to enter into bilateral governmental agreements with the socialist countries. Unfortunately, however, the President's flexibility with respect to MFN negotiations is limited, because of continued congressional unwillingness to give him discretion in this matter.

In negotiations leading to the granting of MFN, the important question is what real concessions could the Eastern countries offer, and how can such concessions be evaluated in terms of the concessions the United States might be willing to make. One assurance that the U.S. should demand is that U.S. exporters be given access to socialist markets, which is in some sense equivalent to the access granted to competing Western nations. Certainly this would mean equivalent rights to exhibit, to advertise and to hire local sales representatives, as well as other sales promotion privileges. Furthermore, any such agreement should attempt to include guarantees of patent rights and provisions for arbitration of commercial disputes, as well as protection against "dumping" of Eastern products on the U.S. market.[12] The recent U.S. agreements with Poland and the U.S.S.R. have explicitly covered a number of these issues, including market access, arbitration, and assurances from the Eastern signatories concerning dumping and "market disruption."[13]

Recently, Samuel Pisar has developed a comprehensive outline for a new legal and institutional "charter" for expanded East-West relations.[14] Pisar suggests that "East-West trade problems can best be handled by an internationally sponsored but *independent* system of regulation...."[15] A joint study group comprised of the Committee for Economic Development (C.E.D.) and organizations from five other major Western countries has gone further, in suggesting the creation "of a new global economic organization representative of the countries of both East and West in order to develop a new and comprehensive framework for resolving the problems of East West trade," although "discussions of course should continue in existing organizations on ways in which concepts of fair trading can be developed and eventually applied"[16]. Such multilateral approaches, if effective, would presumably enhance the chances for the U.S. to assure for itself fair treatment in its trading relations with the Eastern countries.

A fourth strategy would consist simply of unilateral liberalization of the remaining U.S. barriers to East-West trade. As we have suggested, this seems generally inappropriate with respect to MFN, but makes considerable sense in regard to the extra-COCOM control list. Our examination of U.S. East-West trade policies has shown the impossibility of fulfilling the optimal trade policy requirements for those extra COCOM products that are available from other foreign suppliers. Continued control of these products, unless the control procedure is *greatly* streamlined, only has the effect of handing over potential U.S. exports to Western competitors. Consequently the U.S. list should be shortened so as to approximate the restrictiveness of the COCOM embargo. This is basically the mandate laid down by the Export Administration Act of 1969. Presumably, in accordance with this legislation, the Commerce Department is proceeding to "decontrol" all items except those embargoed by COCOM and those not on the COCOM list but still deemed to be "strategic" and not generally available elsewhere in the West. The rising tide of exports to the East, together with the quarterly reports of the OEC, suggest that decontrolling is continuing. The large number of *validated* licenses recently granted by the OEC also implies, however, that a considerable list of products and technology are still subject to control, although not being embargoed.

Congress emphasized its continued dissatisfaction with the pace of export decontrol when it extended and amended the Export Administration Act in 1972. The new legislation required prompt removal of unilateral export controls on goods available from other countries except where it is determined that such action would be detrimental to the national security. Furthermore, the Secretary of Commerce is now required to obtain approval from the Secretary of Agriculture before placing any restrictions on the export of agricultural products.[17]

At the same time that U.S. export controls are reduced on extra-COCOM items, the need will persist for the U.S. to continue to take a strong position in the continuing COCOM discussions. There is little indication that the international diseconomies experienced by Americans with respect to Communist consumption of (investment in) military goods or highly "strategic" nonmilitary products have diminished. Indeed, in an era of possible de-escalation of the numerical arms race, in which the United States agrees to limit its own armaments production and in which the technological sophistication of permitted weaponry becomes all important, it is definitely in the national interest to continue a strict embargo on an inner core of truly "strategic" goods and technology.[e] Since any type of cartel arrangement is inherently unstable, as only one of its members has to decide to break the pact and the restriction of output (in this case sales to the East) comes to an end, the U.S. must remain vigilant over such slippage within the COCOM group, and convince its fellow members that relaxation of U.S. controls only extends to the extra-COCOM list. This is not meant to suggest, however, that periodic reviews of the COCOM list should not continue.

In general, Eximbank credit support for exports to the socialist countries should also be granted on a unilateral basis; that is, without regard to political or economic quid pro quos. Exceptions to this rule would be cases in which these countries still are in default on debt to the U.S. Government, as it is difficult to justify extension of new credits when old credits are in default.

---

[e] The reader will observe that we have steadfastly avoided throughout this book a discussion of precisely what is "strategic" and what is not.

The lend-lease debts of the Soviet Union are a case in point. It could be argued that credit support in the form of guarantees or insurance is justifiable in such situations, however, considering the extremely good payment experience on trade credit extended to these countries in the postwar period by other Western countries, and that the cost to the U.S. taxpayer from such support would be minimal. Any Eximbank credit support, of course, should be granted only in the overall perspective of the Eastern countries' ability to honor their debts.

So far the Nixon Administration has chosen to exercise its new discretionary authority under the Export Expansion Finance Act of 1971 only with respect to exports to Rumania, although the recent trade agreements with Poland and the Soviet Union also provide for their eligibility for Eximbank support. This suggests that the Administration may be shifting away from the "polycentric" policies of its predecessors. As we have observed before, the relatively diminished collective disutility parameters to be associated with consumption in apparently "polycentric" countries seem hardly to be justified by past experience. A policy stressing the positive results for U.S. export expansion rather than the dubious political advantages of Eximbank activity would seem to be a higher payoff strategy.

As we concluded in Chapter 5, the Johnson Act prohibition on the export of private capital to most of the socialist countries is a clear case of a non-optimal policy. To the extent that several of the Eastern countries may be coming around to the idea of allowing foreign investment on highly regulated terms, and to the degree that joint ventures or other types of so-called "industrial cooperation" offer perhaps the best opportunity for breaking the isolation of East and West, this ban on U.S. investment in these countries seems particularly unfortunate. Simple repeal of this obsolete law is advisable. U.S. companies can then decide whether or not to invest on a basis of commercial criteria and their own willingness to work together with the socialist regimes. Repeal of this provision would also be consistent with the recently announced intentions of OPIC to underwrite private investments in certain Eastern countries,[18] as well as enabling these countries to float bond issues in the United States.

In the context of expanded commerce with the East implied by the foregoing strategies, the United States should increasingly turn its attention to *defensive* economic warfare considerations. Because of the large size of the internal market in the U.S., the e_{ij}^k consideration, which reflects American dependence on certain foreign countries as export markets, should not be a major factor in U.S. national security thinking. On the other hand, the m_{ij}^k collective good, embodying the notion of the dependence on foreign supplies of strategic products, does warrant increased consideration. While the import of crude petroleum has been subject to this kind of attention for some time, it is certain to receive even more attention in the future. This is because of the rapid depletion of U.S. domestic reserves of conventional sources of oil, and therefore probable growing dependence on foreign crude.[f] Massive imports of liquified natural gas from the Soviet Union would likewise suggest that greater attention be focused on this national security consideration. Increased reliance on foreign sources for various metals and other raw materials should also be seen within the defensive national security context outlined in Part I. As we suggested earlier in this chapter, however, strictly protectionist arguments should be carefully delineated from national security arguments in the debate over the formation of trade policies designed to deal with these defensive considerations.

In this connection, it should also be observed that maintenance of an adequate merchant marine is probably essential to national security. Indeed, as we have seen, this was the argument of President Roosevelt in urging passage of the merchant marine subsidy legislation of the 1930s.[19] In view of the spillover complications which an implicit or explicit tax policy on the import of shipping services is seen to create, however, it might be advisable to formulate the m_{ij}^k consideration in this case as simply domestic production of such services ($m_{ij}^k = X_i$). This would imply a subsidization policy which would maintain the merchant marine at some minimum level, while at the same time avoiding the complicating intervention into foreign trade implied by defining m_{ij}^k as the *relative* dependence upon foreign shipping. Once again, the arguments for subsidization should be examined carefully, so as to not allow protectionist forces to establish a case for a larger and more expensive U.S. merchant marine than deemed necessary for purposes of national security.

As our discussion of these various trade policy alternatives suggests, there is yet a fifth U.S. East-West trade strategy that would seem to be optimal. This would be a "mixed strategy," which would seek to use that particular approach in any given situation that seems most appropriate in the light of the underlying national security considerations and the expected economic gains to be realized by the United States. A return to near maximal or maximum economic warfare would seem advisable only in the event of a "hot" war, and even then its effectiveness might be limited.

While being skeptical of the strategy that seeks to swap economic concessions for political quid pro quos, we have not altogether ruled out its appropriateness, particularly in the case of relations with the Soviet Union. Mutual bargaining for economic concessions seems particularly appropriate in the context of expanding mutual access to the American and Eastern markets. Unilateral liberalization would appear to be the optimal course with respect to extra-COCOM export controls, Eximbank credit support, and foreign

[f] Higher cost substitutes for conventional crude petroleum (e.g., shale oil) are also an alternative.

private investment, since in these cases the "principle of relative gain" would seem to be strongly in the favor of the United States, given the competition it faces on world export markets from its Western European and Japanese competitors. Provision of Eximbank support without political or economic strings attached (other than a reasonable assurance of creditworthiness) would not rule out, of course, joining in some kind of new initiative of the Western countries to regulate exaggerated competition in the provision of credit to the East.[20]

We are led to conclude that an aggressive policy of economic warfare designed to "contain" the Communist countries would be ineffective and even inappropriate given the present international emphasis on detente, the lack of cohesion of the Western countries with respect to economic warfare policies, and the relative economic strength of the socialist countries. Furthermore, an aggressive trade policy that seeks to induce internal reforms and polycentrism within the socialist world is also of dubious utility. There is little evidence that in a world of fast-moving economic and political currents such a policy could yield any calculable and predictable political advantages.

Much more realistic would seem to be a strategy that cautiously expands economic contacts with the East, with its conscious objective being to jointly maximize current economic welfare and national security. This would be a more subtle variant of the "building bridges" approach of the sixties, which would operate on a longer time horizon, and would rest on the confidence of the West in the belief that increased contacts and a higher level of economic development will ultimately serve as stimuli for an expansion of personal freedom in the East. Moreover, the new policy would entail a basic shift from an offensive policy geared to bipolar confrontation, to a defensive strategy suited to a multipolar world of more subtle threats to the United States' military and economic strength.

Appendixes

Appendix A
The Maximization Problem

Goods Entering Individual Utility Functions

A. *Private Goods*

(1) Matrix of the x_i^k ($i = m + 1, \ldots, n$; $k = 1, \ldots, s$), where x_i^k is the consumption of the ith private good[a] by the kth individual in the home country, and where:[b]

$$\sum_{k=1}^{s} x_i^k \leq X_i + \sum_{j=1}^{P} z_{ij}$$

X_i = Total Home production of the ith private good.

z_{ij} = Net Home import of the ith private good from the jth foreign country (negative z_{ij} means net export from Home to jth country).

B. *Relative Military Strength*

(2) Matrix of the x_h^k ($h = 1, \ldots, m$; $k = 1, \ldots, s$), where x_h^k is consumption of the hth military collective good in Home; and where:

$$x_h^k \leq X_h + \sum_{j=1}^{P} z_{hj} \qquad \text{(for all } k = 1, \ldots, s)$$

X_h = Total Home production of the hth military good.

z_{hj} = Net Home import of the hth military good from the jth foreign country (negative z_{hj} means net export).

(3) Matrix of the y_{hj}^k ($h = 1, \ldots, m$; $j = 1, \ldots, p$; $k = 1, \ldots, s$), where y_{hj} is consumption of the hth military good by the jth country; and where

[a] We make the conventional assumption that the services of productive factors are negative commodities.

[b] This and following equality-inequality relationships in this Appendix reflect our simplifying assumption that there are no "stocks" of goods, either in the short or long run. All consumption is assumed to be from current domestic or foreign (imported) production, an unimportant assumption at this level of abstraction.

$y_{hj} = y^k_{hj}$; that is, y_{hj} is a collective good from the standpoint of Home citizens; and where:

$$y^k_{hj} \leq Y_{hj} - z_{hj} - z_{hw}$$

Y_{hj} = Total production of the hth military good in the jth country.

z_{hw} = Net export of the hth military good by the jth foreign country to the rest of the world (excluding Home).

C. *Economic Warfare: Offensive*

(4) Matrix of the y^k_{ij} ($i = m + 1, \ldots, n$; $j = 1, \ldots, p$; $k = 1, \ldots, s$), where y_{ij} is consumption of the ith nonmilitary good by the jth country; and where $y_{ij} = y^k_{ij}$; that is, y_{ij} is a collective good from the standpoint of individuals in Home; and where:

$$y^k_{ij} \leq Y_{ij} - z_{ij} - z_{iw}$$

Y_{ij}= Total production of the ith nonmilitary good in the jth country.

z_{iw} = Net export of the ith nonmilitary good by the jth country to the rest of the world (excluding Home).

(5) F^k = Matrix of the (f^k_{hj}, f^k_{ij}) $(h = 1, \ldots, m; i = m + 1, \ldots, n; j = 1, \ldots, p; k = 1, \ldots, s)$, where $f_{hj} = p_{hj} z_{hj}$ and $f_{ij} = p_{ij} z_{ij}$, the net foreign exchange earned by the jth foreign country from its net export to Home of the hth and ith goods, respectively. p_{hj} and p_{ij} are the export prices (in terms of Home currency) of the jth country for the hth and ith goods, respectively; and $f_{hj} = f^k_{hj}$ and $f_{ij} = f^k_{ij}$ for all $k = 1, \ldots, s$; that is, f_{hj} and f_{ij} are collective goods from the standpoint of individuals in Home.

(6) S^k = Matrix of the (s^k_{hj}, s^k_{ij}) $(h = 1, \ldots, m; j = 1, \ldots, p; k = 1, \ldots, s)$, where

$$s_{hj} = \frac{(-z_{hj})}{y_{hj}} \quad \text{and} \quad s_{ij} = \frac{(-z_{ij})}{y_{ij}},$$

that proportion of the jth country's consumption of the hth and ith good respectively, imported from Home. (This is a measure of the jth country's dependence on Home as a source of supply for the hth or ith good.) $s_{hj} = s^k_{hj}$ and $s_{ij} = s^k_{ij}$; that is, s_{hj} and s_{ij} are collective goods.

D. *Economic Warfare: Defensive*

(7) M^k = Matrix of the (m_{hj}^k, m_{ij}^k) $(h = 1, \ldots, m;\ i = m + 1, \ldots, n;\ j = 1, \ldots, p;\ k = 1, \ldots, s)$, where:

$$m_{hj} = \frac{z_{hj}}{X_h} \quad \text{and} \quad m_{ij} = \frac{z_{ij}}{X_i},$$

Home's net import from the jth country of the hth and ith goods, respectively, as a proportion of domestic production of these goods. (This is a measure of Home dependence on the jth country as a source of supply for the hth or ith good.) $m_{hj} = m_{hj}^k$ and $m_{ij} = m_{ij}^k$; that is m_{hj} and m_{ij} are collective goods.

(8) E^k = Matrix of the (e_{hj}^k, e_{ij}^k) $(h = 1, \ldots, m;\ i = m + 1, \ldots, n;\ j = 1, \ldots, p;\ k = 1, \ldots, s)$, where:

$$e_{hj} = \frac{(-z_{hj})}{x_h^k} \quad \text{and} \quad e_{ij} = \frac{(-z_{ij})}{\sum_{k=1}^{s} x_i^k}$$

the proportion of Home exports to the jth country of the hth and ith goods, respectively, to domestic consumption of these goods. (This is a measure of Home dependence on the jth country as an export market for the hth or ith good.) $e_{hj} = e_{hj}^k$ and $e_{ij} = e_{ij}^k$; that is, e_{hj} and e_{ij} are collective goods.

In general, when the jth country is either considered a direct threat to Home national security, or for other foreign policy reasons increased influence over the jth country is desired, we may assume for the kth individual, where U^k = utility function of the kth individual and $U^k = U^k(\bar{x}^k, Y^k, F^k, S^k, M^k, E^k)$, $[\bar{x}^k = (x_h^k, x_i^k),\ Y^k = (y_{hj}^k, y_{ij}^k)]$ that:

$$\frac{\partial U^k}{\partial x_i^k} > 0; \quad \frac{\partial^2 U^k}{\partial x_i^{k2}} < 0 \qquad (1)$$

The kth individual experiences diminishing positive marginal utility from consumption of private goods.

$$\frac{\partial U^k}{\partial x_h^k} > 0; \quad \frac{\partial^2 U^k}{\partial x_h^{k2}} < 0 \qquad (2)$$

The kth individual experiences diminishing positive marginal utility from consumption of military goods.

$$\frac{\partial U^k}{\partial y_{hj}^k} < 0; \quad \frac{\partial^2 U^k}{\partial y_{hj}^{k2}} < 0 \tag{3}$$

The kth individual experiences increasing negative marginal utility from the consumption of military goods in the jth country.[c]

$$\frac{\partial U^k}{\partial y_{ij}^k} \leq 0; \quad \frac{\partial^2 U^k}{\partial y_{ij}^{k2}} < 0 \quad \text{if} \quad \frac{\partial U^k}{\partial y_{ij}^k} < 0 \tag{4}$$

The kth individual is either unaffected or experiences increasing negative marginal utility from the consumption of the ith nonmilitary good in the jth country (see previous footnote).

$$\frac{\partial U^k}{\partial f_{ij}^k} \leq 0; \quad \frac{\partial^2 U^k}{\partial f_{ij}^{k2}} < 0 \quad \text{if} \quad \frac{\partial U^k}{\partial f_{ij}^k} < 0 \tag{5}$$

The kth individual is either unaffected or experiences increasing negative marginal utility from the earning of foreign exchange by the jth country through exports of the ith good to Home (Similar conditions hold for f_{hj}.)

$$\frac{\partial U^k}{\partial s_{ij}^k} \geq 0; \quad \frac{\partial^2 U^k}{\partial s_{ij}^{k2}} < 0 \quad \text{if} \quad \frac{\partial U^k}{\partial s_{ij}^k} > 0 \tag{6}$$

The kth individual is either unaffected or experiences diminishing positive marginal utility from increased dependence of the jth country on Home as a source of supply for the ith good. (Similar conditions hold for s_{hj}.)

$$\frac{\partial U^k}{\partial m_{ij}^k} \leq 0; \quad \frac{\partial^2 U^k}{\partial m_{ij}^{k2}} < 0 \quad \text{if} \quad \frac{\partial U^k}{\partial m_{ij}^k} < 0 \tag{7}$$

The kth individual is either unaffected or experiences increasing negative marginal utility from increased Home dependence on the jth country as a

---

[c] As pointed out in footnote d in Chapter 1, our assumption of negative second partial derivatives for (2) and (3) above introduces an apparent asymmetry into the model. That is, we assume that the marginal satisfaction experienced by the kth individual from increased domestic consumption of the hth military good rises at a diminishing rate, whereas his marginal dissatisfaction from an enemy's consumption of the hth good rises at an increasing rate. This apparent asymmetry seems to be more realistic than a symmetrical relationship between x_h and y_{hj}, however, when we plot in x_h, y_{hj} commodity space, the locus of points which give the kth individual a given utility level (U°). Our assumption of negative second partial derivatives in both (2) and (3) result in a U° curve which is concave from below when y_{hj} is plotted on the vertical and x_h on the horizontal axis. This seems more realistic, in most cases, than a convex U° curve, which has the general shape of a backward-bending supply curve. That is to say, our assumption would appear to correspond more closely with the observed "arms races" among nations.

source of supply for the ith good. (Similar conditions hold for m_{hj}.)[d]

$$\frac{\partial U^k}{\partial e_{ij}^k} \leq 0; \quad \frac{\partial^2 U^k}{\partial e_{ij}^{k2}} < 0 \quad \text{if} \quad \frac{\partial U^k}{\partial e_{ij}^k} < 0 \tag{8}$$

The kth individual is either unaffected or experiences increasing negative marginal utility from increased Home dependence on the jth country as an outlet for Home production of the ith good. (Similar conditions hold for e_{hj}. See footnote d.)

The Social Welfare Function

We assume that the foreign economic policy maker has complete knowledge of each U^k individual utility function ($k = 1, \ldots, s$), and that his social welfare function is of the Paretian type; that is, a *ceteris paribus* increase in any kth individual's utility increases social welfare.[1]

We also assume that no external effects exist in domestic consumption. This assumption, combined with the fact that our social welfare function is of the Paretian type, will enable us to derive first order conditions for the general welfare maximum which are independent of interpersonal comparisons.[2] Finally, we shall assume the social welfare function, $W(U^1, \ldots, U^s)$, is a strictly concave function. This assumption corresponds to the conventional notion of a social welfare function convex to the origin in the two-individual case. Taking this function over the closed convex set formed by the several constraints, we may conclude that $W(U^1, \ldots, U^s)$ will take on its global maximum over this set at a unique point provided the first order conditions are satisfied.[3]

The economic policy maker's objective is to maximize the social welfare function subject to the constraints embodied in: (a) the domestic transformation function, and (b) the foreign trade transformation function.

Constraints

Domestic Transformation Function

We define the domestic transformation function as $T(\overline{X}) = 0$, where $\overline{X}$ is the vector of the (X_h, X_i) ($h = 1, \ldots, m$; $i = m + 1, \ldots, n$). X_h is output of the hth military good and X_i is output of the ith nonmilitary good.[e] We shall assume for simplicity that there are no external effects in domestic

---

[d] Most likely the second partial derivative will be negative only over a certain range of values for m_{ij}^k.

[e] We make the conventional assumption that inputs are negative outputs.

production, and we shall ignore the fact that $T(\overline{X})$ will in general be dependent upon the distribution of wealth. We shall assume that the domestic transformation function forms a convex set.[f]

Foreign Trade Transformation Function

We define the foreign trade transformation function as $F(Z) = 0$, where Z is the matrix of the (z_{hj}, z_{ij}) $(h = 1, \ldots, m; i = m + 1, \ldots, n; j = 1, \ldots, p)$. z_{hj} is the net import of the hth military good from the jth country. z_{ij} is the net import of the ith nonmilitary good from the jth country.[g] Our definition of $F(Z)$ follows from the general formulation of Graaff, but our function is not identical to his formulation:[4]

$$F(Z) = \sum_{j=1}^{p} \sum_{h=1}^{m} p_{hj} z_{hj} + \sum_{j=1}^{p} \sum_{i=m+1}^{n} p_{ij} z_{ij} - D = 0$$

p_{hj} and p_{ij} $(h = 1, \ldots, m; i = m + 1, \ldots, n; j = 1, \ldots, p)$ are the import or export prices of the hth and ith goods respectively, either imported from or exported to the jth country. Whenever there is just one world price for the hth or ith good, p_{hj} and p_{ij} are the world prices for these goods (i.e., $p_h = p_{hj}$ for all j; $p_i = p_{ij}$ for all j). p_{hj} and p_{ij} are expressed in terms of Home currency, at the official foreign exchange rate for the jth country's currency in terms of Home currency.

D is the deficit on current account for a given time period. Alternatively it may be defined as the sum of Home's current net capital inflow and the net decrease over that period in Home's international monetary reserve position (expressed in terms of Home currency at the prevailing exchange rates).

D is considered as a constant or, for purposes of this model, to be exogeneously determined. If D is constrained to be zero, Home's current account always must balance. We assume a system of fixed foreign exchange rates, although provided certain conditions were fulfilled we could just as well assume flexible exchange rates.[h] We shall assume that the foreign trade

---

[f] See Appendix B for a discussion of this assumption.

[g] As noted previously, we assume that exports are negative imports.

[h] Assume that each foreign exchange rate (units of Home currency per unit of jth country's currency), R_j, is sensitive to any excess supply or demand for Home currency on the "world" foreign exchange market—i.e., perfect arbitrage. We have $\frac{\partial R_j}{\partial(-D)} < 0$ for very small changes in D. Then if the usual conditions assuring $\frac{\partial D}{\partial R_j} < 0$ (improvement in balance of payments follows from devaluation of Home currency) are met, we will have a stable equilibrium value for each R_j, which approximates a fixed exchange rate system. For a discussion of these conditions, see Kindleberger.[5]

transformation function forms a convex set. This assumption is elaborated in Appendix B.

The Optimization Problem

Summarizing, our problem is to:

$$\text{Maximize: } W = W(U^1(\bar{x}^1, Y^1, F^1, S^1, M^1, E^1), \ldots, U^s(\bar{x}^s, Y^s, F^s, S^s, M^s, E^s))$$

$$\text{Subject to: } T(\bar{X}) = 0$$
$$F(Z) = 0$$

where the goods entering the kth utility function are defined as earlier in this Appendix.

This constrained maximization problem differs from the welfare maximization model underlying conventional optimum tariff theory in two important respects: (1) we have introduced collective goods into the individual utility functions, and (2) we have allowed for external effects in international consumption differentiated according to trading partner.

Appendix B
Second Order Conditions

We can most easily examine the curvature conditions sufficient for a welfare maximum by rewriting the two *implicit* functions, $T(\overline{X})$ and $F(Z)$, as *explicit* functions for each X_h, X_i, z_{hj} and z_{ij}. We have:

$$X_h = T_h'(\overline{X}^*) \qquad h = 1, \ldots, m$$

$$X_i = T_i'(\overline{X}^*) \qquad i = m+1, \ldots, n$$

where $\overline{X}^*$ = Vector of the X_t ($t = 1, \ldots, m, m+1, \ldots, n$; $t \neq i$ or $t \neq h$ as the case may be).

$$z_{hj} = F_{hj}'(Z^*) \qquad h = 1, \ldots, m, j = 1, \ldots, p$$

$$z_{ij} = F_{ij}'(Z^*) \qquad i = m+1, \ldots, n, j = 1, \ldots, p$$

where Z^* = Matrix of the (z_{iv}, z_{hv}, z_{tj}) ($v = 1, \ldots, p$; $v \neq j$; $t = 1, \ldots, m, m+1, \ldots, n$; $t \neq i$ or $t \neq h$ as the case may be).

An alternative formulation of our problem, but one that will not be used in our derivation of the first order conditions because of our desire to work with $F(Z)$ for illustrative purposes, could then be written as follows:

Maximize: $W = W[U^1(\ ), \ldots, U^s(\ )]$

Subject to:

$$\sum_{k=1}^{s} x_i^k \leq T_i'(\overline{X}^*) + F_{ij}'(Z^*) \tag{1}$$

$$x_h^k \leq T_h'(\overline{X}^*) + F_{hj}'(Z^*) \tag{2}$$

$$y_{hj}^k \leq Y_{hj} - z_{hj} - z_{hw} \tag{3}$$

$$y_{ij}^k \leq Y_{ij} - z_{ij} - z_{iw} \tag{4}$$

with the other variables entering the utility function defined as in (5) through (8) in Appendix A. Some subset of the (x_h, x_i) is restricted to be nonnegative (commodities consumed) and some subset is restricted to be nonpositive (productive services rendered). Similar restrictions apply to the (X_h, X_i) and (z_{hj}, z_{ij}).

We are assured of finding a unique global maximum for $W(\ )$ only if this function is strictly concave and our constraints form a convex closed set. This latter condition means that our functions $T_i'(\bar{X}^*)$, $T_h'(\bar{X}^*)$, $F_{ij}'(Z^*)$ and $F_{hj}'(Z^*)$ must be strictly concave, since constraints (1) and (2) are both "less than or equal to" conditions.[1] We shall demonstrate that when we make the usual economic assumptions the conditions for a convex set are met by both $T_i'(\bar{X}^*)$ and $F_{ij}'(Z^*)$. The same conclusions of course follow for $T_h'(\bar{X}^*)$ and $F_{hj}'(Z^*)$.

Addressing ourselves initially to the domestic transformation function, when X_i and X_{i+1} represent outputs of the ith and $(i + 1)$th goods respectively, $T_i'(\bar{X}^*)$ will be strictly concave if we make the usual assumption of diminishing returns to varying factor proportions in production.[2] In a two-commodity economy $T_i'(\bar{X}^*)$ gives us the usual concave transformation curve. In the case where X_i is the output of the ith good and X_{i+1} the input of the $(i + 1)$th factor, the same assumption again gives us a concave function.

When X_i is an input and X_{i+1} is the output of the $(i + 1)$th good, however, $T_i'(\bar{X}^*)$ is convex under the same assumption of diminishing returns to varying factor proportions. And in the case where X_i and X_{i+1} are both inputs in the production of, say, X_{i+2}, we have the familiar production isoquant curve, which is convex when visualized as $X_i = T_i'(X_{i+1})$. We have noted in Appendix A, however, that $X_i < 0$ when X_i is an input. Hence $T_i'(\bar{X}^*)$ is also negative, since $X_i = T_i'(\bar{X}^*)$. And since the negative of a convex function is a concave function,[3] the explicit domestic transformation function, $(-T_i'(\bar{X}^*))$, is concave.

Focusing now on the function $F_{ij}'(Z^*)$, we initially observe under usual conditions of international trade $F_{ij}'(Z^*)$ will be concave when z_{ij} represents the net import of the ith good from the jth country. Specifically, if we assume that the price elasticity of the jth country's demand for Home's exports approaches zero from the negative side (i.e., absence of Giffen effects), the foreign offer curve will be concave when considered in the form $z_{ij} = F_{ij}'(Z^*)$.

For example, in the typical two-commodity case we have the usual well behaved foreign offer curve:[a]

[a] The jth country's offer curve may be derived directly from the jth country's demand function for the $(i+1)$th good (Home's export) when the price of the $(i+1)$th good is expressed in terms of the quantity of the ith good that the jth country is willing to give up in exchange for the $(i+1)$th good. See, for example, Heller.[4]

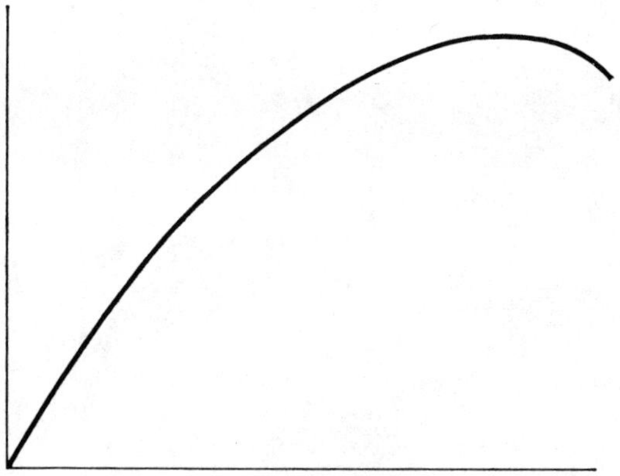

Figure B–1

When Home export revenue is expressed in terms of the import commodity (z_{ij}), this conventional foreign offer curve expresses the notion of diminishing positive marginal export revenue earned by Home, due to its monopoly power (in the general case) in the *j*th market.[5] When Home faces a fixed world price for its exports (i.e., no monopoly power), $F'_{ij}(Z^*)$ becomes straight line, which is both a concave and convex function, but not strictly concave.

When z_{ij} represents the net export of the *i*th good, $z_{ij} < 0$ and therefore $F'_{ij}(Z^*)$ is negative. Even though $F'_{ij}(Z^*)$ is convex in this case, as can be seen in Figure B-1, its negative, $(-F'_{ij}(Z^*))$, will be concave, as required. Similar results can also be shown to hold when z_{ij} and z_{i+1j} are both imported, or exported, and in the case of z_{ij} and z_{ij+1} if conventional economic assumptions are made.

Having just shown that both the domestic and foreign transformation constraints as represented in the alternative formulation are concave if we make the usual simplifying economic assumptions, and applying the rule that the sum of concave functions is concave,[6] we may conclude that constraints (1) and (2) form convex sets, along with (3) and (4). Furthermore, since the intersection of convex sets is convex, our constraints together form a convex set.[7] We have already assumed our social welfare function, $W(\ )$, is concave (see Appendix A). Therefore satisfaction of the first order conditions for a welfare extremum will give us a *unique* global welfare *maximum*.

Appendix C
First Order Conditions[1]

Conventional Optimum Tariff Theory

In conventional optimum tariff analysis we assume the following constrained maximization problem:

Maximize: $W = W[U^1(\bar{x}^1), \ldots, U^s(\bar{x}^s)]$

where: $\sum_{k=1}^{s} x_i^k \leq X_i + z_i$

Subject to: $T(\bar{X}) = 0$ (Domestic Transformation Function)
$F(\bar{z}) = 0$ (Foreign Trade Transformation Function)

where W represents Home social welfare, U^k ($k = 1, \ldots, s$) represents the utility of the kth individual in Home, $\bar{x}^k$ is a vector representing consumption of each ith private good by the kth individual ($i = 1, \ldots, n$), $\bar{X}$ is a vector composed of the aggregate domestic output of each ith good, and $\bar{z}$ is a vector representing the net aggregate Home import of each ith good from the rest of the world. Productive services are considered as negative commodities, inputs as negative outputs, and exports as negative imports.

We assume throughout this and subsequent sections that (1) foreign countries do not retaliate; (2) none of the derived optimal conditions are in actuality constrained to nonsatisfaction; that is, "second best" considerations do not apply; and (3) that the optimum tariff (export tax) proceeds are redistributed internally in some optimal manner; that is, in accordance with the social welfare function $W(\ )$.

Let us also assume that $W(\ )$ is a strictly concave Paretian social welfare function, that there are no external effects in domestic production and consumption, that both $T(\bar{X})$ and $F(\bar{z})$ form convex sets, and that $T(\bar{X})$ is independent of the distribution of wealth. Using the method of Lagrange multipliers, the following first order conditions are easily derived for all $i = 1, \ldots, n$, the satisfaction of which will assure attainment of a unique welfare maximum:

$$\text{(I)}\quad \frac{\dfrac{\partial U^k}{\partial x_i^k}}{\dfrac{\partial U^k}{\partial x_{i+1}^k}} = \frac{\dfrac{\partial T}{\partial X_i}}{\dfrac{\partial T}{\partial X_{i+1}}} \qquad \text{(II)}\quad \frac{\dfrac{\partial U^k}{\partial x_i^k}}{\dfrac{\partial U^k}{\partial x_{i+1}^k}} = \frac{\dfrac{\partial F}{\partial z_i}}{\dfrac{\partial F}{\partial z_{i+1}}}$$

This result embodies the usual notion that the general optimum requires the equality of the domstic rate of commodity substitution, the domestic rate of product transformation, and the rate of foreign trade transformation.

Following Graaff,[2] we define the foreign trade transformation function $F(\bar{z})$, as:

$$F(\bar{z}) = \sum_{i=1}^{n} p_i z_i - D = 0$$

where p_i is the foreign price of the ith import (or export), $p_i = p_i(\bar{z})$, z_i represents Home's net import of the ith good, and D is the net deficit on current account for the given accounting period. We assume that D is either a constant or exogenously determined.

Now let us totally differentiate $F(\bar{z})$:

$$dF = \sum_{i=1}^{n} \left[\frac{\partial \sum_{s=1}^{n} p_s z_s}{\partial z_i} \right] dz_i$$

$$= \sum_{i=1}^{n} \left[p_i + \sum_{s=1}^{n} \frac{\partial p_s}{\partial z_i} z_s \right] dz_i$$

Considering the total derivative for the ith import, z_i, we have (where $t = 1, \ldots, n$, $t \neq i$):

$$\frac{\partial F}{\partial z_i} = p_i + \sum_{s=1}^{n} \frac{\partial p_s}{\partial z_i} z_s$$

$$\frac{\partial F}{\partial z_i} = p_i + z_i \frac{\partial p_i}{\partial z_i} + \sum_{\substack{t=1 \\ t \neq i}}^{n} z_t \frac{\partial p_t}{\partial z_i}$$

$$= p_i \left[1 + \frac{\partial p_i}{p_i} \frac{z_i}{\partial z_i} + \sum_{\substack{t=1 \\ t \neq i}}^{n} \frac{\partial p_t}{p_i} \frac{z_t}{\partial z_i} \right]$$

$$= p_i \left[1 + \eta_i + \sum_{\substack{t=1 \\ t \neq i}}^{n} \eta_{ti}^{c} \frac{p_t z_t}{p_i z_i} \right]$$

where η_i represents the *quantity* elasticity of foreign supply of (demand for) the ith good, and η_{ti}^{c} is the *quantity* cross elasticity for the ith and tth goods.[a]

[a] The *quantity* elasticity is the reciprocal of the *price* elasticity.

If we define $t_i = \left[\eta_i + \sum_{\substack{t=1 \\ t \neq i}}^{n} \eta_{ti}^c \frac{p_t z_t}{p_i z_i}\right]$, our fundamental condition of Pareto optimality (combining conditions (I) and (II)) becomes:[b]

$$\frac{\Pi_i}{\Pi_{i+1}} = \frac{\dfrac{\partial U^k}{\partial x_i^k}}{\dfrac{\partial U^k}{\partial x_{i+1}^k}} = \frac{\dfrac{\partial T}{\partial X_i}}{\dfrac{\partial T}{\partial X_{i+1}}} = \frac{p_i(1 + t_i)}{p_{i+1}(1 + t_{i+1})}$$

where Π_i is the domestic price for the ith good.

The social welfare maximum is attainable only if the Home government intervenes in foreign trade with optimum tax rates (t_i and t_{i+1}) determined by the above condition. The ith tax rate will typically, but not necessarily, be positive if the ith good is imported by Home, and negative if the ith good is exported.

"Natural" Separation of Foreign Markets

Our maximization problem remains the same as in the case of conventional optimum tariff theory, except that now we have $\sum_{k=1}^{s} x_i^k \leq X_i + \sum_{j=1}^{p} z_{ij}$ for all $i = 1, \ldots, n$ and $F(Z) = 0$, where Z is the $n \times p$ matrix of the z_{ij}. Making the same assumptions as before as to concavity-convexity and other properties, we have the following first order conditions using the method of Lagrange multipliers:

$$\text{(I)}' \quad \frac{\dfrac{\partial U^k}{\partial x_i^k}}{\dfrac{\partial U^k}{\partial x_{i+1}^k}} = \frac{\dfrac{\partial T}{\partial X_i}}{\dfrac{\partial T}{\partial X_{i+1}}}$$

$$\text{(II)}' \quad \frac{\dfrac{\partial U^k}{\partial x_i^k}}{\dfrac{\partial U^k}{\partial x_{i+1}^k}} = \frac{\dfrac{\partial F}{\partial z_{ij}}}{\dfrac{\partial F}{\partial z_{i+1j}}}$$

[b] This is the algebraic formulation of expression (1) in Chapter 2.

$$(\text{III})' \quad \frac{\dfrac{\partial U^k}{\partial x_i^k}}{\dfrac{\partial U^k}{\partial x_i^k}} = 1 = \frac{\dfrac{\partial F}{\partial z_{ij}}}{\dfrac{\partial F}{\partial z_{ij+1}}}$$

Condition (I)′ is identical with condition (I) in the previous section. Condition (II)′ expresses the notion that optimally the rate of commodity substitution between the ith and $(i+1)$th goods (which by condition (I)′ should equal the rate of domestic product transformation for these goods) should equal the rate of transformation through trade with *each* foreign market. Condition (III)′ indicates that the marginal social cost of (revenue from) foreign trade in the ith good must be equal for trade with each foreign market.

To understand what this means in the way of an optimum tariff policy we must once again examine carefully the foreign trade transformation function. Since we now allow for the possibility of *separate* foreign markets, our foreign trade transformation function is as follows:

$$F(Z) = \sum_{j=1}^{p} \sum_{i=1}^{n} p_{ij} z_{ij} - D = 0$$

where z_{ij} represents Home's net import of the ith good from the jth market, and p_{ij} is the jth foreign price of the ith import or export. As before, D is constant or exogenously determined.

Now let us totally differentiate $F(Z)$:

$$dF = \sum_{j=1}^{p} \sum_{i=1}^{n} \left[\frac{\partial \sum_{g=1}^{p} \sum_{s=1}^{n} p_{sg} z_{sg}}{\partial z_{ij}} \right] dz_{ij}$$

$$= \sum_{j=1}^{p} \sum_{i=1}^{n} \left[p_{ij} + \sum_{g=1}^{p} \sum_{s=1}^{n} \frac{\partial p_{sg}}{\partial z_{ij}} z_{sg} \right] dz_{ij}$$

Considering the total derivative for trade in the ith good with the jth country, z_{ij}, we have (where $t = 1, \ldots, n$, $t \neq i$; and $v = 1, \ldots, p$, $v \neq j$):

$$\frac{\partial F}{\partial z_{ij}} = p_{ij} + \sum_{g=1}^{p} \sum_{s=1}^{n} \frac{\partial p_{sg}}{\partial z_{ij}} z_{sg}$$

$$\frac{\partial F}{\partial z_{ij}} = p_{ij} + z_{ij} \frac{\partial p_{ij}}{\partial z_{ij}} + \sum_{\substack{v=1 \\ v \neq j}}^{p} z_{iv} \frac{\partial p_{iv}}{\partial z_{ij}} + \sum_{j=1}^{p} \sum_{\substack{t=1 \\ t \neq i}}^{n} z_{tj} \frac{\partial p_{tj}}{\partial z_{ij}}$$

$$= p_{ij}\left[1 + \frac{\partial p_{ij}}{p_{ij}}\frac{z_{ij}}{\partial z_{ij}} + \sum_{\substack{v=1\\v\neq j}}^{p}\frac{\partial p_{iv}}{p_{ij}}\frac{z_{iv}}{\partial z_{ij}} + \sum_{j=1}^{p}\sum_{\substack{t=1\\t\neq i}}^{n}\frac{\partial p_{tj}}{p_{ij}}\frac{z_{tj}}{\partial z_{ij}}\right]$$

$$= p_{ij}\left[1 + \eta_{ij} + \sum_{\substack{v=1\\v\neq j}}^{p}\eta_{iv}^{c}\frac{p_{iv}z_{iv}}{p_{ij}z_{ij}} + \sum_{j=1}^{p}\sum_{\substack{t=1\\t\neq i}}^{n}\eta_{itj}^{c}\frac{p_{tj}z_{tj}}{p_{ij}z_{ij}}\right]$$

where η_{ij} represents the quantity elasticity of jth foreign supply of (demand for) the ith good, η_{iv}^{c} is the quantity country cross elasticity for the ith good and vth country and η_{itj}^{c} is the quantity cross elasticity for the ith and tth goods for each jth country.

If we define

$$t_{ij} = \left[\eta_{ij} + \sum_{\substack{v=1\\v\neq j}}^{p}\eta_{iv}^{c}\frac{p_{iv}z_{iv}}{p_{ij}z_{ij}} + \sum_{j=1}^{p}\sum_{\substack{t=1\\t\neq i}}^{n}\eta_{itj}^{c}\frac{p_{tj}z_{tj}}{p_{ij}z_{ij}}\right]$$

our fundamental condition of Pareto optimality (combining conditions (I)′ and (II)′) becomes:

$$\frac{\Pi_i}{\Pi_{i+1}} = \frac{\dfrac{\partial U^k}{\partial x_i^k}}{\dfrac{\partial U^k}{\partial x_{i+1}^k}} = \frac{\dfrac{\partial T}{\partial X_i}}{\dfrac{\partial T}{\partial X_{i+1}}} = \frac{p_{ij}(1 + t_{ij})}{p_{i+1j}(1 + t_{i+1j})}$$

Condition (III)′ becomes:[c]

$$\frac{\dfrac{\partial U^k}{\partial x_i^k}}{\dfrac{\partial U^k}{\partial x_i^k}} = 1 = \frac{p_{ij}(1 + t_{ij})}{p_{ij+1}(1 + t_{ij+1})} \quad \text{or} \quad \frac{p_{ij}}{p_{ij+1}} = \frac{(1 + t_{ij+1})}{(1 + t_{ij})}$$

Now it is evident that when there is one world price for the ith good (one world market), $t_{ij} = t_i$ for all $j = 1, \ldots, p$; in other words, we have the result of conventional optimum tariff analysis. When the jth and $(j+1)$th markets are isolated from one another however, η_{ij} will not in general be equal to η_{ij+1}, nor will the respective cross elasticities in general be exactly offsetting. Consequently t_{ij} will not in general be equal to t_{ij+1}, which also means that optimally p_{ij} should be different than p_{ij+1}.

---

[c] This is the basis for expression (3) in Chapter 2.

Policy Differentiation Among Foreign Markets

We now assume that initially the jth and $j+1$th markets constitute one foreign market from the standpoint of Home. We further assume, however, that the national security consideration $y_{ij}(j = 1, \ldots, p)$ is operative in the kth individual's utility function. Our constrained maximization problem now takes the following form:

Maximize: $W = W[U^1(\bar{x}^1, Y^1), \ldots, U^s(\bar{x}^s, Y^s)]$

where
$$\sum_{k=1}^{s} x_i^k \leq X_i + \sum_{j=1}^{p} z_{ij}$$
$$y_{ij} \leq Y_{ij} - z_{ij} - z_{iw}$$

Subject to: $T(\bar{X}) = 0$

$$F(Z) = 0$$

where W, $\bar{x}^k$, $\bar{X}$ and Z are defined as before and Y^k is the $n \times p$ matrix of the y_{ij}, consumption of the ith good in the jth country; Y_{ij} represents the aggregate production of the ith good in the jth country; and z_{iw} represents the jth country's net export of the ith good to the rest of the world (excluding Home). We continue to make the same concavity-convexity assumptions and to assume the absence of external effects in domestic consumption and production, and that $T(\bar{X})$ is independent of the distribution of wealth. We also assume separability of the kth utility function as between $\bar{x}$ and Y. Now we form the following Lagrangean function (for simplicity we merely consider the ith nonmilitary good and jth country; this has no effect on the outcome):

$$\begin{aligned} L = {} & \alpha W[U^1(\bar{x}^1, Y^1), \ldots, U^s(\bar{x}^s, Y^s)] \\ & + \beta_i\left(X_i + \sum_{j=1}^{p} z_{ij} - \sum_{k=1}^{s} x_i^k\right) \\ & + \lambda(-T(X)) + \mu(-F(Z)) \\ & + \gamma_i^1(Y_{ij} - z_{ij} - z_{iw} - y_{ij}^1), + \cdots, \\ & \gamma_i^s(Y_{ij} - z_{ij} - z_{iw} - y_{ij}^s) \end{aligned}$$

where α, β, λ, μ and γ are Lagrangean multipliers associated with $W(\ )$ and the constraints and identities. As the second order conditions have been shown in Appendix B to be satisfied in the case of conventional simplifying assumptions, maximization of this Lagrangean function will give the necessary conditions for a global welfare maximum.

Now we set equal to zero the partial derivative of L with respect to each of the ith or ijth independent variables:

$$\frac{\partial L}{\partial X_i} = \beta_i - \lambda \frac{\partial T}{\partial X_i} = 0 \tag{1}$$

$$\frac{\partial L}{\partial z_{ij}} = \beta_i - \mu \frac{\partial F}{\partial z_{ij}} - \gamma_i^1, - \cdots, \gamma_i^s = 0 \tag{2}$$

$$\frac{\partial L}{\partial x_i^1} = \alpha \left[\frac{\partial W}{\partial U^1} \frac{\partial U^1}{\partial x_i^1} \right] - \beta_i = 0 \tag{3.1}$$

$$\vdots$$

$$\frac{\partial L}{\partial x_i^s} = \alpha \left[\frac{\partial W}{\partial U^s} \frac{\partial U^s}{\partial x_i^s} \right] - \beta_i = 0 \tag{3.s}$$

$$\frac{\partial L}{\partial y_{ij}^1} = \alpha \left[\frac{\partial W}{\partial U^1} \frac{\partial U^1}{\partial y_{ij}^1} \right] - \gamma_i^1 = 0 \tag{4.1}$$

$$\vdots$$

$$\frac{\partial L}{\partial y_{ij}^s} = \alpha \left[\frac{\partial W}{\partial U^s} \frac{\partial U^s}{\partial y_{ij}^s} \right] - \gamma_i^s = 0 \tag{4.s}$$

Next we will simplify these equations to several equations describing the first order conditions necessary for a welfare maximum:

from (3.1) $$\beta_i = \alpha \left[\frac{\partial W}{\partial U^1} \frac{\partial U^1}{\partial x_i^1} \right]$$

and (3.s) $$\beta_i = \alpha \left[\frac{\partial W}{\partial U^s} \frac{\partial U^s}{\partial x_i^s} \right]$$

therefore: $$\frac{\dfrac{\partial W}{\partial U^1} \dfrac{\partial U^1}{\partial x_i^1}}{\dfrac{\partial W}{\partial U^s} \dfrac{\partial U^s}{\partial x_i^s}} = 1$$

or $$\frac{\dfrac{\partial W}{\partial U^k} \dfrac{\partial U^k}{\partial x_i^k}}{\dfrac{\partial W}{\partial U^r} \dfrac{\partial U^r}{\partial x_i^r}} = 1 \qquad (k = 1, \ldots, s;\ r = 1, \ldots, s;\ r \neq k) \tag{5}$$ [3]

Equation (5) will help us simplify the following argument:

$$\text{from (1) and (2): } \beta_i = \lambda \frac{\partial T}{\partial X_i} = \mu \frac{\partial F}{\partial z_{ij}} + \gamma_i^1, + \cdots, \gamma_i^s$$

$$\text{from (5): } \qquad \beta_i = \alpha \left[\frac{\partial W}{\partial U^k} \frac{\partial U^k}{\partial x_i^k} \right]$$

$$\text{hence: } \qquad \beta_i = \alpha \left[\frac{\partial W}{\partial U^k} \frac{\partial U^k}{\partial x_i^k} \right] = \lambda \frac{\partial T}{\partial X_i} = \mu \frac{\partial F}{\partial z_{ij}} + \gamma_i^1, + \cdots, \gamma_i^s$$

and substituting from (4.1), ..., (4.s):

$$\alpha \left[\frac{\partial W}{\partial U^k} \frac{\partial U^k}{\partial x_i^k} \right] = \lambda \frac{\partial T}{\partial X_i} = \mu \frac{\partial F}{\partial z_{ij}} + \alpha \sum_{k=1}^{s} \left[\frac{\partial W}{\partial U^k} \frac{\partial U^k}{\partial y_{ij}^k} \right] \tag{6}$$

Using (5) and (6), we can further show that our first order conditions for a welfare maximum are, under our various assumptions,[d] independent of interpersonal comparisons; in other words, independent of the $\frac{\partial W}{\partial U^k}$ ($k = 1, \ldots, s$). This is accomplished by postulating that the ith good has the "collective good" characteristics we have been discussing, but that the $(i+1)$th good is merely a private good; that is, without collective good characteristics.

Looking at the kth individual, and first considering equation (6):

$$\alpha \left[\frac{\partial W}{\partial U^k} \frac{\partial U^k}{\partial x_i^k} - \sum_{k=1}^{s} \frac{\partial W}{\partial U^k} \frac{\partial U^k}{\partial y_{ij}^k} \right] = \mu \frac{\partial F}{\partial z_{ij}}$$

$$\alpha \left[\frac{\partial W}{\partial U^k} \frac{\partial U^k}{\partial x_{i+1}^k} \right] = \mu \frac{\partial F}{\partial z_{i+1\,j}}$$

For the $(i+1)$th good, equation (5) is:

$$\frac{\dfrac{\partial W}{\partial U^k} \dfrac{\partial U^k}{\partial x_{i+1}^k}}{\dfrac{\partial W}{\partial U^r} \dfrac{\partial U^r}{\partial x_{i+1}^r}} = 1 \qquad \text{or} \qquad \frac{\partial W}{\partial U^r} = \frac{\dfrac{\partial W}{\partial U^k} \dfrac{\partial U^k}{\partial x_{i+1}^k}}{\dfrac{\partial U^r}{\partial x_{i+1}^r}}$$

---

[d] See Appendix A.

Since $r = 1, \ldots, s, r \neq k$, we can substitute the latter rendering of equation (5) into equation (6) for the ith good, for all $r \neq k$:

$$\alpha\left[\frac{\partial W}{\partial U^k}\frac{\partial U^k}{\partial x_i^k} - \frac{\partial W}{\partial U^k}\frac{\partial U^k}{\partial y_{ij}^k} - \sum_{\substack{r=1\\ r\neq k}}^{s}\frac{\dfrac{\partial W}{\partial U^k}\dfrac{\partial U^k}{\partial x_{i+1}^k}\dfrac{\partial U^r}{\partial y_{ij}^r}}{\dfrac{\partial U^r}{\partial x_{i+1}^r}}\right] = \mu\frac{\partial F}{\partial z_{ij}}$$

Now we divide through equation (6) for the ith good and $(i + 1)$th goods by $\frac{\partial W}{\partial U^k}$, and then we divide equation (6) for the ith good by equation (6) for the $(i + 1\text{th})$ good, getting:[4]

$$\text{(I)}'' \quad \frac{\dfrac{\partial U^k}{\partial x_i^k}}{\dfrac{\partial U^k}{\partial x_{i+1}^k}} = \frac{\dfrac{\partial T}{\partial X_i}}{\dfrac{\partial T}{\partial X_{i+1}}} \qquad {}^{e}\text{(II)}'' \quad \frac{\dfrac{\partial U^k}{\partial x_i^k}}{\dfrac{\partial U^k}{\partial x_{i+1}^k}} = \frac{\dfrac{\partial F}{\partial z_{ij}}}{\dfrac{\partial F}{\partial z_{i+1j}}} + \sum_{k=1}^{s}\frac{\dfrac{\partial U^k}{\partial y_{ij}^k}}{\dfrac{\partial U^k}{\partial x_{i+1}^k}}$$

As in the previous section we are also very interested in the expression $\frac{\partial F}{\partial z_{ij}}\Big/\frac{\partial F}{\partial z_{ij+1}}$. This may be derived in analogous fashion to equations (I)″ and (II)″ by using our equation (5) for the ith good, where $k = 1, \ldots, s$; $r = 1, \ldots, s, r \neq k$:

$$\frac{\partial W}{\partial U^r} = \frac{\dfrac{\partial W}{\partial U^k}\dfrac{\partial U^k}{\partial x_i^k}}{\dfrac{\partial U^r}{\partial x_i^r}}$$

We can substitute the latter expression for (5) into equation (6) for the ith good traded with the jth country. Then analogously to the foregoing derivations, we divide through equation (6) (for both the ith good traded with the jth country and the ith good traded with the $(j + 1)$th market) by $\frac{\partial W}{\partial U^k}$, and then divide the former by the latter, getting:[f]

$$\text{(III)}'' \quad 1 = \frac{\dfrac{\partial F}{\partial z_{ij}}}{\dfrac{\partial F}{\partial z_{ij+1}}} + \sum_{k=1}^{s}\frac{\dfrac{\partial U^k}{\partial y_{ij}^k}}{\dfrac{\partial U^k}{\partial x_i^k}}$$

[e] This is the algebraic formulation of expression (4) in Chapter 2.

[f] This is the algebraic formulation of expression (5) in Chapter 2.

We should point out here that in deriving these first order conditions we have, for the sake of simplicity, employed only equalities. A perfectly general formulation of these conditions, however, which recognizes that some of the elements of $\bar{x}$, $\bar{X}$ and Z will be negative (the cases of productive services rendered, production inputs, and exports, respectively) and some will be equal to zero, must be stated in terms of inequalities. Implicit in our formulation are the Kuhn–Tucker conditions.[5]

Optimal condition (I)″ is identical to conditions (I) and (I)′ in the previous sections. Condition (II)″ is interpreted analogously to condition (II)′ in the last section: at the welfare maximum the domestic rate of commodity substitution equals the ratio of the marginal social costs of importing (revenue from exporting) the ith and $(i + 1)$th goods. In this case, however, we have an additional component $\left[\sum_{k=1}^{s} \frac{\frac{\partial U^k}{\partial y_{ij}^k}}{\frac{\partial U^k}{\partial x_{i+1}^k}}\right]$ of the marginal social cost of (revenue from) foreign trade with the jth country in the ith good. This term represents the sum, over all s individuals in Home, of the ratio of their marginal utility (or disutility) experienced as a result of jth consumption of the ith good, to their marginal utility from consumption of the $(i + 1)$th good not subject to external effects in international consumption. Condition (III)″ has a similar but not identical term and is interpreted as in the previous section.

Let us assume that collectively individuals in Home receive disutility from jth country consumption of the ith good; in other words, for a preponderant number of individuals $\frac{\partial U^k}{\partial y_{ij}^k}$ is negative. As indicated by the following rewriting of conditions (II)″ and (III)″ in accordance with our examination of $F(Z)$ in the last section, Home should now optimally impose a pattern of foreign trade taxes different from those derived in both the cases of conventional optimum tariff theory and "natural" separation of foreign markets:

$$\text{(II)}'' \qquad \frac{\frac{\partial U^k}{\partial x_i^k}}{\frac{\partial U^k}{\partial x_{i+1}^k}} = \frac{p_{ij}(1 + t_{ij})}{p_{i+1j})1 + t_{i+1j})} + \sum_{k=1}^{s} \frac{\frac{\partial U^k}{\partial y_{ij}^k}}{\frac{\partial U^k}{\partial x_{i+1}^k}}$$

$$\text{(III)}'' \qquad \frac{\frac{\partial U^k}{\partial x_i^k}}{\frac{\partial U^k}{\partial x_i^k}} = 1 = \frac{p_{ij}(1 + t_{ij})}{p_{ij+1}(1 + t_{ij+1})} + \sum_{k=1}^{s} \frac{\frac{\partial U^k}{\partial y_{ij}^k}}{\frac{\partial U^k}{\partial x_i^k}}$$

The specific form of policy intervention implied by the foregoing conditions depends upon whether the ith and $(i+1)$th goods are exported to or imported from the jth and $(j+1)$th markets. For illustrative purposes let us suppose that Home normally exports both goods to both markets. Before taking into account external effects in international consumption (y_{ij}), Home optimally should impose a single optimum export tax on trade with both markets for each good $(t_i = t_{ij} = t_{ij+1};\ t_{i+1} = t_{i+1j} = t_{i+1j+1})$. Taking y_{ij} into consideration, the summed term in each expression becomes negative. Condition (II)″ can now only be satisfied by some combination of a lower $\dfrac{\partial U^k / \partial x_i^k}{\partial U^k / \partial x_{i+1}^k}$ ratio and higher $\dfrac{p_{ij}(1+t_{ij})}{p_{i+1j}(1+t_{i+1j})}$ ratio than formerly. The most direct policy action to achieve this change in domestic and foreign price ratios would be some combination of a higher export tax on z_{ij} and/or a lower export tax on z_{i+1j}.[g]

Similarly, condition (III)″ can now be satisfied by some combination of a higher export tax on z_{ij} and a lower export tax on z_{ij+1}. Significantly, this means that Home must now insure that p_{ij} is greater than p_{ij+1}; Home must somehow break up the *one* world market so as to be able to sell at different prices in the jth and $(j+1)$th markets. Elimination of arbitrage between these markets will also mean that in general t_{ij} will differ from t_{ij+1}.

A Dynamic Consideration

The potential vulnerability of a discriminatory optimum tariff policy in a situation with product differentiation-by-origin, in which only the *transshipment* requirement is satisfied, is illustrated in the partial equilibrium diagram below (see the final section of Chapter 2).

In the diagram we consider only the ith export to the jth market. The free trade price for the ith good in trade between Home and the jth market would be π_0. The curves (straight lines for convenience) $S^1_{j+\text{excess}\,j+1}$ and $D^1_{\text{Home}+\text{excess}\,j}$ represent the effective supply of the ith good available to the

[g] This is *sufficient* policy action for satisfaction of condition (II)″ under the assumptions that F(Z) forms a convex set and that demand and supply curves have the usual curvature. It is theoretically not a *necessary* policy action, however, as the required change in the ratio $C = \dfrac{p_{ij}(1+t^{ij})}{p_{ij+1}(1+t_{i+1j})}$ could be effected by export tax changes which diminished the $p_{ij} - p_{i+1j}$ differential, provided $\dfrac{\partial t_{ij}}{\partial p_{ij}}$ and $\dfrac{\partial t_{i+1j}}{\partial p_{i+1j}}$ were significantly enough different. Similar reasoning applies to our interpretation of condition (III).″

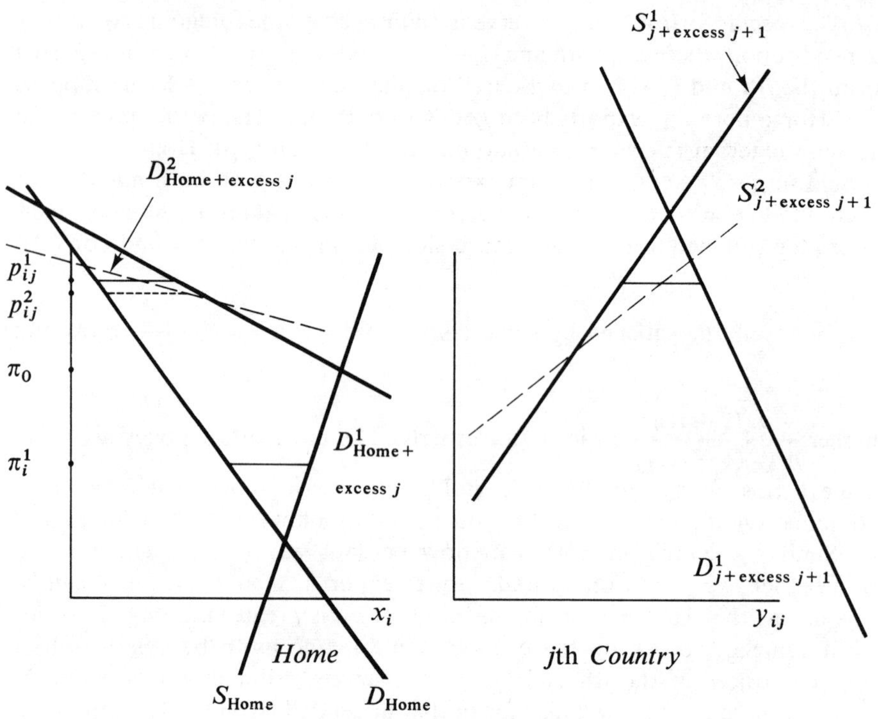

Figure C–1

*j*th market and effective demand for Home's production of the *i*th good after taking into account the excess supply of the $(j + 1)$th market at each price.

Based on the elasticity of *j*th excess demand for Home's export of the *i*th good, let us assume that Home levies an optimum export tax resulting in a domestic price π^1_i and *j*th foreign price p^1_{ij}. Now we may represent an increase in supplies of $(j + 1)$th exports of the *i*th good by the new curves $S^2_{j+\text{excess } j+1}$ and $D^2_{\text{Home}+\text{excess } j}$. Home can only maintain its export volume (quantity) by reducing its export tax from $(p^1_{ij} - \pi^1_i)$ to $(p^2_{ij} - \pi^1_i)$. Alternatively, Home could maintain its original export tax of $(p^1_{ij} - \pi^1_i)$ by reducing its volume (quantity of) exports of the *i*th good. In actuality, pursuit of an optimum tariff policy will lead to a reduced optimum export tax rate but export volume may increase or decrease.

Also, were the *j*th supply curve $S^1_{j+\text{excess } j+1}$ to merely shift rightward in such a way as to maintain the price elasticity of *j*th excess demand for Home exports of the *i*th good at each price, similar results would follow (and similar reasoning can be applied to imports). If we introduce national security variables but assume that they are unaffected by changes in $(j + 1)$th supply, maintenance of an optimum export tax based on, say, an unchanged

$$\sum_{k=1}^{s}\left[\frac{\dfrac{\partial U^k}{\partial y_{ij}^k}}{\dfrac{\partial U^k}{\partial x_{i+1}^k}}\right]$$

(and a diminished t_{ij} arising from an increase in $(j+1)$th excess supply) will lead to diminished export volume ($dz_{ij} > 0$) and possibly to an effective embargo on Home exports to the jth country. In other words, with an unchanged value for $\sum_{k=1}^{s}\left[\frac{\partial U^k / \partial y_{ij}^k}{\partial U^k / \partial x_{i+1}^k}\right]$, Home exporters may be priced out of the jth market.

Appendix D
Extensions to Other National Security Variables

First order conditions for the other national security considerations may be easily derived in a fashion similar to that already demonstrated in Appendix C for the collective good y_{ij}^k. Consequently, rather than repeat the same derivation procedure here for each of the other national security variables, we shall content ourselves with merely showing the derived first order conditions in each case, followed by a short interpretation of these conditions in terms of policy recommendations. The Roman-numerated expressions in each case (I, II, and III) have a general meaning similar to the respective conditions in Appendix C.

Relative Military Strength

Only optimal condition (I) is affected by the x_h^k consideration:

$$\text{(I)} \quad \sum_{k=1}^{s} \frac{\dfrac{\partial U^k}{\partial x_h^k}}{\dfrac{\partial U^k}{\partial x_{i+1}^k}} = \frac{\dfrac{\partial T}{\partial X_h}}{\dfrac{\partial T}{\partial X_{i+1}}}$$

The implications of this condition for policy makers can be seen in Figure D-1. Without policy intervention the equilibrium commodity bundle (x_h, x_{i+1}) will be produced and consumed at point C_0.

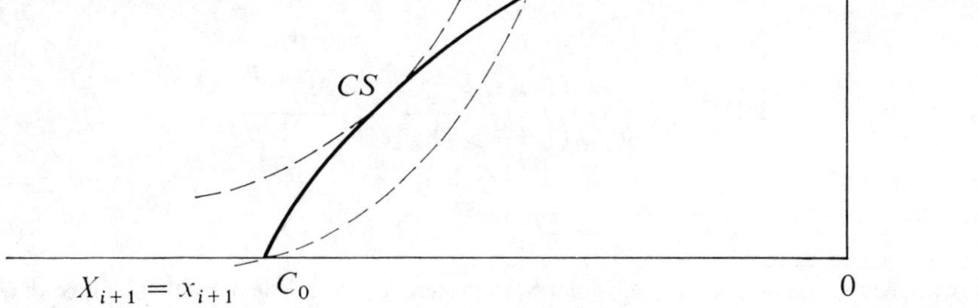

Figure D–1

This boundary solution results from the fact that participants in the market effectively have no private demand for x_h.[a] Home policy makers recognize, however, that x_h is desired by individuals as a collective good. The policy makers' family of Bergson contours (W^*) will therefore have a flatter slope than the domestic transformation curve at C_0.[2] In seeking to maximize social welfare, policy makers will subsidize the production of x_h at the point at which the highest possible Bergson contour is achieved. The new production-consumption position will be at CS, the point of tangency between W_1^* and the domestic transformation curve. At this point the sum over all s individuals of their actual rates of commodity substitution (not reflected in their *private* purchases) will equal the ratio of marginal private costs of producing both goods.[3] The ratio of the production subsidy for the hth good to the marginal private cost of producing the $i + 1$th good at this point will equal $\dfrac{\frac{\partial T}{\partial X_h}}{\frac{\partial T}{\partial X_{i+1}}}$.

Economic Warfare: Offensive

F^k is the matrix of the (f_{hj}^k, f_{ij}^k) where $f_{hj}^k = p_{hj} z_{hj}$ and $f_{ij}^k = p_{ij} z_{ij}$, the net foreign exchange earned by the jth foreign country from its export to Home of the hth and ith goods respectively. Focusing on just nonmilitary goods (f_{ij}^k), conditions (II) and (III), but not condition (I), are affected by the f_{ij}^k consideration:

$$\text{(II)} \quad \frac{\frac{\partial U^k}{\partial x_i^k}}{\frac{\partial U^k}{\partial x_{i+1}^k}} = \frac{p_{ij}(1 + t_{ij})}{p_{i+1j}(1 + t_{i+1j})} - \sum_{k=1}^{s} \frac{\frac{\partial U^k}{\partial f_{ij}^k} \cdot p_{ij}}{\frac{\partial U^k}{\partial x_{i+1}^k}}$$

$$\text{(III)} \quad 1 = \frac{p_{ij}(1 + t_{ij})}{p_{ij+1}(1 + t_{ij+1})} - \sum_{k=1}^{s} \frac{\frac{\partial U^k}{\partial f_{ij}^k} \cdot p_{ij}}{\frac{\partial U^k}{\partial x_i^k}}$$

[a] It will be in each individual's self-interest to pretend to have little or no demand for the jth good under the assumption that others will finance its purchase, in spite of the fact that everyone will share in "consumption" of this collective good (see Samuelson[1]).

When the Home community on balance is pained by the jth country's earning foreign exchange in trade with Home, the expressions

$$\sum_{k=1}^{s} \frac{\frac{\partial U^k}{\partial f_{ij}^k} \cdot p_{ij}}{\frac{\partial U^k}{\partial x_{i+1}^k}} \quad \text{and} \quad \sum_{k=1}^{s} \frac{\frac{\partial U^k}{\partial f_{ij}^k} \cdot p_{ij}}{\frac{\partial U^k}{\partial x_i^k}}$$

will be negative.[b]

Condition (II) will be satisfied by policy intervention which results in some combination of a higher

$$\frac{\frac{\partial U^k}{\partial x_i^k}}{\frac{\partial U^k}{\partial x_{i+1}^k}} = \frac{\Pi_i}{\Pi_{i+1}}$$

and lower foreign price ratio $\frac{p_{ij}}{p_{i+1j}}$ than in the absence of national security considerations. The implied policy action is some combination of a higher tariff on the ith import from the jth country and higher export tax on the $(i+1)$th good if it is exported or a lower tariff on the $(i+1)$th good imported from the jth country.

Condition (III) will be satisfied by policy intervention which is successful in raising the price of the ith good in the $(j+1)$th market relative to the price of the ith good in the jth market. The implied policy action is some combination of a higher tariff on the ith good imported from the jth market and a higher export tax on the ith good if it is exported to the $(j+1)$th market or a lower tariff on the ith good if it is imported from the $(j+1)$th market. Furthermore, the usual enforced transshipment or isolation requirement must be met, depending upon whether or not there is product differentiation-by-origin in $(j+1)$th consumption.

We turn now to S^k, which is the matrix of the (s_{hj}^k, s_{ij}^k), where $s_{hj}^k = \frac{(-z_{hj})}{y_{hj}}$ and $s_{ij}^k = \frac{(-z_{ij})}{y_{ij}}$, representing the relative dependence of the jth country

[b] We might note in passing that these expressions would also be negative in the case of exports of the ith good if Home were pursuing a "mercantilist" objective of adding to its stock of international reserves by assuring itself of a "favorable" trade balance with foreigners.

on Home as a source of supply for the *h*th and *i*th goods respectively. Focusing only on nonmilitary goods (s_{ij}^k), once again conditions (II) and (III), but not condition (I), are affected:

$$\text{(II)} \quad \frac{\dfrac{\partial U^k}{\partial x_i^k}}{\dfrac{\partial U^k}{\partial x_{i+1}^k}} = \frac{p_{ij}(1 + t_{ij})}{p_{i+1j}(1 + t_{i+1j})} + \sum_{k=1}^{s} \frac{\dfrac{\partial U^k}{\partial s_{ij}^k} \dfrac{(z_{ij} + y_{ij})}{(y_{ij})^2}}{\dfrac{\partial U^k}{\partial x_{i+1}^k}}$$

$$\text{(III)} \quad 1 = \frac{p_{ij}(1 + t_{ij})}{p_{ij+1}(1 + t_{ij+1})} + \sum_{k=1}^{s} \frac{\dfrac{\partial U^k}{\partial s_{ij}^k} \dfrac{(z_{ij} + y_{ij})}{(y_{ij})^2}}{\dfrac{\partial U^k}{\partial x_i^k}}$$

Except in the unlikely case where Home exports of the *i*th good to the *j*th country are greater than *j*th consumption of this good (i.e., negative z_{ij} greater than positive y_{ij}), the national security term in this case will be positive, as we have stipulated that increased *j*th dependence on Home exports of the *i*th good gives the *k*th individual in Home positive marginal utility.

The implications for optimal policy intervention in this case are the opposite of those when y_{ij}^k is the national security consideration. Now, instead of imposing a higher export tax on z_{ij} so as to deprive the *j*th country of the *i*th good, the Home policy maker will lower the export tax (or possibly grant an export subsidy) so as to induce the *j*th country to purchase more of the *i*th good from Home.[c]

Economic Warfare: Defensive

M^k is the matrix of the (m_{hj}^k, m_{ij}^k) $(h = 1, \ldots, m; i = m + 1, \ldots, n; j = 1, \ldots, p)$ where $m_{hj}^k = \dfrac{z_{hj}}{X_h}$ and $m_{ij}^k = \dfrac{z_{ij}}{X_i}$, representing Home's dependence on the *h*th and *i*th goods respectively. This concern with the *relative* magnitudes of z_{ij} and X_i means that *both* the first order condition relating to the domestic economy, condition (I), and the conditions relating to foreign trade, (II) and (III), are affected:

[c] Analogous to our earlier discussions of y_{ij}^k and f_{ij}^k, optimal policy intervention to satisfy condition (II) will actually consist of some *combination* of a lower export tax on the *i*th export to the *j*th country and a lower tariff on the $(i+1)$th good if imported or a higher export tax on the $(i+1)$th good if exported to the *j*th country.

$$\text{(I)}\quad \frac{\dfrac{\partial U^k}{\partial x_i^k}}{\dfrac{\partial U^k}{\partial x_{i+1}^k}} = \frac{\dfrac{\partial T}{\partial X_i}}{\dfrac{\partial T}{\partial X_{i+1}}} + \sum_{j=1}^{p}\sum_{k=1}^{s} \frac{\dfrac{\partial U^k}{\partial m_{ij}^k}\cdot\dfrac{z_{ij}}{X_i^2}}{\dfrac{\partial U^k}{\partial x_{i+1}^k}}$$

$$\text{(II)}\quad \frac{\dfrac{\partial U^k}{\partial x_i^k}}{\dfrac{\partial U^k}{\partial x_{i+1}^k}} = \frac{p_{ij}(1+t_{ij})}{p_{i+1j}(1+t_{i+1j})} - \sum_{k=1}^{s} \frac{\dfrac{\partial U^k}{\partial m_{ij}^k}\cdot\dfrac{1}{X_i}}{\dfrac{\partial U^k}{\partial x_{i+1}^k}}$$

$$\text{(III)}\quad 1 = \frac{p_{ij}(1+t_{ij})}{p_{ij+1}(1+t_{ij+1})} - \sum_{k=1}^{s} \frac{\dfrac{\partial U^k}{\partial m_{ij}^k}\cdot\dfrac{1}{X_i}}{\dfrac{\partial U^k}{\partial x_i^k}}$$

First of all, we observe that if the m_{ij}^k national security consideration is operative with respect to *any* jth country, the national security expression in condition (I) will in general be nonzero. This is because the national security term, which is negative, is summed over all $j = 1, \ldots, p$ as well as over all $k = 1, \ldots, s$. In this case condition (I) will be satisfied only by policy intervention that results in some combination of a lower $\dfrac{\partial U^k / \partial x_i^k}{\partial U^k / \partial x_{i+1}^k}$ (= domestic price ratio) and a higher $\dfrac{\partial T / \partial X_i}{\partial T / \partial X_{i+1}}$. The implied policy action is some combination of a production subsidy for the ith good and/or a production tax on the $(i + 1)$th good.

When this national security consideration is operative for the jth country, condition (II) will be satisfied by policy intervention that results in some combination of a higher domestic price ratio and a lower foreign price ratio than in the absence of national security considerations. The implied policy action is some combination of a higher tariff on the import of the ith good from the jth country and a lower tariff on the $(i + 1)$th good if imported from the jth country or a higher export tax on the $(i + 1)$th good if exported to the jth country.

Condition (III) will be satisfied by policy intervention which is successful in lowering the price of the ith good in the jth market relative to the price of the ith good in the $(j+1)$th market. The implied actions will be similar to those required in the case of f_{ij}^k.

That policy intervention in the domestic sector in this case must be in the form of some subsidy-tax combination relating to production rather than consumption is made clear by the partial equilibrium diagram in Figure D-2. This diagram shows Home and jth country supply and demand for the ith good, with the $(i+1)$th good considered as *numéraire* for illustrative purposes.

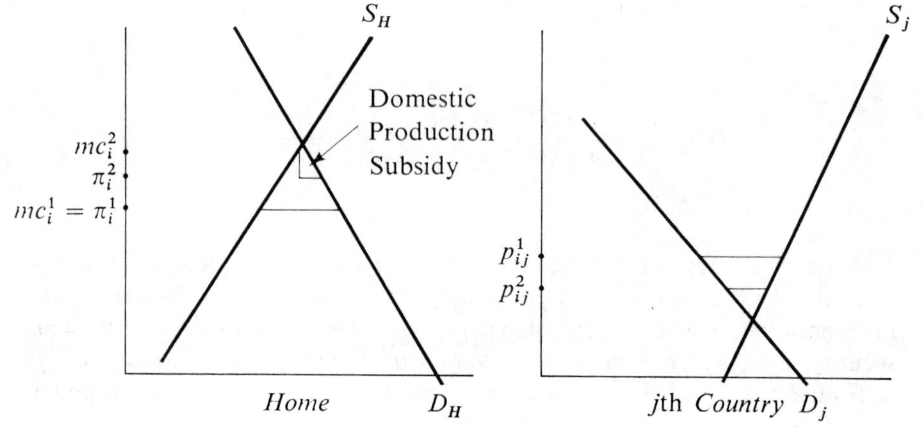

Figure D–2

Before taking into account the national security consideration embodied in m_{ij}^k, Home would levy an optimum tariff equal to $\pi_i^1 - p_{ij}^1$ ($mc_i^1 = \pi_i$; mc_i^1 being the domestic marginal cost of producing the ith good) on the import of the ith good from the jth country (and, indeed, from the rest of the world). After taking this defensive economic warfare consideration into account, Home would levy a higher optimum tariff equal to $\pi_i^2 - p_{ij}^2$ on the import of the ith good from the jth country. This new tariff would satisfy condition (II). In addition, a subsidy equal to $mc_i^2 - \pi_i^2$ (the difference between domestic marginal cost and price for the ith good) would apply to this good in satisfaction of condition (I). The diagram shows that if all domestic consumption were subsidized at the rate implied by condition (I), this would imply that domestic marginal cost (mc_i^2) would optimally equal the foreign price including the tariff but before the subsidy. But this implies that condition (II) be:

$$\frac{\dfrac{\partial T}{\partial X_i}}{\dfrac{\partial T}{\partial X_{i+1}}} = \frac{p_{ij}(1+t_{ij})}{p_{1+ij}(1+t_{i+1j})} - \sum_{k=1}^{s} \frac{\dfrac{\partial U^k}{\partial m_{ij}^k}\dfrac{1}{X_i}}{\dfrac{\partial U^k}{\partial x_{i+1}^k}}$$

whereas in reality conditions (I) and (II) give:

$$\frac{\frac{\partial T}{\partial X_i}}{\frac{\partial T}{\partial X_{i+1}}} > \frac{\frac{\partial U^k}{\partial x_i^k}}{\frac{\partial U^k}{\partial x_{i+1}^k}} = \frac{p_{ij}(1+t_{ij})}{p_{i+1j}(1+t_{i+1j})} - \sum_{k=1}^{s} \frac{\frac{\partial U^k}{\partial m_{ij}^k}\frac{1}{X_i}}{\frac{\partial U^k}{\partial x_{i+1}^k}}$$

Consequently both conditions (I) and (II) can only be met through a subsidy to domestic *producers* of the ith good, combined with a higher tariff on the import of this good from the jth country.

Finally, let us turn to E^k, the matrix of the (e_{hj}^k, e_{ij}^k) $(h = 1, \ldots, m;$ $i = m+1, \ldots, n;$ $j = 1, \ldots, p)$ where $e_{hj}^k = \frac{(-z_{hj})}{x_h^k}$, and $e_{ij}^k = \frac{(-z_{ij})}{\sum_{k=1}^{s} x_i^k}$, representing Home's dependence on the jth country as a market for the hth and ith goods produced in Home respectively. This concern with the relative magnitudes of z_{ij} and $\sum_{k=1}^{s} x_i^k$ means once again that *both* the first order condition relating to the domestic sector, condition (I), and the conditions relating to foreign trade, (II) and (III), are affected:

$$\text{(I)} \quad \frac{\frac{\partial U^k}{\partial x_i^k}}{\frac{\partial U^k}{\partial x_{i+1}^k}} = \frac{\frac{\partial T}{\partial X_i}}{\frac{\partial T}{\partial X_{i+1}}} - \sum_{j=1}^{p}\sum_{k=1}^{s}\left[\frac{\frac{\partial U^k}{\partial e_{ij}^k}\frac{z_{ij}}{\left(\sum_{k=1}^{s} x_i^k\right)^2}}{\frac{\partial U^k}{\partial x_{i+1}^k}}\right]$$

$$\text{(II)} \quad \frac{\frac{\partial U^k}{\partial x_i^k}}{\frac{\partial U^k}{\partial x_{i+1}^k}} = \frac{p_{ij}(1+t_{ij})}{p_{i+1j}(1+t_{i+1j})} + \sum_{k=1}^{s} \frac{\frac{\partial U^k}{\partial e_{ij}^k}\frac{1}{\sum_{k=1}^{s} x_i^k}}{\frac{\partial U^k}{\partial x_{i+1}^k}}$$

$$- \sum_{k=1}^{p}\sum_{k=1}^{s} \frac{\frac{\partial U^k}{\partial e_{ij}^k}\frac{z_{ij}}{\left(\sum_{k=1}^{s} x_i^k\right)^2}}{\frac{\partial U^k}{\partial x_{i+1}^k}}$$

$$(\mathrm{III})\quad 1 = \frac{p_{ij}(1+t_{ij})}{p_{ij+1}(1+t_{ij+1})} + \frac{\displaystyle\sum_{k=1}^{s}\left[\frac{\dfrac{\partial U^k}{\partial e^k_{ij}}\dfrac{1}{\sum_{k=1}^{s} x^k_i}}{\dfrac{\partial U^k}{\partial x^k_i}}\right]}{\left[1+\displaystyle\sum_{j=1}^{p}\sum_{k=1}^{s}\frac{\dfrac{\partial U}{\partial e^k_{ij}}\dfrac{z_{ij}}{\left(\sum_{k=1}^{s} x^k_i\right)^2}}{\dfrac{\partial U^k}{\partial x^k_i}}\right]}$$

With respect to condition (I) we observe that if the e^k_{ij} national security consideration is operative with respect to *any* jth country, the double-summed expression will in general be nonzero. This is because the national security term is summed over all $j = 1, \ldots, p$ as well as over all $k = 1, \ldots, s$. In this case condition (I) will be satisfied only by policy intervention that results in some combination of a lower $\dfrac{\partial U^k / \partial x^k_i}{\partial U^k / \partial x^k_{i+1}}$ and a higher $\dfrac{\partial T / \partial X_i}{\partial T / \partial X_{i+1}}$ than in the absence of national security considerations, because we assume that $\dfrac{\partial U^k}{\partial e^k_{ij}}$ will be negative for the preponderant number of individuals.[d] The implied policy is some combination of a subsidy on domestic consumption of the ith good and a tax on domestic consumption of the $(i+1)$th good.

When e^k_{ij} is operative for the jth country, condition (II) will be satisfied by policy intervention that results in some combination of a lower domestic price ratio and a higher foreign price ratio than in the absence of national security considerations. The implied policy action is some combination of a higher export tax on the export of the ith good to the jth country and a lower export tax on the $(i+1)$th good if exported to the jth country or a higher tariff on the $(i+1)$th good if imported from the jth country.

Condition (III) will be satisfied only by policy intervention which is successful in raising the price of the ith good in the jth market relative to the price of the ith good in the $(j+1)$th market. The implied policy actions will be similar to those required in the case of a negative

[d] It will be recalled that z_{ij} is negative when the ith good is exported to the jth country.

$$\sum_{k=1}^{s} \frac{\dfrac{\partial U^k}{\partial y_{ij}^k}}{\dfrac{\partial U^k}{\partial x_i^k}}.$$

That policy intervention in the domestic sector in this case must be in the form of some subsidy-tax combination relating to consumption rather than production is made clear by the partial equilibrium diagram in Figure D-3. This diagram shows Home and *j*th country supply and demand for the *i*th good, with the $(i + 1)$th good once again considered as *numéraire* for illustrative purposes.

Before taking into account the national security consideration embodied in e_{ij}^k, Home would levy an optimum export tax equal to $p_{ij}^1 - \pi_i^1(\pi_i^1 = mc_i^1)$ on the export of the *i*th good to the *j*th country (and, indeed, to the rest of the world). After taking this particular defensive economic warfare consideration into account, Home would levy a higher optimum export tax equal to $p_{ij}^2 - mc_i^2$ on the export of the *i*th good to the *j*th country. That this would satisfy condition (II) is seen if we substitute condition (I) into condition (II) obtaining:

$$\frac{\dfrac{\partial T}{\partial X_i}}{\dfrac{\partial T}{\partial X_{i+1}}} = \frac{p_{ij}(1 + t_{ij})}{p_{i+1j}(1 + t_{i+1j})} + \sum_{k=1}^{s} \frac{\dfrac{\partial U^k}{\partial e_{ij}^k} \dfrac{1}{\sum_{k=1}^{s} x_i^k}}{\dfrac{\partial U^k}{\partial x_{i+1}^k}}$$

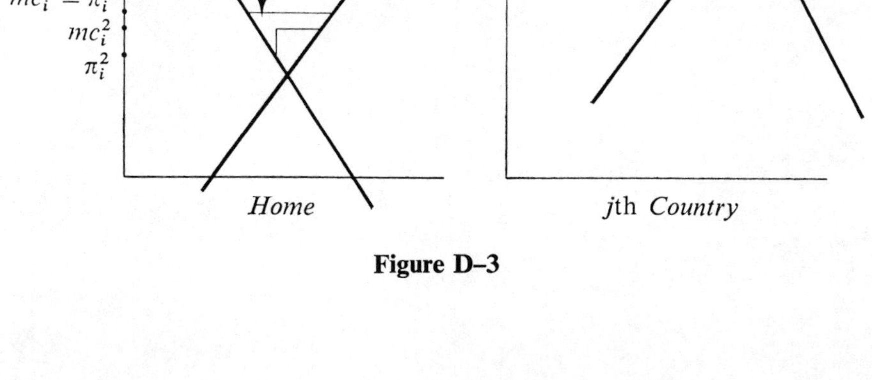

Figure D–3

In addition, a subsidy equal to $mc_i^2 - \pi_i^2$ (the difference between domestic marginal cost and price for the *i*th good) would apply to this good in satisfaction of condition (I). We can see by the diagram that if domestic production were to be subsidized at the rate implied by condition (I), this would imply that the domestic price (π_i^2) would optimally equal the foreign price less the export tax but before subsidy. But we know from condition (II) that the domestic price will be less than this amount by the amount of the subsidy. Consequently, it is clear that the optimal conditions can only be met through a subsidy on domestic *consumption* of the *i*th good, together with a higher export tax on the export of the *i*th good to the *j*th country.

Notes

Notes to Introduction

1. Richard E. Caves, *Trade and Economic Structure* (Cambridge, Mass.: Harvard University Press, 1967), p. 238.

2. Albert O. Hirschman, *National Power and The Structure of Foreign Trade* (Berkeley: University of California Press, 1945).

3. Murray, C. Kemp, *The Pure Theory of International Trade* (Englewood Cliffs, N.J.: Prentice-Hall, 1964); and Kemp *The Pure Theory of International Trade and Investment* (Englewood Cliffs, N.J.: Prentice-Hall, 1969).

4. Charles P. Kindleberger, *Power and Money* (New York: Basic Books, 1970).

5. See, for example, Harry G. Johnson, "The Cost of Protection and the Scientific Tariff." *Journal of Political Economy*, LXVIII, 4 (August 1960), pp. 327–345; Harry G. Johnson, "A Theoretical Model of Economic Nationalism in New and Developing States," *Political Science Quarterly*, LXXX, 2 (June 1965), pp. 169–185; Harry G. Johnson "An Economic Theory of Protectionism, Tariff Bargaining and the Formation of Customs Unions," *Journal of Political Economy*, LXXIII, 3 (June 1965), pp. 256–283; and J. Bhagwati and T. N. Srinivasan, "Optimal Intervention to Achieve Non-Economic Objectives," *Review of Economic Studies*, XXXVI (1), 105 (January 1969), pp. 27–38.

6. Harry G. Johnson, "An Economic Theory of Protectionism, Tariff Bargaining and the Formation of Customs Unions."

7. Benjamin J. Cohen, "American Foreign Economic Policy: Some General Principles of Analysis," in Cohen (Ed)., *American Foreign Economic Policy* (New York: Harper & Row, 1968), pp. 1–20.

8. J. de V. Graaff, "On Optimum Tariff Structures," *Review of Economic Studies*, 17 (1949) as revised and reprinted in Kenneth Arrow and Tibor Scitovsky (Eds.), *Readings in Welfare Economics* (Homewood, Ill.: Irwin, 1969), pp. 523–540.

9. See R. G. Lipsey and K. J. Lancaster, "The General Theory of Second Best," *Review of Economic Studies*, XXIV(1), 63 (1956–1957).

10. Gunnar Adler-Karlsson, *Western Economic Warfare 1947–1967* (Stockholm: Almqvist and Wiksell, 1968).

Notes to Chapter 1

1. Benjamin J. Cohen, "American Foreign Economic Policy: Some General Principles of Analysis," in Cohen (Ed.), *American Foreign Economic Policy* (New York: Harper & Row, 1968), pp. 1–2.

2. Ibid., p. 4.

3. Ibid., p. 8.

4. Ibid., p. 9.

5. Ibid., p. 10.

6. Harry G. Johnson, "An Economic Theory of Protectionism, Tariff Bargaining and the Formation of Customs Unions," *Journal of Political Economy*, LXXIII, 3 (June 1965), pp. 256–283.

7. Cohen, *American Foreign Economic Policy*, pp. 16–20.

8. This definition of a nonoptional collective good may be found in E. J. Mishan, "The Relationship Between Joint Products, Collective Goods, and External Effects," *Journal of Political Economy*, LXXVII, 3 (May–June 1969), p. 335. Since national security is not by and large the unintended by-product of the pursuit of other objectives, its designation as a collective good rather than as an external effect seems appropriate.

9. See Robert Loring Allen, *Soviet Economic Warfare* (Washington: Public Affairs Press, 1960), p. 29: "Economic warfare is defined as the conscious attempt to increase the relative economic, military, and political position of a country through foreign economic relations. Several aspects of the definition require amplification. The action must be purposeful; otherwise a nation merely in pursuit of the benefits of trade would be considered engaging in economic warfare if the action should improve its relative position. Economic warfare does not imply success."

10. See, for example, James M. Henderson and Richard E. Quandt, *Microeconomic Theory: A Mathematical Approach* (New York: McGraw-Hill, 1958), Chapter 2.

11. See J. de V. Graaff, *Theoretical Welfare Economics* (Cambridge, England: Cambridge University Press, 1967 paperback edition), p. 57.

12. Ibid., p. 57; p. 72.

13. Ibid., pp. 125–126.

14. Graaff, ibid. (pp. 125–126 and 140–141) allowed for this "international external effect in consumption" in his later refinements of a mathematical formulation of optimum tariff theory, but he defined foreign consumption of the *i*th good simply as y_i. In other words, he made no attempt to allow for the more realistic situation in which individuals in Home will differentiate *among* foreign countries for national security reasons.

15. See, for example, Albert O. Hirschman, *National Power and the Structure of Foreign Trade* (Berkeley: University of California Press, 1945), Chapter 2.

16. See, for example, P. J. D. Wiles *Communist International Economics* (New York: Praeger Publishers, 1969), Chapter XVI.

Notes to Chapter 2

1. J. de V. Graaff, "On Optimum Tariff Structures," *Review of Economic Studies*, 17 (1949), revised and reprinted in Kenneth J. Arrow and Tibor Scitovsky (Eds.), *Readings in Welfare Economics* (Homewood, Ill.: Irwin, 1969), pp. 523–540.

2. Ibid.

3. Tibor Scitovsky, "A Reconsideration of the Theory of Tariffs," *Review of Economic Studies*, IX (1942), reprinted in Howard S. Ellis and Lloyd A. Metzler (Eds.), *Readings in the Theory of International Trade* (Homewood, Ill.: Irwin, 1950), pp. 358–389.

4. Joan Robinson, *The Economics of Imperfect Competition* (London: MacMillan, 1965 edition), Chapter 15.

5. J. de V. Graaff, *Theoretical Welfare Economics* (Cambridge, England: Cambridge University Press, 1967 paperback edition), pp. 140–141.

6. The presence of summed ratios of marginal utilities in the first order conditions is, of course, the characteristic feature of all problems involving so-called collective goods or external effects. See, for example, Paul A. Samuelson, "The Pure Theory of Public Expenditure," *Review of Economics and Statistics*, XXXVI (1954), reprinted in Arrow and Scitovsky (Eds.), *Readings in Welfare Economics*, pp. 179–182.

Notes to Chapter 3

1. Note that this result represents a hybrid case of the generally accepted theoretical principle that *optimal* policy intervention in the case of divergence between domestic prices and marginal social costs in domestic production will be limited to domestic tax-subsidy combinations, and that *optimal* policy intervention in the case of divergence between foreign prices and marginal social costs of (revenue from) trade will be restricted to taxes on foreign trade. See Jagdish Bhagwati and V. K. Ramaswami, "Domestic Distortions, Tariffs, and the Theory of Optimum Subsidy," *Journal of Political Economy*, LXXI, 1 (February 1963), reprinted in Richard E. Caves and Harry G. Johnson (Eds.), *Readings in International Economics* (Homewood, Ill.: Irwin, 1968), pp. 230–239.

Notes to Chapter 4

1. J. de V. Graaff, "On Optimum Tariff Structures," *Review of Economic Studies*, XVII (1949), as revised and reprinted in Kenneth J. Arrow and Tibor Scitovsky (Eds.), *Readings in Welfare Economics* (Homewood, Ill.: Irwin, 1969), pp. 523–540.

2. S. K. Nath, *A Reappraisal of Welfare Economics* (London: Routledge & Kegan Paul, 1969), p. 202.

3. R. G. Lipsey and K. J. Lancaster, "The General Theory of Second Best," *Review of Economic Studies*, XXIV (1), 63 (1956–1957).

4. For example, see Jagdish Bhagwati and T. N. Srinivasan, "Optimal Intervention to Achieve Non-Economic Objectives," *Review of Economic Studies*, XXXVI (1), 105 (January 1969), pp. 27–38.

5. Nath, *A Reappraisal of Welfare Economics*, pp. 48–55.

6. See, for example: E. J. Mishan, "Second Thoughts on Second Best," *Oxford Economic Papers*, N.S. XIV (October 1962), pp. 205–217, revised and reprinted in Mishan, *Welfare Economics: Ten Introductory Essays*, Second Edition (New York: Random House, 1969); O. Davis and A. B. Whinston, "Welfare Economics and the Theory of Second Best," *Review of Economic Studies*, XXXII (1965), pp. 1–13. For a summary of the recent debate over this question, see Takashi Negishi, *General Equilibrium Theory and International Trade* (Amsterdam: North-Holland, 1972), Chapter 10.

7. See Robert Loring Allen and Ingo Walter, *The Formation of United States Trade Policy: Retrospect and Prospect*, Bulletin No. 70–71 (New York: Institute of Finance, New York University Graduate School of Business Administration, 1971), pp. 28–29.

8. Tibor Scitovsky, "A Reconsideration of the Theory of Tariffs," *Review of Economic Studies*, IX (1942): reprinted in Howard S. Ellis and Lloyd A. Metzler (Eds.), *Readings in the Theory of International Trade* (Homewood, Ill.: Irwin, 1950), pp. 358–389.

9. Allen and Walter, *The Formation of United States Trade Policy*, pp. 29–33. For a theoretical discussion of the conditions making reciprocal tariff reduction beneficial to both parties, see Scitovsky, ibid; also see Ingo Walter, *International Economics: Theory and Policy* (New York: Ronald Press, 1968), pp. 184–188.

10. Harry G. Johnson, "An Economic Theory of Protectionism, Tariff Bargaining, and the Formation of Customs Unions," *Journal of Political Economy*, LXXIII, 3 (June 1965), pp. 256–283.

11. Harry G. Johnson, "Optimum Tariffs and Retaliation," *Review of Economic Studies*, XXI (2) 55 (1953–1954).

Notes to Chapter 5

1. Act of July 2, 1940 (54 Stat. 714).

2. See *Comprehensive Export Schedule*, Nos. 23 and 24, Department of Commerce, Office of International Trade, Export Supply Branch (Washington, D.C., 1946, 1947); also see testimony of Thomas C. Blaisdell, Acting

Assistant Secretary of Commerce, before *Hearings on Export Control Act of 1949*, U.S. Congress, House, Committee on Banking and Currency, 81st Congress, 1st Session, January 31–February 2, 1949 (Washington, D.C., 1949), pp. 6–7.

3. See Gunnar Adler-Karlsson, *Western Economic Warfare*, 1947–1967 (Stockholm: Almqvist & Wiksell, 1968), p. 22, and his reference to the celebrated "first" published declaration of a "containment policy" in 'The Sources of Soviet Conduct," *Foreign Affairs* (July 1947).

4. Benjamin J. Cohen, "American Foreign Economic Policy: Some General Principles of Analysis," in Cohen (Ed.), *American Foreign Economic Policy* (New York: Harper & Row, 1968), pp. 31–32.

5. See, for example, Adler-Karlsson, *Western Economic Warfare*, pp. 31–33.

6. Ibid., p. 44; and Josef Wilczynski, *The Economics and Politics of East-West Trade* (New York: Praeger Publishers, 1969), pp. 275–278. For a theoretical discussion of "attacking" the enemy's "welfare contours," see Richard Gift, "Trading in a Threat System: The U.S.-Soviet Case," *Journal of Conflict Resolution*, XIII, 4 (December 1969).

7. Adler-Karlsson, *Western Economic Warfare*, pp. 22–23.

8. Statement of Jack W. Behrman, Assistant Secretary of Commerce for International Affairs, before *Hearings on Extension of the Export Control Act-1962*, U.S. Congress, Senate, Committee on Banking and Currency, 87th Congress, 2nd Session, May 2, 1962 (Washington, D.C., 1962), p. 27; and Adler-Karlsson, *Western Economic Warfare*, p. 22.

9. Export Control Act of 1949, Section 2 (63 Stat. 7). Emphasis added.

10. Ibid., Section 3(a). Emphasis added.

11. Ibid., Section 4(a).

12. Testimony of Lawrence C. McQuade, Assistant Secretary for Domestic and International Business, U.S. Department of Commerce, before *Hearings on East-West Trade*, U.S. Congress, Senate, Committee on Banking and Currency, 90th Congress, 2nd Session, June 4–July 25, 1968 (Washington D.C., 1968), pp. 221–222.

13. Ibid., p. 220; also James Henry Giffen, *The Legal and Practical Aspects of Trade with the Soviet Union* (New York: Praeger Publishers, 1969), pp. 9–10.

14. On this see Adler-Karlsson, *Western Economic Warfare*, pp. 69–70.

15. Giffen, *Legal and Practical Aspects*, pp. 28–35 and pp. 260–266.

16. Current regulations in this regard are to be found in *Export Control Regulations*, U.S. Department of Commerce (Washington, D.C.), Parts 376.12, 370.9, and 379.8.

17. Adler-Karlsson, *Western Economic Warfare*, Chapter 5.

18. Foreign Assistance Act of 1948, Section 117(d) (62 Stat. 153); also see Adler-Karlsson, ibid., p. 23–24.

19. Adler-Karlsson, *Western Economic Warfare*, pp. 40–45.

20. Nicholas Spulber, "Effects of the Embargo on Soviet Trade," *Harvard Business Review*, XXX (1952), pp. 125–126, as quoted in ibid., p. 44.

21. Mutual Defense Assistance Control Act of 1951, Title I, Section 101 (22 U.S.C. 1611).

22. Adler-Karlsson, *Western Economic Warfare*, p. 53.

23. Ibid., p. 56.

24. Peter J. Wiles, *Communist International Economics* (New York: Praeger Publishers, 1969), Chapter 15.

25. See Adler-Karlsson, *Western Economic Warfare*, p. 66.

26. Ibid., pp. 56–59.

27. Mutual Defense Assistance Control Act of 1951, Title I, Section 103(b) (65 Stat. 644) as amended by the Foreign Assistance Act of 1961 (75 Stat. 424).

28. Transaction Control Regulations (31 CFR Part 505.10).

29. See, for example, *Hearings on East-West Trade*, U.S. Congress, Senate, Committee on Banking and Currency, 90th Congress, 2nd Session, June 4–July 25, 1968 (Washington, D.C., 1968).

30. See Adler-Karlsson, *Western Economic Warfare*, p. 30.

31. For example, see ibid., p. 33.

32. Senator Eugene D. Millikin before *Hearings on the Trade Agreements Extension Act of 1951*, Part I, U.S. Congress, Senate, Committee on Finance, 82nd Congress, 1st Session, February 22–March 13, 1951 (Washington, D.C., 1951), p. 52.

33. Ibid., pp. 50–52.

34. Testimony of Dean Acheson, Secretary of State, before *Hearings* on the *Trade Agreements Extension Act of* 1951, pp. 8–9

35. See Adler-Karlsson, *Western Economic Warfare*, Chapter 5.

36. Trade Agreements Extension Act of 1951, Section 5 (65 Stat. 72).

37. Statement submitted by the Department of State to the *Hearings on East-West Trade*, p. 85.

38. This information is based on conversations the author had with several officials in the Departments of Commerce and State, in the spring of 1971.

39. Trade Agreements Extension Act of 1951, Section 11 (65 Stat. 72). The seven types of fur skins were ermine, fox, kolinsky, marten, mink, musk-rat, and weasel. With respect to the motivations involved, see comments of

Senator Eugene D. Millikin before *Hearings on the Trade Agreements Extension Act of 1951*, p. 52.

40. U.S. Department of State, "Legislative Provisions Relevant to Trade with Communist Countries" (mimeo., Washington, D.C., 1970).

41. Tariff Act of 1930, Section 307.

42. Samuel Pisar, *Co-existence and Commerce* (New York: McGraw-Hill, 1970), p. 101. Apparently this embargo was lifted on March 25, 1961 (See U.S. Department of State, "Legislative Provisions . . .").

43. See, for example, Robert Loring Allen and Ingo Walter, *The Formation of United States Trade Policy: Retrospect and Prospect*, Bulletin No. 70–71, (New York: Institute of Finance, New York University Graduate School of Business Administration, 1971), pp. 28–29.

44. *Tariff Schedules of the United States Annotated*, U.S. Tariff Commission (Washington, D.C., 1971), Headnote 3 (e).

45. Raymond F. Mikesell, *United States Economic Policy and International Relations* (New York: McGraw-Hill, 1952), pp. 44–46.

46. See *Hearings on the Sale of Foreign Bonds and Securities in the United States*, U.S. Congress, Senate, Committee on Finance, 72nd Congress, 1st and 2nd Sessions (Washington, D.C., 1931, 1932).

47. Takashi Negishi, *General Equilibrium Theory and International Trade* (Amsterdam: North-Holland, 1972), p. 129.

48. Murray C. Kemp, *The Pure Theory of International Trade and Investment* (Englewood Cliffs, N.J.: Prentice-Hall, 1969), pp. 297–298.

49. Senate Report No. 20, U.S. Congress, Senate, Judiciary Committee, 73rd Congress, 1st Session, April 6, 1933 (Washington, D.C., 1933).

50. Mikesell, *United States Economic Policy*, p. 46.

51. 19 U.S.C. 955 (1965). Emphasis added.

52. U.S. Department of State, "Legislative Provisions . . ."

53. 42 Opinions Attorney General No. 27 (May 9, 1967).

54. See interpretations by Pisar, *Coexistence and Commerce*, pp. 108–109, and U.S. Department of State, "Legislative Provisions . . ." For a more cautious interpretation, see Giffen, *Legal and Practical Aspects*, p. 207.

55. 42 Opinions Attorney General No. 15 (October 9, 1963).

56. Giffen, *Legal and Practical Aspects*, pp. 204–205, who cites 39 Opinions Attorney General 401 (1939).

57. Pisar, *Coexistence and Commerce*, p. 109.

58. Cohen, "American Foreign Economic Policy . . .," in Cohen (Ed.), *American Foreign Economic Policy*, p. 132.

59. See testimony of Winthrop G. Brown, Director, Office of International Trade Policy, Department of State, before *Hearings on the Trade*

Agreements Extension Act of 1951, Part II, U.S. Congress, Senate, Committee on Finance, 82nd Congress, 1st Session, March 16–April 16, 1951 (Washington, D.C., 1951), pp. 998–999. This point was confirmed informally in several interviews the author had with Department of State officials.

60. Under the influence of mercantilist ideas, eighteenth and nineteenth century belligerents were often quite anxious to export to their enemies. See, for example, Wiles, *Communist International Economics*, pp. 455–462.

61. Adler-Karlsson, *Western Economic Warfare*, p. 201.

62. *Foreign Assets Control Regulations and Related Documents* (31CFR 500.101–500.808).

63. Adler-Karlsson, *Western Economic Warfare*, p. 202.

64. Ibid., pp. 203–204.

65. Ibid., pp. 201–202.

66. *Foreign Assets Control Regulations*, Subpart B, Section 500.204.

Notes to Chapter 6

1. Gunnar Adler-Karlsson, *Western Economic Warfare*, 1947–1967 (Stockholm: Almqvist & Wiksell, 1968), p. 54.

2. Ibid., Chapter 9.

3. Ibid., Chapter 8.

4. Ibid., pp. 83–84.

5. Ibid., p. 87.

6. Ibid., p. 87.

7. Ibid., p. 92.

8. *Fourteenth Battle Act Report to Congress*, U.S. Secretary of State (Washington, D.C., 1960); also ibid., p. 202.

9. Adler-Karlsson, *Western Economic Warfare*, p. 99.

10. The "Polish constituency" interpretation was conveyed to the writer in the course of several interviews with officials at the Departments of Commerce and State, as well as with several outside observers of the American policy making process.

11. (73 Stat. 212).

12. *New York Times*, October, 2, 1960, quoted in Adler-Karlsson, *Western Economic Warfare*, p. 105.

13. See Agricultural Trade Development and Assistance Act of 1954 (PL 480), Section 2 (68 Stat. 454).

14. See, for example, Foreign Assistance Act of 1961, Section 102 ("Statement of Policy") (75 Stat. 424).

15. 7 U.S.C. 1691.

16. U.S. Department of State, "Legislative Provisions Relevant to Trade with Communist Countries" (mimeo, Washington, D.C., 1970).

17. Ibid.

18. Adler-Karlsson, *Western Economic Warfare*, p. 100.

19. U.S. Department of State, "Legislative Provisions . . .".

20. Adler-Karlsson, *Western Economic Warfare*, p. 100.

21. See testimony of Lawrence C. McQuade, Assistant Secretary for Domestic and International Business, U.S. Department of Commerce, before *Hearings on East-West Trade*, U.S. Congress, Senate, Committee on Banking and Currency, 90th Congress, 2nd Session, June 4–July 25, 1968 (Washington, D.C., 1968), p. 221; also ibid., p. 100.

22. This was the unanimous interpretation given to the author in interviews with several Department of Commerce and State officials (Spring 1971).

23. Statement submitted by the Department of State to the 1968 *Hearings on East-West Trade*, p. 85.

24. Adler-Karlsson, *Western Economic Warfare*, pp. 208–209.

25. Based on interviews with several Department of State officials (January 1971); also ibid., p. 208.

26. As quoted in Adler-Karlsson, *Western Economic Warfare*, p. 210.

27. See, for example, testimony of Peter J. Wiles before *Hearings on a Foreign Economic Policy for the 1970s*, U.S. Congressional Joint Economic Committee, 91st Congress, 2nd Session, December 7–9, 1970 (Washington, D.C., 1971), pp. 1244–1245.

28. Ibid., p. 210.

29. *Export Control*, Fifty-Fifth Quarterly Report, First Quarter 1961, Secretary of Commerce (Washington, D.C., 1961).

30. *Cuban Assets Control Regulations* (31 CFR 515.101–515.808).

31. Based on interviews with several Department of State officials (January 1971); also *Tariff Schedules of the United States* (*Annotated*), U.S. Tariff Commission (Washington, D.C., 1971), "General Headnotes and Rules of Interpretation," footnote 1 to Headnote 3(e).

32. Ibid., "General Headnotes and Rules of Interpretation," footnote 1 to Headnote 3(e).

33. 31 CFR 515.101–515.808.

34. Adler-Karlsson, *Western Economic Warfare*, p. 210.

35. Ibid., p. 213.

36. See Robert Loring Allen and Ingo Walter, *The Formation of United States Trade Policy: Retrospect and Prospect*, Bulletin No. 70–71 (New York:

Institute of Finance, New York University Graduate of Business Administration, 1971); also, for a study of the interaction of "trade-biased" and "protectionist" elements in the political process, see Ingo Walter, "The Formation of International Trade Policy" (Working Paper, Center for International Studies, New York University, December 1970).

37. For a concise statistical series on the economic growth of the eastern European countries, see Andrea Boltho, *Foreign Trade Criteria in Socialist Economies* (Cambridge, England: Cambridge University Press, 1971), Appendix.

38. See, for example, Mose L. Harvey, *East-West Trade and United States Policy* (New York: National Association of Manufacturers, 1966), pp. 77–85.

39. See testimony of Congressman Paul A. Kitchin, Chairman, House Select Committee on Export Control, before *Hearings on Extension of the Export Control Act of 1949*, U.S. Congress, House of Representatives, Committee on Banking and Currency, 87th Congress, 2nd Session, May 8, 1962 (Washington, D.C., 1962), pp. 21–27.

40. Amendments to the Export Control Act of 1949, Section 1(b) (76 Stat. 127). Emphasis added.

41. Ibid., Section 2(3).

42. Ibid., Section 3(a). Emphasis added.

43. Ibid., Section 5(a).

44. *Export Control*, Sixty-First Quarterly Report, Third Quarter 1962, Secretary of Commerce (Washington, D.C., 1962), pp. 6–7.

45. Adler-Karlsson, *Western Economic Warfare*, p. 105.

46. Nathaniel McKitterick, *East-West Trade, The Background of U.S. Policy* (New York: Twentieth Century Fund, 1966), p. 31, as quoted in ibid., p. 235.

47. President's Message submitted to the *Hearings on the Trade Expansion Act of 1962*, U.S. Congress, House of Representatives, Committee on Ways and Means, 87th Congress, 2nd Session (Washington, D.C., 1962), p. 15.

48. *Hearings on H.R. 11970, The Trade Expansion Act of 1962*, Part IV, U.S. Congress, Senate, Committee on Finance, 87th Congress, 2nd Session (Washington, D.C., 1962).

49. Testimony of George W. Ball, Under Secretary of State, ibid., p. 2209.

50. Trade Expansion Act of 1962, Section 231(a) (76 Stat. 872).

51. Based on several interviews with Department of State officials (Spring 1971).

52. Foreign Assistance Act of 1963, Section 402 (77 Stat. 379). Emphasis added.

53. Based on a conversation with a Department of State legal advisor (Spring 1971).

54. *United States Constitution*, Article 1, Section 8.

55. For a discussion of the interaction of various forces in the formation of U.S. trade policy, see Allen and Walter, *The Formation of United States Trade Policy: Retrospect and Prospect.*

Notes to Chapter 7

1. Gunnar Adler-Karlsson, *Western Economic Warfare*, 1947–1967 (Stockholm: Almqvist & Wiksell, 1968), p. 101.

2. For a more extensive discussion of the new course launched by the Kennedy and Johnson administrations, see Samuel Pisar, *Coexistence and Commerce* (New York: McGraw-Hill, 1970), pp. 87–93.

3. See President Kennedy's Inaugural Address, January 20, 1960; and President Johnson's State of the Union message, January 12, 1966.

4. See, for example, statement of Peter Wiles, before *Hearings on a Foreign Economic Policy for the 1970s*, U.S. Congress, Joint Economic Committee, 91st Congress, 2nd Session, December 7–9, 1970 (Washington, D.C., 1971), p. 1242.

5. "Report to the President of the Special Committee on U.S. Trade Relations with East European Countries and the Soviet Union" (Washington, D.C., 1965), p. 9; reprinted in *Hearings on a Foreign Economic Policy for the 1970s*, p. 1158.

6. See Michael Kaser, *Comecon* (London: Oxford University Press, Second Edition, 1967), Chapter 2.

7. See Adler-Karlsson, *Western Economic Warfare*, pp. 86–89.

8. For a theoretical discussion of "attacking" a foreign country's welfare levels (or, more formally, its "Scitovsky contours"), see Richard Gift, "Trading in a Threat System: The U.S.-Soviet Case," *Journal of Conflict Resolution*, XII, 4 (December 1969).

9. Nathaniel McKitterick, *East-West Trade, The Background of U.S. Policy* (New York: The Twentieth Century Fund, 1966), p. 28, as quoted in Adler-Karlsson, *Western Economic Warfare*, p. 105.

10. "Report to the President of the Special Committee . . .," pp. 2 and 8; reprinted in *Hearings on a Foreign Economic Policy for the 1970's* p. 1151 and pp. 1157–1158; on the "internal liberalization" issue, see also testimony of Ota Sik, former Deputy Premier, Czechoslovak Socialist Republic, before ibid., pp. 1182–1190.

11. See Gift, "Trading in a Threat System . . ." for a discussion of the distinction between these two concepts.

12. See Pisar, *Coexistence and Commerce*, p. 134; also see Adler-Karlsson, *Western Economic Warfare*, pp. 135–136, on the extent of the U.S. extraterritorial control machinery.

13. For specific examples of extraterritoriality disputes, see testimony of George W. Ball, Permanent Representative-Designate to the United Nations, before *Hearings on East-West Trade*, U.S. Congress, Senate, Committee on Banking and Currency, 90th Congress, 2nd Session, June 4–July 25, 1968 (Washington, D.C., 1968), pp. 39–40; and Pisar, *Coexistence and Commerce*, pp. 135–137.

14. See testimony of George W. Ball before *Hearings on East-West Trade*, pp. 39–40.

15. See Adler-Karlsson, *Western Economic Warfare*, pp. 105–106.

16. On the commercial profitability of the wheat deal, see Louis de Alessi, "The Sale of Wheat to the USSR: A Change in U.S. Policy," *Kyklos*, XVIII, 1 (1965), pp. 116–129.

17. Adler-Karlsson, *Western Economic Warfare*, p. 102.

18. Philomene von Herberg, "Our Befuddled Maritime Policy," *Wall Street Journal*, March 2, 1971.

19. Public Resolution 17, March 26, 1934 (48 Stat. 500). Emphasis added.

20. "Message from the President," March 4, 1935, H. Doc. No. 18, in *Hearings on the Merchant Marine Act of 1935*, U.S. Congress, Senate, Commerce Committee, 74th Congress, 1st Session, (Washington, D.C., 1935), pp. 1–2.

21. Ibid., p. 3.

22. (49 Stat. 1985).

23. Ibid., Section 1(a). Emphasis added.

24. Ibid., Title V and Title VI.

25. Cargo Preference Law of 1954 (68 Stat. 832). Emphasis added.

26. Testimony of Kenneth N. Davis, Jr., Assistant Secretary for Domestic and International Business, U.S. Department of Commerce, before *Hearings on the Cargo Preference Provision of the Export Expansion and Regulation Act*, U.S. Congress, Senate, 91st Congress, 1st Session, July 1969 (Washington D.C., 1969).

27. *Comprehensive Export Schedule* U.S. Department of Commerce (Washington, D.C.), Part 376.3.

28. Testimony of Kenneth N. Davis, Jr., *Hearings on the Cargo Preference Provision of the Export Expansion and Regulation Act*.

29. Raymond F. Mikesell, *Public International Lending for Development* (New York: Random House, 1966 paperback edition), pp. 12–13; 84–85.

30. Ibid., pp. 12–13; 46–48; 84–91.

31. See statement of the Department of State to the *Hearings on East-West Trade*, pp. 78–84.

32. U.S. Department of State, "Legislative Provisions Relevant to Trade with Communist Countries" (Washington, D.C., 1970).

33. Testimony of Harold F. Linder, President and Chairman, Export-Import Bank of the United States, before *Hearings on East-West Trade*, pp. 127–130. The sales were ultimately paid for in gold and hard currencies.

34. (78 Stat. 1022). Emphasis added.

35. Testimony of Warren W. Glick, Assistant General Counsel, Export-Import Bank of the United States, before *Hearings on East-West Trade*, p. 147.

36. Testimony of Harold F. Linder, ibid., pp. 130–134.

37. Testimony of Lawrence C. McQuade, Assistant Secretary for Domestic and International Business, U.S. Department of Commerce, before *Hearings on East-West Trade*, p. 221.

38. For a comprehensive discussion of the intra-Comecon tensions and the protagonist role of Rumania, see Kaser, *Comecon*, Chapter 6.

39. See testimony of Lawrence C. McQuade, *Hearings on East-West Trade*, p. 206; also Adler-Karlsson, *Western Economic Warfare*, p. 104.

40. See Adler-Karlsson, ibid., p. 103.

41. Proposed "East-West Trade Relations Act," Section 2. The full text of this bill is reprinted in James Henry Giffen, *The Legal and Practical Aspects of Trade with the Soviet Union* (New York: Praeger, 1969), pp. 292–298; also see Giffen's discussion of this bill, pp. 97–102.

42. Proposed "East-West Trade Relations Act," Section 3.

43. Ibid., Section 4.

44. Ibid., Sections 5, 6, and 9.

45. See Adler-Karlsson, *Western Economic Warfare*, p. 104.

46. *Export Control*, Fifty-Fifth Quarterly Report, First Quarter 1961, Secretary of Commerce (Washington, D.C., 1961).

47. *Foreign Assets Control Regulations and Related Documents* (31 CFR 500.101–500.808).

48. For an examination of Soviet economic warfare against China, as well as studies of Soviet economic warfare directed against Albania and Yugoslavia, see Robert Owen Friedman, *Economic Warfare in the Communist Bloc* (New York: Praeger Publishers, 1970).

49. Adler-Karlsson, *Western Economic Warfare*, p. 109.

50. U.S. Department of State, "Legislative Provisions. . ."

51. See Pisar, *Coexistence and Commerce*, pp. 91, 110; and Adler-Karlsson, *Western Economic Warfare*, p. 104.

52. Export-Import Bank Act of 1945 (as amended), Section 2(b). Emphasis added.

53. Pisar, *Coexistence and Commerce*, p. 110.

54. See Thomas A. Wolf and Robert G. Hawkins, "The Evolving Policy on East-West Trade," in Hawkins and Ingo Walter (Eds.), *The United States and International Markets: Commercial Policy Options in an Age of Controls* (Boston: D. C. Heath, 1972).

55. See testimony of Hugh D. Donaghue, Assistant to the President, Control Data Corporation, and A. R. Fredrikson, Division Vice President, Minnesota Mining and Manufacturing Co., before *Hearings on East-West Trade*, pp. 149–162 and pp. 296–306, respectively; also see letter from David Packard, Chairman, Hewlett-Packard Co., submitted to *Hearings on East-West Trade*, pp. 1040–1041.

56. For an account of early activities of private business aimed at liberalizing U.S. restrictions, see Adler-Karlsson, *Western Economic Warfare*, pp. 105–106.

57. For a discussion of these various antitrade groups, see ibid., pp. 106–108; and Pisar, *Coexistence and Commerce*, pp. 79–87.

58. See various testimony, statements, and letters introduced into the 1968 and 1969 Senate and House hearings on East-West Trade.

59. See speech by Senator Walter F. Mondale, *Congressional Record*, May 9, 1968; also testimony of Hugh P. Donaghue and A. R. Fredrikson, and letter from David Packard, before *Hearings on East-West Trade*.

60. See testimony of Thomas A. Christiansen, Manager, International Planning, Hewlett-Packard Co., before *Hearings on the Export Expansion and Regulation Act of 1969*, U.S. Congress, Senate, Committee on Banking and Currency, 91st Congress, 1st Session (Washington, D.C., 1969).

61. See speech by Senator Walter F. Mondale, *Congressional Record*, May 9, 1968; also testimony of Hugh P. Donaghue and A. R. Fredrikson before *Hearings on East-West Trade* (1968), pp. 150 and 296, respectively.

62. For example, see Herbert E. Meyer, "What It's Like to Do Business with the Russians," *Fortune*, LXXXV, 5 (May 1972).

63. Export Administration Act of 1969, (PL 91-184), Section 2. Emphasis added.

64. Ibid., Section 3. Emphasis added.

65. Ibid., Section 4(a).

66. Ibid., Section 4(b). Emphasis added.

67. Ibid., Section 5(a).

68. Ibid., Section 7(d).

69. Ibid., Section 9.

70. *Export Control*, Secretary of Commerce (Washington, D.C.), various issues, 1970–1971.

71. Export Control, Ninety-Sixth Quarterly Report, Second Quarter 1971, Secretary of Commerce (Washington, D.C., 1971), p. 4.

72. For a varied group of arguments for expanded economic relations with the P.R.C., see testimony of John C. Campbell, Uri Ra'anan, J. Irwin Miller, Alexander Eckstein, and Peter Wiles before the *Hearings on a Foreign Economic Policy for the 1970s*; also see Joint Economic Committee, U.S. Congress, *An Economic Profile of Mainland China* (New York: Praeger Publishers, 1968).

73. *Foreign Assets Control Regulations* (31 CFR Parts 500.541 and 500.543).

74. *Wall Street Journal*, April 15, 1971.

75. *Export Control*, Ninety-Sixth Quarterly Report, Second Quarter 1971, pp. 14–15.

76. *New York Times*, June 10, 1971.

77. *International Herald Tribune*, February 15, 1972.

78. Proposed "Export Expansion and Regulation Act of 1969," S. 1940, Section 4(f).

79. See, for example, various testimony before *Hearings on The Cargo Preference Provision of the Export Expansion and Regulation Act*, U.S. Congress, Senate, 91st Congress, 1st Session, July 1969 (Washington, D.C., 1969); also, see testimony of Roy F. Hendrikson, Executive Secretary, National Federation of Grain Cooperatives, before *Hearings on East-West Trade* (1968), pp. 366–377; also see statement of N.R. Danielian, President, International Economic Policy Association, submitted to *Hearings on East-West Trade* (1968).

80. Testimony of Paul Hall, President, Seafarers International Union of North America, AFL-CIO, before *Hearings on Cargo Preference. . .*, pp. 37–40.

81. Testimony of Phillip H. Trezise, Assistant Secretary for Economic Affairs, U.S. Department of State; and of Kenneth N. Davis, Jr., Assistant Secretary for Domestic and International Business, U.S. Department of Commerce, before *Hearings on Cargo Preference. . ..*

82. *Congressional Record*, October 22, 1969.

83. *New York Times*, June 10, 1971; *International Herald Tribune*, November 6, 1971.

84. *International Herald Tribune*, November 18–19, 1972 and November 24, 1972.

85. See speech of Senator Walter F. Mondale, *Congressional Record*, January 25, 1971; also see letter of Thomas A. Christiansen, Manager, International Trade Relations, Hewlett-Packard Corp., submitted to *Hearings on the Export Expansion Finance Act of 1971*, U.S. Congress, House of Representatives, Committee on Banking and Currency, 92nd Congress, 1st Session, May 18–26, 1971 (Washington, D.C., 1971), pp. 640–642.

86. Statement of Phillip H. Trezise, Assistant Secretary of State for Economic Affairs, to *Hearings on the Export Expansion Finance Act of 1971*, pp. 598–599.

87. *Congressional Record*, January 25, 1971.

88. *Congressional Quarterly*, "Weekly Report," August 21, 1971, p. 1819.

89. *International Herald Tribune*, December 2, 1971; October 19, 1972; and November 9, 1972.

90. Notable exceptions have been Roy F. Hendrikson, *Hearings on East-West Trade* (1968), p. 373; and Thomas A. Christiansen, *Hearings on the Export Expansion Finance Act of 1971*, pp. 641–642.

91. See, for example, Pisar, *Coexistence and Commerce*, p. 77.

92. Ibid., Chapter 5.

93. The interaction of trade-biased and protection-biased groups in the policy formulation process is examined in some detail by Ingo Walter, "The Formation of International Trade Policy" (Working Paper, Center for International Studies, New York University, December, 1970).

94. Giffen, *Legal and Practical Aspects of Trade with the Soviet Union*, p. 101.

95. *International Herald Tribune*, October 2, 1971.

96. *International Herald Tribune*, March 27, 1972.

97. *International Herald Tribune*, October 19, 1972.

Notes to Chapter 8.

1. United Nations, *Yearbook of International Trade Statistics, 1969*, (New York: United Nations, 1971).

2. Josef Wilczynski, *The Economics and Politics of East-West Trade* (New York: Praeger Publishers, 1969), p. 52.

3. United Nations, *Economic Bulletin for Europe*, XXII, 1 (1971), p. 27.

4. See, for example, United Nations, Economic Commission for Europe, *Analytical Report on the State of Intra-European Trade* (New York: United

Nations, 1970); also, Rudolf Nötel, "Future Development of East-West Trade," *Economia Internationale*, XXIII (1970), pp. 212–235. For a summary discussion of the structure of East-West trade, see Thomas A. Wolf and Robert G. Hawkins, "The Evolving Policy on East-West Trade," in Hawkins and Ingo Walter (Eds.), *The United States and International Markets: Commercial Policy Options in an Age of Controls* (Boston, D. C. Heath, 1972).

5. Based on "Trade of NATO Countries with Communist Countries, 1966 to 1969," *Research Study* (unclassified), Bureau of Intelligence and Research, Department of State (Washington, D.C., 1970).

6. Based on Wilczynski, *Economics and Politics of East-West Trade*, p. 290.

7. Gunnar Adler-Karlsson, *Western Economic Warfare*, 1947–1967 (Stockholm: Almqvist & Wiksell, 1968), Chapter 14.

8. Ibid., pp. 158–160.

9. Ibid., p. 166.

10. Ibid., p. 186. Also see his quote from the 1961 study by Pisar on this question, ibid., p. 145.

11. See Thomas A. Wolf. "A Note on the Restrictive Effect of Unilateral United States Export Controls," *Journal of Political Economy*, LXXXI, 1 (January/February 1973).

12. Testimony of Michael W. Blumenthal, President of Bendix International, before *Hearings on the Export Expansion and Regulation Act of 1969*, U.S. Congress, Senate, Committee on Banking and Currency, 91st Congress, 1st Session (Washington, D.C., 1969), p. 89.

13. Samuel Pisar, *Coexistence and Commerce* (New York, McGraw-Hill, 1970), p. 78. Emphasis added.

14. Statement submitted by Thomas A. Christiansen, Manager of International Planning, to *Hearings on the Export Expansion and Regulation Act of 1969*.

15. Letter submitted by Thomas A. Christiansen to *Hearings on the Export Expansion Finance Act of 1971*, U.S. Congress, House of Representatives, Committee on Banking and Currency, 92nd Congress, 1st Session, May 18–26, 1971 (Washington, D.C., 1971), p. 642.

16. Statement of John M. Montias to the *Hearings on a Foreign Economic Policy for the 1970s*, U.S. Congress, Joint Economic Committee, 91st Congress, 2nd Session, December 7–9, 1970 (Washington, D.C., 1971), pp. 1231–1241.

17. Testimony of Dr. N. R. Danielian, President, International Economic Policy Association, before *Hearings on the Export Expansion and Regulation Act of 1969*.

18. Wolf, "A Note on the Restrictive Effect of Unilateral United States Export Controls."

19. Thomas A. Wolf, "The Quantitative Impact of Liberalization of United States Unilateral Restrictions on Trade with the Socialist Countries of Eastern Europe," *External Research Study*, XR/RECS-3, U.S. Department of State (Washington, D.C., 1972).

20. Ibid.

21. Calculated from *Battle Act Report*, U.S. Department of State (Washington, D.C.), various issues.

22. *International Herald Tribune*, December 1, 1971.

23. *International Herald Tribune*, November 4–5, 1972.

24. *The Times* (London), July 19, 1972.

25. See Wolf and Hawkins, "The Evolving Policy on East-West Trade."

26. *Export Control*, Ninety-Seventh Quarterly Report, Third Quarter 1971, Secretary of Commerce (Washington, D.C., 1971); and *U.S. Foreign Trade: Highlights of Exports and Imports*, U.S. Department of Commerce (Washington, D.C., December, 1971).

27. *International Herald Tribune*, July 26, 1972.

28. *International Herald Tribune*, August 11, 1972.

29. *International Herald Tribune*, November 18, 1971, February 18, 1972; and November 4–5, 1972.

30. See, for example, *New York Times*, November 11, 1971; *International Herald Tribune*, November 27–28, 1971; December 9, 1971; May 27, 1972.

31. Robert F. Dernberger, "The Prospects for Trade with the People's Republic of China," in Arvind V. Phatak (Ed.), *Building Business Bridges to Eastern Europe and Mainland China*, Occasional Paper Series, No. 4 (Philadelphia: Temple University, School of Business Administration, 1972), pp. 8–18.

Notes to Chapter 9.

1. See Gunnar Adler-Karlsson, *Western Economic Warfare*, 1947–1967 (Stockholm): Almqvist & Wiksell, 1968), pp. 24, 32.

2. See the so-called "Miller Report": "Report to the President of the Special Committee on U.S. Trade Relations with East European Countries and the Soviet Union" (Washington, D.C., 1965); reprinted in *Hearings on a Foreign Economic Policy for the 1970s*, U.S. Congress, Joint Economic Committee, 91st Congress, 2nd Session, December 7–9, 1970 (Washington, D.C., 1971), pp. 1147–1171.

3. Quoted in Adler-Karlsson, *Western Economic Warfare*, p. 125.

4. Testimony of John M. Montias before *Hearings on a Foreign Economic Policy for the 1970s*, p. 1253.

5. Stanislaw Wasowski, "Introduction," in *East-West Trade and the Technology Gap* (New York: Praeger Publishers, 1970), pp. 7–8.

6. For the opinions of various academic economists on the subject of political quid pro quos, see *Hearings on a Foreign Economic Policy for the 1970s*, pp. 1241–1259.

7. Robert Loring Allen and Ingo Walter, *The Formation of United States Trade Policy: Retrospect and Prospect*, Bulletin No. 70-71 (New York: Institute of Finance, New York University Graduate School of Business Administration, 1971).

8. See *Hearings on East-West Trade*, U.S. Congress, Senate, Committee on Banking and Currency, 90th Congress, 2nd Session, 1968 (Washington, D.C., 1968), and *Hearings on the Export Expansion and Regulation Act of 1969*, U.S. Congress, Senate, Committee on Banking and Currency, 91st Congress, 1st Session, 1969 (Washington, D.C., 1969).

9. See, for example, testimony of Peter Wiles before ibid., pp. 1247–1248.

10. See, for example, an editorial in the *International Herald Tribune* (reprinted from *The Washington Post*), August 22, 1972.

11. Peter J. D. Wiles, *Communist International Economics* (New York: Praeger Publishers, 1969), pp. 465–466; also see testimony of Wiles before *Hearings on a Foreign Economic Policy for the 1970s*, p. 1245.

12. For an extensive discussion of the problems of selling in the East, and the types of "guarantees" that should be striven for in the context of bilateral agreements, see Samuel Pisar, *Coexistence and Commerce* (New York: McGraw-Hill, 1970).

13. *International Herald Tribune*, November 11–12, 1972.

14. Ibid., Chapter 25.

15. Ibid., p. 481.

16. Committee for Economic Development, *A New Trade Policy Toward Communist Countries* (New York: C.E.D., 1972), p. 44.

17. *Congressional Quarterly Weekly Report*, August 26, 1972; and *The Morgan Guaranty Survey*, September 1972.

18. *International Herald Tribune*, March 22, 1972.

19. See also Albert O. Hirschman, *National Power and the Structure of Foreign Trade* (Berkeley: University of California Press, 1945), Chapter 2.

20. For suggested O.E.C.D. action in this area, see Committee for Economic Development, *A New Trade Policy Toward Communist Countries*, pp. 42–43.

Notes to Appendix A

1. J. de V. Graaff, *Theoretical Welfare Economics* (Cambridge, England: Cambridge University Press, 1967 paperback edition), p. 57.

2. Ibid., p. 57; p. 72.

3. G. Hadley, *Nonlinear and Dynamic Programming* (Reading, Mass.: Addison-Wesley, 1964), Chapters 3 and 6.

4. See J. de V. Graaff, "On Optimum Tariff Structures," *Review of Economic Studies*, 17 (1949), as revised and reprinted in Kenneth J. Arrow and Tibor Scitovsky (Eds.), *Readings in Welfare Economics* (Homewood, Ill.: Irwin, 1969), pp. 523–540.

5. C. P. Kindleberger, *International Economics* (Homewood, Ill.: Irwin, 1968), Appendix F.

Notes to Appendix B

1. G. Hadley, *Nonlinear and Dynamic Programming* (Reading, Mass.: Addison-Wesley, 1964), Chapters 3 and 6. Note that the constraints (3) and (4) form convex sets since they are both linear functions (identities).

2. See Paul A. Samuelson, *Foundations of Economic Analysis* (New York: Atheneum, 1967 paperback edition), pp. 233–234.

3. Hadley, *Nonlinear and Dynamic Programming*, Chapters 3 and 6.

4. H. Robert Heller, *International Trade: Theory and Empirical Evidence* (Englewood Cliffs, N.J.: Prentice-Hall, 1968), pp. 55–56.

5. See, for example, J. Bhagwati and T. N. Srinivasan, "Optimal Intervention to Achieve Non-Economic Objectives," *Review of Economic Studies*, XXXVI (1), 105 (January 1969), pp. 27–38.

6. Hadley, *Nonlinear and Dynamic Programming*, p. 85.

7. Ibid., p. 87.

Notes to Appendix C

1. This Appendix draws heavily on Thomas A. Wolf, "Optimum Tariff Theory and Differentiation Among Foreign Markets" (unpublished paper, 1972).

2. J. de V. Graaff, "On Optimum Tariff Structures," *Review of Economic Studies*, 17 (1949), as revised and reprinted in Kenneth J. Arrow and Tibor Scitovsky (Eds.), *Readings in Welfare Economics* (Homewood, Ill.: Irwin, 1969), pp. 523–540.

3. This is equivalent to Samuelson's celebrated "condition (3)": Paul A. Samuelson, "The Pure Theory of Public Expenditure," *Review of Economics and Statistics*, XXXVI (1954), reprinted in Arrow and Scitovsky (Eds.), *Readings in Welfare Economics*, pp. 179–182.

4. "Condition (II)" is similar to Samuelson's "condition (2)," ibid.

5. See G. Hadley, *Nonlinear and Dynamic Programming* (Reading, Mass.: Addison-Wesley, 1964), pp. 185–187. For a more detailed discussion of these first order conditions in terms of inequalities, see Thomas A. Wolf, "Towards a Theory of Optimum Trade Policy in a National Security Context: The Case of United States Policies with Respect to East-West Trade" (unpublished dissertation: New York University Graduate School of Business Administration, 1971), pp. 47–55.

Notes to Appendix D

1. Paul A. Samuelson, "The Pure Theory of Public Expenditure," *Review of Economics and Statistics*, XXXVI (1954), reprinted in Kenneth J. Arrow and Tibor Scitovsky (Eds.), *Readings in Welfare Economics* (Homewood, Ill.: Irwin, 1969), pp. 179–182.

2. The concept of Bergson welfare contours is discussed extensively in J. de V. Graaff, *Theoretical Welfare Economics* (Cambridge, England: Cambridge University Press, 1967 paperback edition), Chapters III–IV.

3. This exposition is similar to Samuelson's treatment, except that we employ a Bergson social welfare contour in *commodity* space. (See Paul A. Samuelson, "Diagrammatic Exposition of a Theory of Public Expenditure," *Review of Economics and Statistics*, XXXVII (November, 1955), pp. 350–356.

Index

About The Author

Thomas A. Wolf is a postdoctoral Research Fellow at the International Institute of Management, Berlin. He is currently engaged in independent research concerning various aspects of East-West economic relations, including the role of the Western multinational corporation in East-West commerce.

Before completing his doctorate in economics at the New York University Graduate School of Business Administration in 1971, Dr. Wolf had served as an officer of First National City Bank (New York). While completing his doctorate he prepared a special study on East-West trade for the U.S. Department of State. Dr. Wolf also serves as a consultant to the United Nations Conference on Trade and Development (Geneva), and has authored several other articles and research reports concerning East-West economic relations.

In addition to his Ph.D., Dr. Wolf holds an M.B.A. in finance from Columbia University, and a B.A. in English from Amherst College.